FIGHTING POVERTY AND INJUSTICE

A manifesto inspired by Peter Townsend

Edited by Alan Walker, Adrian Sinfield and Carol Walker

First published in Great Britain in 2011 by
The Policy Press
University of Bristol
Fourth Floor
Beacon House
Queen's Road
Bristol BS8 1QU
UK

Tel +44 (0)117 331 4054
Fax +44 (0)117 331 4093
e-mail tpp-info@bristol.ac.uk
www.policypress.co.uk

North American office:
The Policy Press
c/o International Specialized Books Services (ISBS)
920 NE 58th Avenue, Suite 300
Portland, OR 97213-3786, USA
Tel +1 503 287 3093
Fax +1 503 280 8832
e-mail info@isbs.com

© The Policy Press 2011

British Library Cataloguing in Publication Data
A catalogue record for this book is available from the British Library.

Library of Congress Cataloging-in-Publication Data
A catalog record for this book has been requested.

ISBN 978 1 84742 714 4 paperback
ISBN 978 1 84742 715 1 hardcover

The right of Alan Walker, Adrian Sinfield and Carol Walker to be identified as
editors of this work has been asserted by them in accordance with the 1988
Copyright, Designs and Patents Act.

Cover design by The Policy Press.
Front cover: image kindly supplied by Getty Images.
Printed and bound in Great Britain by TJ International,
Padstow.
The Policy Press uses environmentally responsible
print partners.

MIX
Paper from
responsible sources
FSC
www.fsc.org   FSC® C013056

For Peter

First there was Tawney. Then came Titmuss. Now there is Townsend. At least future students of social reform will have an easy key to remembering the most important egalitarian writers of the past 75 years: a convenient triumvirate of 'Ts'.

The Guardian Leader, 31 July 1975

Contents

List of figures and tables

Figures

Tables

Preface

This book was inspired by Peter Townsend and is dedicated to him. The shock of his death, in June 2009, quickly translated into a widely held determination to ensure that his work and, especially, its core message concerning the need for social justice, was not lost to current and future generations of students, and policy makers. Therefore the book serves as an introduction to Peter's work. It is not merely a festschrift because it does more than celebrate Peter's massive contributions. It builds on the sure foundations that he laid in various fields and applies his myriad insights to contemporary policy debates.

The book reflects Peter's triple contributions, to teaching, research and campaigning, which were all, in essence, concerned with combating poverty, inequality and social injustice. It comprises a rallying call to defeat these evils and to create a better, more cohesive society. It also reminds everyone – policy makers, politicians, media and the public – why there is a welfare state and why the case for it must be repeated constantly alongside critiques of its failings and constructive proposals for improvement.

This book would not have been possible without the help and support of various colleagues and friends. First of all the contributors deserve our thanks for their enthusiastic assent to joining this venture and the quality of their chapters, each of which is dedicated, with great affection, to Peter. Alison Shaw, at The Policy Press, was an equally enthusiastic commissioning editor and a great source of support. Karen Tsui and Olga Swales, at the University of Sheffield, provided excellent technical assistance. Last, but not least, Dorothy Sinfield acted as a fourth 'shadow editor'. We are very grateful to all of them.

Alan Walker, University of Sheffield
Adrian Sinfield, University of Edinburgh
Carol Walker, University of Lincoln

Notes on contributors

Sir Tony Atkinson is a Fellow of Nuffield College, of which he was Warden from 1994 to 2005, and is Centennial Professor at the London School of Economics and Political Science. His most recent books are *The changing distribution of earnings in OECD countries* (2008), and *Top incomes: A global perspective* (2010). He can be contacted via Nuffield College, Oxford (www.nuffield.ox.ac.uk/economics/people/atkinson.htm).

Jonathan Bradshaw CBE, FBA, is Professor of Social Policy at the University of York. His main interests are in child poverty, social security policy and comparative social policy. He has recently been working on an edited book on *The well-being of children in the UK* (The Policy Press, 2011). (For more information see www-users.york.ac.uk/~jrb1)

Bob Deacon is Professor of International Social Policy at the University of Sheffield. He also holds the UNESCO-UNU Chair in Regional Integration, Migration and the Free Movement of People at UNUCRIS in Bruges. His most recent books are *Global social policy and governance* (2007) and *World regional social policy and global governance* (co-edited) (2010). (www.sheffield.ac.uk/socstudies/staff/staff-profiles/deacon.html)

Danny Dorling is Professor of Human Geography at the University of Sheffield. With a group of colleagues he helped create the website www.worldmapper.org which shows who has most and least in the world. His recent books include: (in 2010) *Injustice: Why social inequalities persist* and (in 2011) *So you think you know about Britain?*. (www.sheffield.ac.uk/geography/staff/dorling_danny)

Conor Gearty is Professor of Human Rights Law, at the London School of Economics and Political Science. Recent publications include *Debating social rights* (with Virginia Mantouvalou) (Hart Publishing, 2011), and *The rights future* (2011) (web publication: www. therightsfuture.com). His main research fields are in civil liberties, human rights and terrorism. He is currently undertaking research into liberty and security (for publication as a book for Polity Press) and also the law relating to human rights in the UK. (www.conorgearty. com and www.therightsfuture.com)

Hilary Land is Emerita Professor of Family Policy at the University of Bristol. Publications include *Large families in London* (Bell, 1969) (pilot for national poverty survey); *Change, choice and conflict in social policy* (with Hall, P., Parker, R. and Webb, A.) (Heinemann, 1975) and *Lone motherhood in twentieth century Britain* (with Kiernan, K. and Lewis, J.) (Oxford University Press, 1998).

Ruth Lister is Emeritus Professor of Social Policy, Loughborough University, and a member of the House of Lords. Key research interests are poverty, citizenship, social security, gender and children. Publications include: *Citizenship: Feminist perspectives* (Macmillan Palgrave, 1997/2003); *Poverty* (Polity Press, 2004); *Understanding theories and concepts in social policy* (The Policy Press, 2010). (www. lboro.ac.uk/departments/ss/staff/lister.html)

Chris Phillipson is Professor of Applied Social Studies and Social Gerontology at Keele University. He has published extensively on age-related matters. His books include: *Reconstructing old age* (Sage, 1998); *Social theory and social ageing* (co-authored) (McGraw-Hill, 2003); *Social networks and social exclusion* (co-edited) (Ashgate, 2004); *Ageing, globalisation and inequality* (co-edited) (Baywood, 2006); *Futures of old age* (co-edited) (Sage, 2006) and *Family practices in later life* (co-authored) (The Policy Press, 2009). He is the co-editor (with Dale Dannefer) of the *Sage handbook of social gerontology* (Sage, 2010). (www. keele.ac.uk/sociology/people/chrisphillipson/)

Hilary Rose is Visiting Professor of Sociology at the London School of Economics and Political Science and Emerita Professor of Social Policy at the University of Bradford. The great social movements of the last quarter of the twentieth century – feminism, and the struggle against racism – are transforming the social sciences, but no field has more richly benefited from this than social policy. It has been a privilege to be part of this.

Adrian Sinfield, Professor Emeritus of Social Policy, The University of Edinburgh, has worked on social security, poverty, unemployment and the social division of welfare. Publications include: *The long-term unemployed* (OECD, 1968); *Which way for social work?* (Fabian Society, 1969); *What unemployment means* (Martin Robertson, 1981); *The workless state* (co-edited) (Martin Robertson, 1981); *Excluding youth* (co-authored) (1991); *Comparing tax routes to welfare in Denmark and the United Kingdom* (co-authored) (The Danish National Institute of Social Research, 1996). (www.sps.ed.ac.uk/staff/social_policy/sinfield_adrian)

Carol Thomas is a Professor of Sociology at Lancaster University based in the School of Health and Medicine. She is best known for her publications in Disability Studies – including her books *Female forms: Experiencing and understanding disability* (OU Press, 1997) and *Sociologies of disability and illness: Contested ideas in disability studies and medical sociology* (Palgrave Macmillan, 2007). Carol is currently Director of the Centre for Disability Research (CeDR) at Lancaster University. (www.lancs.ac.uk/shm/dhr/profiles/102/)

Paul Thompson is Professor Emeritus in Sociology at the University of Essex and a Research Fellow at the Young Foundation. He is Founder-Editor of *Oral history* and Founder of the National Life Story Collection at the British Library. He is a pioneer of oral history in Europe and author of the international classic *The voice of the past* (Oxford University Press, 2000). His other books include *The Edwardians* (Weidenfeld and Nicolson, 1975, reprinted 2005), *Growing up in stepfamilies* (co-author) (Oxford University Press, 1998), and most recently, on migrants: *Jamaican hands across the Atlantic* (The

Young Foundation, 2006). His interview in the series on Pioneers of Qualitative Research can be found at www.esds.ac.uk/qualidata/pioneers/thompson.

Alan Walker, Professor of Social Policy and Social Gerontology at the University of Sheffield, has research interests across a broad field of social analysis and social policy. Publications include: *Social planning* (Blackwell, 1984); *The caring relationship* (co-authored) (Macmillan, 1989); *East Asian welfare regimes in transition* (co-edited) (The Policy Press, 2005); and *Social policy in ageing societies* (co-edited) (Palgrave, 2009). He currently directs the New Dynamics of Ageing Research Programme (www.newdynamics.group.shef.ac.uk) and the European Research Area in Ageing (www.era-age.group.shef.ac.uk). Active in the voluntary sector, he co-formed the Disability Alliance (with Peter Townsend) and is patron of the National Pensioners Convention and the Greater London Forum for Older People.

Carol Walker is Professor of Social Policy at the University of Lincoln. She has worked in the areas of poverty and social security, particularly the growth and impact of means-testing, both through research (*Managing poverty: The limits of social assistance*, Routledge, 1993) and as a voluntary welfare rights adviser. More recently her work has been in the area of learning disability, with particular reference to the ageing of this population and the challenge for services presented by the growing numbers of older family carers. She was co-author (with Alan Walker) of *Uncertain futures: People with learning difficulties and their ageing family carers* (Pavilion, 1997), and has subsequently been engaged in a number of projects designed to highlight and address this growing challenge for social care services. (www.lincoln.ac.uk/socialsciences/staff/879.asp)

Margaret Whitehead is the W.H. Duncan Professor of Public Health at the University of Liverpool, where she is also Head of the World Health Organization (WHO) Collaborating Centre for Policy Research on Social Determinants of Health. She has worked extensively on social inequalities in health over the past 30 years. Her books related to the above include: *The health divide*, published together with the seminal Black Report (Penguin Books, 1992); *Tackling inequalities in health: An agenda for action* (King's Fund, 1995) and *Challenging inequities in health: from ethics to action* (Oxford University Press, 2001). Her policy briefing documents for WHO with Göran Dahlgren – *Concepts and principles of equity and health* and *Policies and strategies to promote social equity in health* – have been translated into over 20 languages and won a number of awards.

Nicola Yeates is Professor of Social Policy at The Open University, UK. She has published extensively in the areas of globalisation, migration and social policy, and acted as advisor or consultant to the World Bank, UNICEF, UNRISD and UNESCO. She was section editor ('From welfare state to international welfare') of Walker et al (eds), *The Peter Townsend reader* (The Policy Press, 2010), co-editor (with Chris Holden) of *The Global Social Policy Reader* (The Policy Press, 2009) and editor of *Understanding Global Social Policy* (The Policy Press, 2008). She is a former Co-Editor of *Global Social Policy: An interdisciplinary journal of public policy and social development* (Sage) and is Vice-Chair of the UK Social Policy Association. (www.open.ac.uk/socialsciences/staff/people-profile. php?name=Nicola_Yeates)

ONE

The legacy of Peter Townsend

Adrian Sinfield, Alan Walker and Carol Walker

Introduction

This book aims to encourage and support a concerted campaign against poverty, inequality and social injustice and to provide a reasoned case for a new approach to social policy and politics to achieve this goal. It seeks to do so in the name of one of the 20th-century's great champions of social justice, Peter Townsend. Peter dedicated his professional life to fighting poverty, inequality and injustice, and this book stands as a tribute to that legacy, in partnership with *The Peter Townsend reader* (Walker et al, 2010). It is not intended to reflect back on the work of its central character in the style of a festschrift, but to apply Peter Townsend's analyses to the contemporary debates on different key aspects of social policy and to develop new ideas for achieving a more socially just society. Apart, for obvious reasons, from Chapter Two, those are the tasks that each contributor was set and they have all responded magnificently. Most were friends or colleagues of Peter's (hence the preference for his first name), and shared his mission, even if they disagreed on aspects of analysis or tactics, and where there were such disagreements, these are stated openly. However, the main focus is on current and likely future policy debates.

As well as being an indefatigable campaigner against poverty and injustice, Peter was an outstanding contributor to the social sciences, without question one of a handful of global academic giants of the 20th century. His academic reputation was built on a corpus that is awe-inspiring in both its breadth and quality. It is unusual enough, these days, for academics to span other fields, as Peter did in campaigning and politics, but to contribute seminal texts to so many diverse aspects of social policy is unheard of. Yet, in a career spanning six decades, this is exactly what he did with regard to ageing, disability, poverty, health inequalities, human rights and international social policy. Before the age of 40 he had laid the foundations of the sociology of ageing, or social gerontology, producing texts that are still regarded as classics. In their depth and quality Peter's books and articles are finely written models of empiricism, social analysis and policy relevance. Remarkably he maintained this impressive quality throughout the bulk of his massive production of books, reports and scientific papers: his publication list is nearly 600 items long.

This book uses this academic legacy as the foundation for addressing the present unacceptable levels of poverty and inequality and the need to shape new arguments and policies to combat them. In the rest of this chapter we review Peter's scientific and campaigning biography, in order to provide background to the ones that follow as well as some historical context for those encountering Peter's work for the first time. The chapter concludes with an overview of the rest of the book.

The life of 'a university teacher'

Peter was born in Middlesbrough on 6 April 1928. His grandmother became a key figure in his life as his parents separated before he was two and his mother, a singer and stage performer, often had to work away from home. In 1939 he gained a scholarship from elementary school to University College School, one of the few public schools to remain in London during the blitz, where he became captain of cricket and rugby and head boy, abolishing the school's cadet corps (Holman, 2001, p 129). These early years are examined in more detail in Chapter Two.

After two years of National Service, Peter read Moral Sciences (philosophy, logic, ethics and psychology) at St John's College, Cambridge, completing his BA in the two years then allowable under war and immediate postwar regulations. He spent a third year studying social anthropology, specialising in the West Indies. He was also active as a student journalist, editing *Varsity*. Indeed, Peter told Paul Thompson in an interview: "I thought I was going to be a journalist until I discovered social anthropology". These combined skills were invaluable. While he was at Cambridge he married Ruth Pearce and they had four children, Matthew, Adam, Christian and Ben.

In 1951 he undertook a postgraduate fellowship in sociology at the Free University of Berlin (there was then no sociology teaching at Cambridge). On his return he became Research Secretary of the Social Services Research Section at PEP (Political and Economic Planning – the forerunner of PSI, the Policy Studies Institute). His first pamphlet, 'Poverty – ten years after Beveridge' (1952), challenged both the complacent postwar assumption of success in reducing poverty and the conventional wisdom on the concept of poverty itself. Before it agreed to publish, the PEP Board required a debate – or confrontation – with Commander Lavers, the co-author with Seebohm Rowntree of the influential postwar study of York, who had protested at a draft rejecting their optimistic conclusions on poverty (Rowntree and Lavers, 1951). Another assignment on unemployment and poverty among Lancashire cotton workers provided Peter's first experience of interviewing, and did much to shape an understanding of poverty that had already begun with the experiences of his early years and his memories of the blitz (see Chapters Two and Three, this volume; also Townsend, 1958, 2009; Holman, 2001).

After two years Peter moved to the Institute of Community Studies in Bethnal Green in the East End of London, which had been founded by Michael Young to analyse social change in British society, 'a job the universities were not doing' (Townsend, 1958, p 108). Here he produced *The family life of old people* (1957; revised with theoretical postscript, 1963), interviewing 160 of the 200 people in the study and providing the photographs for the hardback edition. Rejecting stereotypes of older people's withdrawal from urban, industrial society, he demonstrated 'the relevance of kinship networks and relations within the extended family of three or four generations ... and showed how state policies conditioned the "success" or otherwise of ageing' (Townsend, 2008, p 7).

By this time Peter was already actively involved with the Labour Party and the Fabian Society. With Richard Titmuss, the first Professor of Social Administration in the UK, and Brian Abel-Smith, a social economist whom he had met in 1952, he began the work with Harold Wilson and Richard Crossman on the Labour Party's influential *National superannuation* (Labour Party, 1957) that eventually led to the more limited State Earnings-Related Pension Scheme (SERPS) of the 1970s. The original plan for state pensions that were both earnings-related and redistributive 'could have reduced poverty' in retirement 'while consolidating what might be called the psychology of investment in the national economy' (Townsend, 2008, p 8). The historian of occupational pensions, Leslie Hannah, says that 'the clearest public statement of the Titmuss group's blueprint' was provided by Peter and Brian Abel-Smith's Fabian pamphlet, *New pensions for the old* (Abel-Smith and Townsend, 1955; see Hannah, 1986, p 171, n 37).

In 1957 Peter became Research Fellow, and later Lecturer, at the Department of Social Administration and Science at the London School of Economics and Political Science (LSE), led by Richard Titmuss. Funded by the Nuffield Foundation, he began his study of institutional care of older people partly provoked by visiting an ex-workhouse in Stepney and published as *The last refuge* (1962a; revised in paperback, 1964). This included interviews, two weeks working as an attendant and his own photographs. He was already planning and searching for funding for a comparative study with British, Danish and US research teams – *Old people in three industrial societies* (Shanas et al, 1968) – one of the first comparative studies to attempt to use a common set of questions across three countries. He also continued his work on poverty, notably 'The meaning of poverty' (1962b), and began *The poor and the poorest* with his now academic colleague, Brian Abel-Smith – an early independent secondary analysis of official statistics on income and expenditure (Abel-Smith and Townsend, 1965).

In 1958 'A society for people' was Peter's contribution to *Conviction*, a widely discussed book of 'personal declarations' that vigorously challenged left-wing thinking at the time. This chapter and Brian Abel-Smith's 'Whose welfare state?' constituted a powerful critique of widespread complacency in the virtues and successes of the British welfare state. Peter's title identified the dominant theme, not just for that one chapter, but also for his whole working career. By the age of 30 he had very clearly set out the central questions he would continue to pose as a sociologist in social policy for the rest of his life. His concern for 'the cool test of evidence' in 'the analysis of social diversity', and the need to set it in context was accompanied by an insistence on a broad definition of structural social policy. His commitment to a 'faith in people', requiring a single 'standard of social value' for evaluating needs, policies and practice across society, led to rejection of inequalities and the institutions reinforcing them, including the many ways in which policies ordered and set people off from the rest of society.

In 1963 Peter was appointed the founding Professor of Sociology at the new University of Essex, one of its first two professorial appointments. The large department he created at Essex was unique in its multidisciplinary character: staff were drawn from not only sociology and social policy but also anthropology, social history, social psychology, geography, philosophy, the classics and the natural sciences. The excitements, pressures and challenges of establishing sociology in a new university were immense. The innovations that he introduced included much that we now take for granted in the social sciences. From the start he brought in 12-month postgraduate Master's taught courses with a research dissertation in the second part. It took longer negotiations to achieve the University's support for the admission of candidates without first degrees but other qualifications into postgraduate work: in the initial years each case had to be argued through the School and then the Senate with often considerable questioning. At undergraduate level there was active recruitment of mature students, and eventually their direct entry into the second year of the undergraduate degree, and innovations in teaching and more open forms of examination.

What Peter aimed to achieve and how he tackled it he later recalled in papers on the development of sociology at Essex. He starts to consider 'what a University of the people might begin to look like, whom it might recruit and what it might provide' (1990, p 13), giving a vivid sense of what he understood by 'sociology in practice'. That, he said, 'means using principles of social structure and other key concepts to advance an understanding of what a university should be about' (1990, p 4). This included an insistence on a less divisive setting with one single restaurant for students and staff and the rejection of a senior common room, although that fight was lost again many years later. He was very conscious of 'the crushing political domination of higher education by established class interests' (1990, p 3) and the threat that could 'distort and inhibit the intellectual and creative potential in all of us' (1990, p 2), recalling the resistance to many innovations in recruitment, selection, teaching and examining, even in somewhere that prided itself on being a 'new' university.

While Head of Department, Peter carried a full teaching load, writing out his lectures in full in longhand (one late-1970s lecture in text and tape in McDonough, 1978). He also maintained his research – in particular, working on the completion of the massive *Poverty in the UK*, most closely with Phil Holden, Dennis Marsden and Alan Walker. This became an enormous exercise as he had to take over analysis from Brian Abel-Smith when he became a government adviser. In those days the transfer of data from LSE to Essex computers was in itself greatly time-consuming and fraught with difficulties, especially with little research assistance. He also continued to be actively involved in debates about social policy in practice. The publication just before Christmas 1965 of *The poor and the poorest* (Abel-Smith and Townsend, 1965) gave an added impetus to the Child Poverty Action Group (CPAG) that they had helped to set up some nine months before. Four years later Townsend became Chair of CPAG, taking a very active role in its campaigning and lobbying for the next 20 years, until he was made Life President.

Even within the university Peter was involved in much more than teaching and research. In his 30 years of full-time university teaching he was Chair or Head of Department for 18 of them. The year of student demonstrations and challenge to academic and wider political complacency, 1968, he described as 'the most absorbing and exciting year of my university career' (2004, p 10). In 1973–74 Peter played a key role mediating with the Vice-Chancellor, the Deputy Chief Constable and the leader of the students' union to bring about an eventually peaceful end while many sociology and other staff stood for hours between the police and students who had blocked deliveries on the University supply road under the main campus. Tony Atkinson (2009) recalled, 'At a time when the University was trying to repress student demonstrations, Peter provided a locus of sanity. His qualities of wisdom and humanity were later recognised by his colleagues in his election as Pro-Vice-Chancellor, when he stood against the establishment candidate'. During his three years as Pro-Vice-Chancellor (Social) from 1975, Peter was responsible for the University's social facilities including all of its housing and the highly controversial issues of rents and the handling of arrears. He introduced the day nursery and special provision for students with disabilities. Ruth, his wife, had remained living in London, however, and Townsend's weekly commuting led to their drifting apart and eventual divorce. In 1977 he married Joy Skegg and they had one daughter, Lucy. In 1980 he met Jean Corston, then a Labour Party Regional Organiser, whom he fell "head over heels in love with". They married and remained devoted partners to the end of his life.

Disability

At Essex Peter extended his work on disability in *The last refuge*, initiating and directing *Put away*, a study of institutions for those then called 'mentally handicapped' (Lucianne Sawyer, completed by Pauline Morris, with a substantial foreword by Peter, 1969). His lecture on *The disabled in society* (1967b), setting out a sociological approach, was widely regarded as seminal, examining 'the imbalance between the impulses of the disabled towards integration into ordinary social and occupational life and the segregative practices of society.... The fundamental difficulty here for individuals and society is one of recognising diversity without ordering groups of people in superior and inferior social ranks' (1967b, in 1973, pp 109 and 126). In 1974 he established the Disability Alliance with Alan Walker, a campaigning organisation bringing together many large national charities and small self-help groups to argue the case for a comprehensive disability income to be paid regardless of how the disability was caused. Peter was closely involved in it, as Chair and then President, until he died. In 1976 the first edition of its annual *Disability rights handbook* was produced, primarily by Peter. It is now in its 35th edition.

Poverty: campaigning and research

CPAG took up much time, especially when Peter became involved in arguments over the Labour government's impact on child poverty before the 1970 General Election. Frank Field (1982, pp 32-3), then Director, recalled a meeting with the Minister Richard Crossman and civil servants, when Townsend 'quietly argued back against the torrent of abuse'. In 1976 he had to cope with the uproar over the way that Labour abandoned the introduction of child benefit and Field (1976) released an account based on the Cabinet minutes left outside his door. But Peter was also closely involved locally with Colchester CPAG. On many Saturday mornings during the mid-1970s he shared a shift on its welfare rights stall, listening to the experiences of people trying to cope with low or reduced incomes, and giving out advice and leaflets on social security and other issues, working with the editors of this book and many others.

In 1979 *Poverty in the United Kingdom* was published, a massive tome of over 1,200 pages that will long be the key reference on this topic. At a meeting in London, Peter had taken the manuscript back for a few hours while Allen Lane reconsidered their refusal to publish so many tables. It was very much to their credit that they recognised the strength of his arguments: the proceeds from both editions of this best-selling book were donated to campaigning charities while Peter devoted much energy and time to lecturing and lobbying on the evidence from the book 'of which he is most proud' (Holman, 2001, p 147).

Health inequalities

Peter had long been concerned about, and written on, the links between poverty and ill health: for example, 'the trend of growing inequality [in health] is securely established' (Townsend, 1974). His seminal contribution in this field was as a member of a small group set up by the Labour government in 1977, under the Chair of the previous Chief Scientist at the then Department of Health and Social Security, Sir Douglas Black. The Committee's explosive report, *Inequalities in health*, which became known as the Black Report, owed a huge amount to him. The official version was released simply as 250 copies of Xeroxed typescript, with a dismissive ministerial foreword just before a bank holiday weekend: this provoked Peter's media and campaigning skills (Townsend and Davidson, 1982). The impact across the world of that report and its subsequent versions has been immense.

In 1982 Peter moved to the Chair of Social Policy at the University of Bristol, where he continued to be actively involved inside and outside the university. He pursued his analyses of inequalities in health through city, rural and regional studies and developed further editions of *Inequalities in health* that became a standard part of education and training in Medicine, Nursing and the Social Sciences. The press launch at the Health Education Council of one edition, combining it with Margaret Whitehead's *The health divide*, was banned at the very last moment: the evening television news began with pictures of Peter and Sir Douglas Black walking down Oxford Street to hold an impromptu press conference above a record shop – another own goal for a Conservative government that insisted on referring to health 'variations', not 'inequalities' (Townsend et al, 1988).

International social policy

Peter's continuing work on poverty included a study of poverty and living standards in Greater London in the mid-1980s with over 3,000 interviews across the city and additionally in two contrasting boroughs (Townsend, with Corrigan and Kowarzik, 1987). There were increasingly technical exchanges with Amartya Sen on the nature of poverty and its relativity that were never satisfactorily resolved (in Walker et al, 2010, ch 18). It is a pity that their great talents were never combined in the mission to combat poverty that they both agreed on.

At Bristol Peter also began to build much more on earlier work on international and global issues relating to poverty and social policy. Working particularly closely with David Gordon, he produced a series of studies on the *The international analysis of poverty* (1993a), including their two co-edited books, *Breadline Europe* (Gordon and Townsend, 2000) and *World poverty* (Townsend and Gordon,

2002). In 1999 the University of Bristol recognised the scale of his contribution by establishing the Townsend Centre for International Poverty Research, dedicated to multidisciplinary research on poverty in both the industrialised and the developing world.

Peter increasingly took a global perspective towards poverty eradication, which recognised the deep-seated and global nature of unequal resource distribution and the need for international action. He developed a powerful case for what Nicola Yeates and Bob Deacon describe in their chapter (Chapter Thirteen) as 'development-oriented *global social planning* as a prerequisite to the establishment of an international welfare state' (their emphasis). This international perspective in campaigning against poverty and for universal provision in social policy was increasingly strengthened by a developing commitment to human rights that Conor Gearty discusses in Chapter Twelve.

His international work included consultancies to the United Nations (UN) and its constituent bodies. He was much influenced by his experiences on a visit to Georgia in 1994 and was particularly closely involved in the World Summit for Social Development in Copenhagen in 1995, working for clearer definitions of 'absolute' and 'overall' poverty. Subsequently he organised a 'statement by European social scientists', arguing for 'An international approach to the measurement and explanation of poverty' (Gordon and Townsend, 2000, pp 17-18). He was actively working right up until his death with the International Labour Organization (ILO) and UNICEF to improve the human rights of poor adults and children, including campaigning for a global child benefit as a means to reduce poverty (Townsend, 2009, ch 7).

Teacher and public intellectual

Although Peter officially retired from Bristol in 1993, he continued teaching there for five years. In 1998 he returned to LSE as Professor of International Social Policy until his death on 8 June 2009. He designed an MSc option, 'Child Rights, Child Poverty and Development', which he taught until his last year. He also helped establish the LSE Centre for the Study of Human Rights and was its

Acting Director in 2002 and then Chair of its Advisory Committee until 2007.

He was a deeply committed teacher – his autobiography was to be called 'The life of a university teacher'. In his later years his teaching seemed to gain a new edge as evidenced in the comments of many of his students on the LSE tribute website. His ideal working day ended with a trip two stops on the underground to Westminster to eat with his wife, Jean, then Labour MP for Bristol East, before continuing research in the House of Commons Library.

It is impossible to understand Peter's impact without recognising his extraordinary ability to pursue issues in many different ways. 'Research, teaching and participation in public affairs (for us the three always developed together)' – this is how David Donnison (1982, p 18) described working with Richard Titmuss, Brian Abel-Smith, Peter Townsend, Tony Lynes and others at LSE.

Peter had an extraordinary ability to be involved in so much and so effectively at one and the same time. He was 'a consummate juggler', with a remarkable sense of urgency and priority that gave a special edge to his commitment to creating 'a society for people' that informed all his work. 'Is it possible to check the "fairness" of a system by depending upon its principal beneficiaries for information about it?' (Townsend, 1976, in Walker et al, 2010, p 289).

> The aims and priorities of policy must be better formulated. Government ministers are inclined to speak ambiguously, and with different voices. Experts from universities and planning departments shrink too often from "the best view" and they don't like brawling with the public. Time given up to the discussion of the general conclusions that should be drawn from erudite evidence about needs and arguments with the public about priorities and procedures is time well-spent. (Townsend, 1975, p 350; originally in *The Times*, 1971)

He was particularly active through the Fabian Society that he joined during his National Service: he was on various committees and/ or an honorary officer for nearly 40 years. He wrote pamphlets, organised conferences and contributed to and edited books, especially evaluations of Labour in office (Townsend and Bosanquet, *Labour and inequality*, 1972; Bosanquet and Townsend, *Labour and equality*, 1980); on society and social policy principles (Townsend, 1967a, *Poverty, socialism and Labour in power*;Townsend, with others, 1968, *Social services for all?*) and the reform of the personal social services (Townsend, 1970, *The fifth social service*), all much read and discussed at a time when Fabian publications received close attention in public debate and in teaching and research. One of them particularly well illustrates Peter's vigorous and prominent engagement as a public intellectual. His Fabian lecture, *Poverty, socialism and Labour in power* (1967a), was 'critical of the first two years of Labour government', he said, making 'a call for "a more single-minded and large-scale strategy to achieve greater social equality"' (Townsend, 2008, p 14). It was trenchantly responded to in early 1968 by Richard Crossman, then Secretary of State for Social Services, who told Peter that he was under orders from the Prime Minister, Harold Wilson, to do so. The contrasting perspectives on Labour in power over 40 years ago make thought-provoking reading today (Townsend, 1967a; Crossman, 1967).

He was also directly involved with the Labour Party, serving on policy subcommittees for some 30 years, and with Labour governments, including research working parties into mental handicap and into inequalities in health. He maintained, as the work with the Fabians demonstrates, a critical distance. In 1968 he resigned over the introduction of higher fees for overseas students. In 1996 he judged the Labour Party as 'far too impressed with the development of international markets and the difficulties created for politicians in a single country who may want to adopt measures which modify the development of that market' (interview in *Times Higher Education Supplement*, 1996). As early as 1958, he had observed: 'You cannot live like a lord, and preach as a Socialist' (1958, p 117).

He was frequently seeking to stimulate public discussion, especially through the columns of the *New Statesman*, *New Society* and *Tribune*, and by organising and contributing to many debates, responding to Green Papers, giving advice to select committees and interviews with every form of media and participating in radio and television programmes. Particular contributions include his one-hour debate with Sir Keith Joseph, credited as Mrs Thatcher's guru, in the mid-1970s (well worth detailed analysis) and his chairing of the Channel 4 Poverty Commission in the mid-1990s (Holman, 2001, p 154). His high public visibility provoked one of Mrs Thatcher's Secretaries of State for Social Security to launch a particular attack on him in rejecting any scientific concept of poverty (Moore, 1989).

He was disinterested in merely academic contributions and certainly not driven by income: the proceeds from his best-selling *Poverty in the United Kingdom* were donated to campaigning charities. He was proud of his eight honorary doctorates but refused the highest civil honours available in the UK. He experienced many bitter disappointments because of the deeply entrenched vested interests opposing social justice in all societies and globally but, as he saw it, there was no choice. Being pigeonholed as 'committed' was a small price to pay for intellectual integrity and the necessary relentless pursuit of social justice.

Social policy

If social justice defined Peter's life, social policy was the means to achieve it. Throughout his career he argued that the subject could not be conceptualised or practised meaningfully outside of the context of sociology. At his Bristol retiral Peter reflected,

> Sociology and social policy I find difficult to separate. They cannot be separated for reasons of intellectual principle. I believe that professional ideology within universities and within sociology itself, and political ideology in general, obstruct the theoretical analysis of social policy and policy institutions as the primary instruments of social change. (1993b, p 3)

This was a challenge that both subjects have so far failed to respond to. As early as 1958 he had recognised that 'Mine is a Utopian view of the definition and scope of sociology' (in 2009, p 524) and in 1975 'A commitment to social policy ... was felt to be improper in a sociologist' (1975, p 1). His challenge to this view that narrowed social policy to 'welfare administration' was accompanied in both his teaching and research by a firm rejection of sociology as 'value-free' together with criticism of many sociological theories of social change as 'unduly optimistic and facile' (1975, p 1).

His definition of social policy was a sociological one that started with the basic question of what is 'social'. It stands apart from other contemporary and most succeeding ones as well:

> ... the underlying as well as the professed rationale by which social institutions and groups are used or brought into being to ensure social preservation or development. (Townsend, 1975, p 6)

To grasp the paradigm-changing potential of his contribution to social policy, it is necessary to bear in mind the dominant tradition of social administration that not only started with the welfare state as the embodiment of social policy but ended there as well. A 'simple, but crushingly cold and complacent phrase' is how he described the term, echoing his then mentor Richard Titmuss (Townsend, 1958, p 523). Thus his definitions of social policy topics, such as poverty and disability, were sociological definitions derived from first principles concerning the social construction of society rather than taking for granted the administrative categories handed down by welfare state agencies. His broad sociological conception of social policy contrasts starkly with the T.H. Marshall tradition of social policy being concerned only with government policies to promote welfare, which is still the mainstream today.

Drawing on and extending Titmuss's analysis, Peter argued that social policy is not limited only to government or state actions and encompasses both positive and negative intentions: 'Government policy is no more synonymous with social policy than government behaviour is synonymous with social behaviour' (Townsend, 1975, p 3). Thus his definition of social policy, quoted above, brings into play all social institutions and groups and includes the hidden intentions and ideologies as well as the open ones. Unfortunately he did not enlarge on this stunning insight and use it to build a new comprehensive conceptualisation of the social nature of social policy.

His commentary on the relationship between economic and social policy, however, does point to the potentially transcendent nature of his outline model of structural or 'societal' policy:

> It is impossible to have an economic policy which is not also a social policy.... The management of an economy is inseparable from its social effects ... social policy is embedded within economic policy.... Economic policy inevitably specifies support for those in society on whom economic development is believed to depend. Policies on investment, taxation and public expenditure show who it is the government believes are important and who are unimportant. (Townsend, 1981, pp 23-4)

Social development and social planning were essential complements to this vision of a comprehensive social policy. Social planning is 'that system of thought, preparation and organisation that maintains or changes existing, institutionalised policies' (Townsend, 1986, p 28). Peter's concern with social development, also cast in a broader than conventional framework, follows from his emphasis on social planning. Rather than seeing progress in terms of economic development he argued that all societies, not only the less developed ones, should prioritise social development.

It is not surprising that much of his later work engaged with the global and international context. The social quality initiative, which began in Europe and is flourishing in Asia, may be the signal of a breakthrough towards a comprehensive version of social policy in the Townsend mould (Beck et al, 1997, 2001; van der Maesen and Walker, 2011). Certainly Peter's work was influential at the start of this initiative and he was present to take part in its formal launch under the Dutch Presidency of the European Union (EU) in 1997. Peter himself remained optimistic:

> One day ... there will be one of those great leaps in scientific knowledge.... The future is with languages and statistics; and in the context of Europe and the international system. (1993b, p 3)

He emphasised repeatedly that, although it was an essential milestone in social development towards 'a society for people', the eradication of poverty was by no means sufficient to bring it about:

> The central choice in social policy lies ... between a national minimum and equality [and] the source of confusion in choosing between them is that the national minimum has been held to be the badge of equality. The problem for the future is to refuse to tolerate two standards of social value and apply one. (Townsend, 1958, p 529)

The potential of this radical and liberating conception of social policy and the related formulations of planning and development has not yet been taken forward and explored systematically, and that has been a major motivation for this book.

Why Townsend must be read

Our conviction is that Peter's work offers an essential reference point for anyone interested in the practical pursuit of social justice today. This is true not only for those working in the broad field encompassed by social policy but especially for them.

First of all, there is huge scope for the development of the concept of social policy based on the broad formulation he outlined. It is daunting undoubtedly, but the prize is a comprehensive societal or global societal approach that combines the social and economic, and possibly the ecological as well. On this basis we could begin to debate realistically social priorities and how to achieve them.

Second, social planning has been neglected in society as well as in the social sciences and, to some extent, has been 'ghettoised' as a matter for 'state socialist' or 'less developed' countries. Peter argued consistently against the ideological and structural constraints that inhibit social planning. If social justice is going to be achieved, it will not happen by accident: there must be a social plan.

Third, Peter demands to be read because he was the outstanding social policy figure of the second half of the 20th century. He provided, most consistently and originally, an unsurpassed number of fundamental insights into a broader range of key social policy topics than any comparable figure.

Fourth, he provides an inspirational model of what a public intellectual should be: one who uses the best possible scientific research and inquiry to contribute to public debates aimed at social change. For various reasons too few academics choose to adopt public profiles and thereby fail in one of the duties of intellectuals, especially those supported by public money. We argue in the conclusion (Chapter Fourteen) that, if the cause of social justice is to be advanced, this reluctance must be overcome.

Finally, Peter should be read because he was an outstandingly good writer, producing some of the best writing in social policy and sociology. Yet it is the content, more than the style, that is so compelling. You cannot read Peter without thinking about the sort of society we want to live in now and the role that social science can play in helping to create 'a society for people' today.

Overview of the book

The following chapters cover all of the major fields that Peter researched and campaigned in. The starting point is Peter himself and, in Chapter Two, Paul Thompson draws on over 17 hours of interviews conducted with Peter between 1997 and 1999. The chapter reveals clear links between Peter's childhood and education and the kind of sociologist he became and the work he undertook. The 'unusual coherence' in the interviews, which required only 'careful punctuation', is also indicative of Peter's incisive thinking and clarity of expression, which is reflected in the quality of his writing, which led to an example of his work being used in an exam for French students studying English. Through Peter's own words, the chapter 'highlights the combination of high research standards with empathy and passion which drove his work forwards'. This is a common thread that runs through the chapters in this book. For example, Ruth Lister, in Chapter Six refers to his tireless contribution to the campaign to end child poverty. Thompson draws attention to the influence of social anthropology on Peter's research method and on his development of new qualitative techniques, in, for example, *The family life of old people* and *The last refuge*, in which the lived experience of his research subjects is paramount. The mammoth fieldwork undertaken for *Poverty in the United Kingdom* required the development of new skills in the collection and analysis of data (at a time when computer analysis was in its very early stage). However, by including extensive quotes and case studies Peter ensured that the voices of the people were not buried by the statistics. It is this preoccupation with the lived experiences of groups who are marginalised by society, underpinned by his commitment to social justice, which forms the basis for the rest of the book.

These skills as a social researcher are illustrated in Chapter Three by Hilary Land and Hilary Rose, in which they demonstrate both the sociological and methodological significance of Peter's work. Women respondents outnumbered men in both *The family life of old people* and *The last refuge*. In both studies he meticulously illustrated everyday experiences but superimposed on 'his novelist's eye ... a passion for scientific analysis'. In his recognition of the importance of the role of women, and especially grandmothers, in these studies, Land and Rose acknowledge that he was a pioneer and ahead of his time, while being at the same time a man of his time. The revelations he made on both the 'family system of care' and the 'home economy' were unique, and illustrated the women's willingness to share their financial secrets with him: a feat not equalled by much modern research. The chapter goes on to trace some of the key demographic, social and economic features of the period and how official statistics – another of Peter's battles – gave over-simplified pictures both of family and work life. Many of the themes first revealed in *The family life of old people* and *The last refuge* – the nature of the family, the family versus the household, changes in marriage and childbearing, women and the labour market, institutional versus family care, social housing and the social services – informed the fieldwork for his major study of poverty, *Poverty in the UK*. Peter's work has been criticised for not sufficiently acknowledging issues of gender (Williams, 1989). However, Land and Rose argue that, while his research preceded the kind of gendered analysis which subsequent research might have included, he presents 'meticulous descriptions of the gendered division of care and the gendered secrets of money'.

Four chapters consider Peter's seminal contribution to the measurement, analysis and campaigns against poverty. In Chapter Four Tony Atkinson takes up Peter's campaign for a universal child benefit, started over 40 years ago. He makes the case for its retention, against the trend of policy on income-tested benefits increasingly favoured by British governments over the past 30 years, not only for its crucial role in addressing child poverty but 'above all ... [based] ... on a wider view of social justice, concerned to redistribute towards families with children and with gender equity'. This discussion is particularly pertinent given the proposal by the Coalition government to end child benefit for higher rate taxpayers announced in October 2010. This chapter also contains an implicit critique of economists for their failure to address important social issues. Jonathan Bradshaw, in Chapter Five, highlights three key elements in Peter's work on poverty: first, his role as the first person to conceptualise poverty as relative and his seminal influence in the adoption of this approach in most national and international definitions and measurements of poverty, with the notable exceptions of the US and The World Bank. Second, there is the need to treat 'resources' as being beyond solely income. In this, Peter was a pioneer of the use of social indicators to measure poverty, which, after initial criticism, is now a well-established method. Third, Peter considered poverty in the context of *groups*: an approach 'so obvious and simple but it was one of Peter's great contributions'. His campaigning work with CPAG and the Disability Alliance as well as on pensions can be linked to this. In examining Peter's contribution to the anti-child poverty cause, both as a social scientist and as a campaigner, in Chapter Six Ruth Lister stresses that 'he did not separate [child poverty] out from the wider issues of poverty and privilege as a discrete problem, which could be solved without addressing the underlying structures of inequality that maintain social injustice'. This lifelong belief is frequently demonstrated, for example, notably in *Poverty in the UK*, in which he attributes the experience of poverty by women and children to structural disadvantage, not to 'personal characteristics', up until his final work on international poverty (Townsend, 2009) which used the language of human rights to shift the debate from the personal failures of the poor to failures at the macro level of national governments and international organisations. Lister also sets out the major challenges which need to be addressed in the continuing fight to end child poverty. Most of these Peter raised in his lifetime but, despite some important progress, they remain, and, in the climate of austerity likely to pervade UK policy for the foreseeable future, will only become more urgent and more intense.

In Chapter Seven Carol Walker sets out the reasons for Peter's impassioned arguments against means tests and in favour of universalism: a campaign which began in the 1950s, in relation to the failures of the British social security system, and ended with his critique of The World Bank's promotion of selectivity in developing economies in his final book *Building decent societies*. Walker explores the reasons why means-tested benefits systems have consistently been favoured by governments despite, and sometimes because, they do not reach all those for whom they are intended. Peter criticised means tests for creating a hierarchy and a 'division of the population into first-class and second-class citizens' (Townsend, 1958, p 523), between the 'deserving' and the 'undeserving', between different categories of claimants and between claimants and taxpayers. Thus, Walker points out, the case for universalism is based on far more than its technical superiority to means-tested benefits – it has a crucial role to play in the promotion of social justice and solidarity (see also Chapters Four and Fourteen).

In Chapter Eight Danny Dorling picks up the theme of structural inequality by focusing not on the poor but on those who, through their high incomes and their wealth, have disproportionate power and influence: the rich. Dorling shows that the total wealth held by the top half of the population (excluding the top 1% which would make the comparison even less favourable) has consistently been between five and six times greater than that of the bottom half of the population. The top 1% hold riches eight times greater than the total wealth of the bottom 50% put together. This picture of gross inequality between the very rich and the rest and between the rich and the poor has widened not only nationally but also internationally. Furthermore, to a significant extent, the increasing wealth of the super-rich has been at the expense of greater poverty elsewhere. As Dorling points out, Peter's early work on income and wealth inequality was published in the 1970s, a period when Britain was most equal, or at least, relatively, least unequal. Today we live in a society that is grossly more unequal and in which 'our current excesses of wealth inequalities and the flaunting of wealth is obscene, damaging and indefensible'.

In Chapter Nine Margaret Whitehead considers health inequalities, an area in which Peter used 'his science and his art to press for more effective action'. Far from allowing the Conservative government at the time to bury the findings of the Black Report on health inequalities, which focused on the social determinants of health, his efforts turned it into a Penguin best-seller with three editions (1982, 1988 and 1992). Its message has spread internationally and health inequality is now recognised as a global issue. However, the report of the global Commission on Social Determinants of Health reveals that there is still the need to tackle many of the issues raised in the Black Report 30 years ago (CSDH, 2008). As well as considering the link between poverty and health, the chapter draws on Peter's work to discuss both the nature of the national and global challenges that remain.

In Chapter Ten Chris Phillipson assesses Peter's role as the 'founder in the UK of the sociology of ageing' and his influence on the development of critical gerontology. His article published in the first issue of *Ageing and Society* in 1981 represented a systematic attempt to provide a new theoretical framework for the study of ageing. As in his work on poverty and health inequality, Peter sought to shift the debate from individual approaches to the social processes that led to the structured dependency of people in later life. He highlights the ways the welfare state provided 'security' (albeit of a limited kind) in exchange for 'dependency' as older people were defined as a distinct category through retirement and the very structures of the welfare state. This background offered fertile territory for the 'crisis in ageing' that took hold from the 1980s and remains central to the contemporary political discourse on ageing. The chapter then goes on to consider three major issues for structured dependency theory and critical gerontology more generally: the transformation of retirement; the impact of privatisation and deregulation; and, finally, the influence of globalisation. Overall the chapter makes a powerful case for a break with the past and for research and policy on older people to be central to wider debates within social policy, sociology and political science.

In Chapter Eleven Carol Thomas looks at Peter's landmark contribution to the sociological understanding of disability and, through his campaigning, to the acceptance of disability rights as a focus for social policy and grass-roots campaigning. She examines the paradox of why someone who shared so many of its values and influenced many of its ideas is not celebrated in the academic discipline of disability studies. The UPIAS (Union of the Physically Impaired Against Segregation) and the Disability Alliance, with Peter in the lead, could not reach agreement 'on joining forces on the income question' despite agreeing on the social character of disability. Thomas presents the argument from the Disability Studies perspective; the counter argument from Alan Walker, active in the discussions at the time, has been put elsewhere (Walker et al, 2010, p 493). The chapter then assesses the extent to which the campaign for disability rights has been successful (not least through equality legislation and improved benefits). However, the Disability Studies movement feels that this has been at the expense of the cause itself, which has been usurped by the professionalisation of disability rights. Similarly, the positive strategy of independent living initiatives has been sabotaged by inadequate funding. Finally, the chapter considers recent research that confirms the messages behind the Disability Alliance campaign for a disability income, that, in the 21st century, families who experience disability are more likely to be poor and disability is more often found in poor families. The solutions, therefore, lie in addressing the social determinants discussed by Margaret Whitehead in Chapter Nine.

In his chapter Conor Gearty discusses how Peter embraced the framework of human rights to carry on his battles against poverty and in so doing wrested the term from the exclusive appropriation by lawyers. For Peter 'the core of human rights was ... to be found not in the courtroom but on the streets, in the souls of the activists and campaigners who were seeking by their human rights-inspired actions to change society for the better', echoing his earliest research of giving voice to the poor and the socially disadvantaged and excluded. The way human rights has been used to underpin action against poverty, Gearty argues, is a very good example of the energy outside the law that is to be found in this very contemporary way of doing human rights. He argues three propositions. First, the idea of human rights in general (and social rights in particular) is valuable, and such entitlements deserve not just to be protected but also to be respected and promoted. Second, the value of this notion of social rights lies principally in the political arena, this being the world in which the good that these words do can be best concretised, and nowhere more so than in poverty reduction. Third, the least effective way of securing social rights is by an over-concentration on the legal process with the constitutionalisation of such rights being an especial disaster wherever it occurs. Gearty makes an impassioned case for 'why care?' and then 'how should we care?'. This involves the building of alliances in the real world to achieve socially valuable outcomes and to keep it out of the courtroom. While it is kept in the social sphere, then it can unite diverse figures from within civil society, government, trade unions, the poor themselves and even the Pope!

In Chapter Thirteen Nicola Yeates and Bob Deacon address the innovativeness and breadth of coverage of Peter's work on global social policy, which was grounded in a materialist, globalist and sociological analysis of social policy. Again he is shown to be a man ahead of his time in addressing global issues four decades before global social policy became a recognised field of study. As has been implicit in many of the preceding chapters, Peter 'eschewed the conventional division between "domestic" and "overseas" social policy': he saw them not as opposites but as 'inseparable realms of analysis and action'. The chapter illustrates how the conventional distinctions between the 'national' and the 'international', challenged by Peter, become increasingly unsustainable as decisions in one country inevitably have ramifications for others. Peter's concerns (The World Bank) and hopes (UNICEF and ILO) for international agencies are also examined. Yeates and Deacon consider the several campaigns, in which Peter was a key player, including the 1995 UN Copenhagen Summit on Poverty and latterly the campaign for a 'global social floor', a topic covered in his last book. As the authors conclude, Peter left a legacy to the international community of social policy scholars, students, activists and reformers 'to catch up on and – crucially – to act upon'. At the end of the book (Chapter Fourteen) we pull together the main threads linking each of these chapters, summarise their contributions to a policy manifesto inspired by Peter and emphasise the main issues for research, teaching and campaigning intended to promote social justice.

References

Abel-Smith, B. (1958) 'Whose welfare state?', in N. Mackenzie (ed) *Conviction*, London: MacGibbon & Kee.

Abel-Smith, B. and Townsend, P. (1955) *New pensions for the old,* London: Fabian Society.

Abel-Smith, B. and Townsend, P. (1965) *The poor and the poorest*, London: Bell.

Atkinson, A.B. (2009) Contribution to LSE website, 'In memory of Professor Peter Townsend' (http://www2.lse.ac.uk/socialPolicy/newsandevents/PeterTownsendTribute.aspx).

Beck, W., van der Maesen, L. and Walker, A. (eds) (1997) *The social quality of Europe*, Bristol: The Policy Press.

Beck, W., van der Maesen, L., Thomese, F. and Walker, A. (eds) (2001) *Social quality: A vision for Europe*, The Hague: Kluwer International.

Bosanquet, N. and Townsend, P. (eds) (1980) *Labour and equality: A Fabian study of Labour in power 1974–79*, London: Heinemann.

Crossman, R. (1967) 'Socialism and planning', in Fabian Society, *Socialism and affluence*, London: Fabian Society, pp 70-93.

CSDH (Commission on Social Determinants of Health) (2008) *Closing the gap in a generation: Health equity through action on the social determinants of health*, Final report of CSDH, Geneva: World Health Organization.

Donnison, D. (1982) *The politics of poverty*, Oxford: Martin Robertson.

Field, F. (1976) 'Killing a commitment: the cabinet v the children', *New Society*, 17 June [reprinted 24 June].

Field, F. (1982) *Poverty and politics*, London: Heinemann.

Gordon, D. and Townsend, P. (eds) (2000) *Breadline Europe: The measurement of poverty*, Bristol: The Policy Press.

Hannah, L. (1986) *Inventing retirement: The development of occupational pensions in Britain*, Cambridge: Cambridge University Press.

Holman, R. (2001) *Champions for children*, Bristol: The Policy Press, Chapter Six, 'Peter Townsend'.

Labour Party (1957) *National superannuation*, London: Labour Party.

Marshall, G. (1989) *In praise of sociology*, London: Routledge, chapter 4 on Townsend (1979).

McDonough, J. (1978) *Listening to lectures: Sociology*, Oxford: Oxford University Press [text and tape].

Moore, J. (1989) 'The end of the line for poverty', Conservative Party Centre lecture, London, 11 May.

Rowntree, B.S. and Lavers, G.R. (1951) *Poverty and the welfare state: A third social survey of York dealing only with economic questions*, London: Longmans, Green.

Shanas, E., Townsend, P. et al (1968) *Old people in three industrial societies*, London: Routledge and Kegan Paul.

Townsend, P. (various dates) Personal diary extracts included in *Peter Townsend 1928–2009*, prepared for the Memorial Service Celebrating the Life of Peter Townsend, Bristol: The Policy Press.

Townsend, P. (1952) 'Poverty – ten years after Beveridge', *Planning*, no 344, London: Political and Economic Planning.

Townsend, P. (1957) *The family life of old people*, London: Routledge and Kegan Paul [abridged edition with postscript published in 1963 by Pelican Books, Penguin].

Townsend, P. (1958) 'A society for people', in N. Mackenzie (ed) *Conviction*, London: MacGibbon & Kee, pp 93-120 [shortened in *New Statesman*, 18 October, pp 523-30, reprinted in (2009) *Social Policy and Society*, vol 8, no 2, pp 147-58].

Townsend, P. (1962a) *The last refuge: A survey of residential institutions and homes for the aged in England and Wales*, London: Routledge and Kegan Paul [abridged edition published in 1964].

Townsend, P. (1962b) 'The meaning of poverty', *British Journal of Sociology*, vol 13, no 3, pp 210-27.

Townsend, P. (1967a) *Poverty, socialism and Labour in power*, Fabian Tract [also in Fabian Society, *Socialism and affluence*, London: Fabian Society, pp 39-69; and reprinted in Townsend, 1975, chapter 20].

Townsend, P. (1967b) *The disabled in society*, London: Greater London Association for the Disabled [reprinted in Townsend, 1973, chapter 7].

Townsend, P. (1969) 'Social planning for the mentally handicapped', Foreword to P. Morris, *Put away: A sociological study of institutions for the mentally handicapped*, London: Routledge and Kegan Paul [reprinted in Townsend, 1975, chapter 10].

Townsend, P. (1973) *The social minority*, London: Allen Lane.

Townsend, P. (1974) 'Inequality and the Health Service', *The Lancet*, 15 June, pp 1179-90.

Townsend, P. (1975) *Sociology and social policy*, London: Allen Lane.

Townsend, P. (1976) 'How the rich stay rich', *New Statesman*, 1 October, pp 341-3.

Townsend, P. (1979) *Poverty in the United Kingdom: A survey of household resources and standards of living*, London: Penguin Books and Allen Lane.

Townsend, P. (1981) 'Imprisoned in a casualty model of welfare', *Community Care*, 3 September, pp 22-5.

Townsend, P. (1986) 'Social planning: ideology and instruments', in P. Bean and D. Whynes (eds) *Barbara Wootton: Social science and public policy, Essays in her honour*, London: Tavistock, pp 19-39.

Townsend, P. (1990) 'Sociology in university practice: sociology and social policy at Essex 1964–1982', Unpublished [a 2004 revised and shortened version is available at www.essex.ac.uk/sociology/documents/TownsendonEssex.pdf].

Townsend, P. (1993a) *The international analysis of poverty*, Hemel Hempstead: Harvester Wheatsheaf.

Townsend, P. (1993b) *Retiral reflections*, Bristol: University of Bristol.

Townsend, P. (2008) *Peter Townsend: Complete list of publications 1948–2008*, London and Bristol: London School of Economics and Political Science and University of Bristol.

Townsend, P. (ed) (2009) *Building decent societies: Rethinking the role of social security in state building*, Geneva: International Labour Organization/ Palgrave Macmillan.

Townsend, P. and Bosanquet, N. (1972) *Labour and inequality*, London: Fabian Society.

Townsend, P. and Davidson, N. (eds) (1982) *Inequalities in health*, London: Penguin [edited version of 1980 report for Department of Health and Social Security by Sir Douglas Black, Jerry Morris, Cyril Smith and Peter Townsend].

Townsend, P. and Gordon, D. (eds) (2002) *World poverty: New policies to defeat an old enemy*, Bristol: The Policy Press.

Townsend, P. with Corrigan, P. and Kowarzik, U. (1987) *Poverty and labour in London*, London: Low Pay Unit.

Townsend, P., Whitehead, M. and Davidson, N. (eds) (1988) *Inequalities in health: The Black Report and the health divide*, London: Penguin [new edn revised and updated, 1992].

Townsend, P. with others (1968) *Social services for all?*, London: Fabian Society.

Townsend, P. with others (1970) *The fifth social service*, London: Fabian Society.

van der Maesen, L. and Walker, A. (eds) (2011) *Social quality: From theory to indicators*, Houndmills: Palgrave.

Walker, A., Gordon, D., Levitas, R., Phillimore, P., Phillipson, C., Salomon, M.E. and Yeates, N. (eds) (2010) *The Peter Townsend reader*, Bristol: The Policy Press.

Welshman, J. (2007) *From transmitted deprivation to social exclusion*, Bristol: The Policy Press, pp 192-9, 'Relative deprivation: Peter Townsend'.

Williams, F. (1989) *Social policy: A critical introduction*, Oxford: Polity Press.

TWO

The making of a pioneer researcher: reflections from Peter Townsend's life story

Paul Thompson

Peter Townsend was in no doubt as to how much of his development as a major researcher he owed to his direct personal social experience. 'Nowadays, I reflect a lot on the question of being an only child and what that means. It led, in part, to my enormous interest in family relations and extended family life, and the structure of families' (p 5),[1] he remarked early in the first session of the life story interview which I recorded with him. It seems too that he grew up with a family tradition of telling stories about the personal past. He said of his mother, 'You can tell she has been an enormous influence on me, because she has a huge sense of narrative and wit, and regales every audience with most extraordinarily pointed and revealing stories about past experience' (p 4).

With this life story interview, Peter's reflection on his own past was so thorough that we needed five long sessions to complete it, with altogether 17 hours recorded.[2] For each session he prepared thoughts on new themes, and throughout he continued to speak with such unusual coherence that it only needed careful punctuation to turn his oral discourse into a publishable form. This means that in this discussion I will be able, to an unusual extent, cite directly from the interview and so to give Peter's account of his development in his own voice.

Childhood roots: the extended family

Peter saw three fundamental influences as running through his childhood and early adulthood. The first, and the most precise, was the experience – at a time when divorce was very rare – of being 'the only child of a lone parent family' (p 2). Interestingly, he did not see being an only child as in itself a disadvantage: on the contrary, 'that isolation … the intensity of depending on your own resources, which I had to experience as an only child … I think those were very productively creative things, as far as I was concerned' (p 9). Still more significant, however, was the consequence of his parents' break-up for the family structure.

Born in 1928 in Middlesbrough, Peter had lived less than two years with both of his parents before his mother and father separated. His mother then moved in with his grandmother. 'My father, I'd better just say, very quickly, became a commercial traveller of a kind, for much of the rest of his life.... And I didn't have much to do with him' (p 4). Then at the age of four they moved to London. This was because his mother was a singer, in light opera and at clubs, and in the summer round the coastal seaside resorts, and in wartime to the armed forces. Inevitably this work frequently took her away from home, so Peter's main childhood carer was his grandmother. She became for him the symbol from his own childhood experience of what was to be a major theme in his later research, the strength of the extended family:

> My grandmother was the key figure in my early life, because she was left by her husband, with three small children, in a very tiny terraced house in Middlesbrough, and she took in washing, and she rented out the two rooms upstairs, in order to get by and make a living. She was also a woman who was a kind of midwife for the local area.... (p 2)
>
> She rang true as a bell all her life.... She worked for others all her life.... (p 10)
>
> My grandmother was perfect, an absolute rock, in terms of emotional solidity. (p 6)

Schooling

The second strand of crucial influences was through Peter's education, from his schooling through to the University of Cambridge. Here there is an important contrast between school influences, which were more about personal development, and university influences – to which we will need to return later – which were primarily intellectual.

From his schooling Peter singled out two teachers. With both, the underlying message was, be ambitious, you can do it! The first was 'dear Miss Sard' at Fleet Road Elementary School, through whose encouragement and influence he decided to apply for various secondary school scholarships. These included University College School, where he was successful, becoming a scholarship boy. Peter flourished at this school – 'I used to do very well at sport' – and eventually served for two years as head boy, and school captain. In the course of these later years at school he developed a close relationship with the school's headmaster, Cecil Walton, whom he describes as 'a colossal influence' (p 11).

> The really big influence was ... C.S. Walton.... He was a very young headmaster before the War, and he was there all through the War, when I was at that school (1939–46). He was an extraordinary example of a person who taught not only moral values, but a whole approach to keeping open doors on experiences. Let me give you one example....
>
> He devised the "Commando Exams", where, through the day, we had to indulge in a number of other activities, [rather] than all sitting in a quiet environment, writing papers.... We had to run a three-mile cross-country race around Hampstead Heath, and if we did it fast, we then had more time than everybody else to write the maths paper. But if we ran it too fast, and got so exhausted we were incapable of writing the maths paper. So we had to make some judgements about this.... And so the whole

idea was, how could you perform in the most trying experiences of life?...

He taught me to think about values in a very acute way.... I was two years Captain of the School, and I like to think there were one or two innovations which were my responsibility, like the abandonment of the University Cadet Corps.... We set up various charitable activities, raising money for ... the Royal National Institute for the Blind. (pp 10-11)

Another influence from Walton that proved much less lasting was Peter's phase of religious activism. He describes this as 'like a little rocket in the sky that went up' – and then quickly faded (p 13).

Class difference and social mixing

The third key influence from his earlier life, which grew stronger as Peter became older, was his direct experience of social class differences. He described himself as coming 'from a very mixed-class background in the North of England' (p 2), and referred later to 'this class mixture' (p 9) in his early childhood. This class mixture started within the family. While Peter's parents were both lower middle class – his mother with aspirations of rising to fame – his grandmother, his main carer, was thoroughly working class both in her occupations and her attitudes to life. Peter took from her an admiration of traditional working-class culture.

In later years Peter was repeatedly able to relate with equal ease to people at contrasting social levels. Thus at school, where he was one of only four scholarship boys in a sea of middle-class pupils, he rose to the top. While Peter lived in a cramped attic flat, his first wife Ruth, whom he met at 16 while snowballing on Hampstead Heath, was a comfortably housed dentist's daughter.

Beginning with the war, he also developed a knack for reaching out to neighbours:

The important thing was sociability ... even at the age of 13, I was an Air Raid Warden, and helped shovel one or two incendiaries off the rooftops of the street, and was sitting with mugs of tea, around the clock, into the night shift sometimes, with other people from the surrounding houses. And people met each other through hiding in air raid shelters. (p 9)

He recalled similar experiences after leaving school during National Service in the Army:

I remember vividly that, in the next two beds to me, when I was doing my compulsory training ... were Geordies, who were illiterate.... I wrote their love letters home to Newcastle. And, of course, that was a very vivid experience of ... [becoming] quite familiar with the problems that they had encountered and the lives they'd experienced, and this was, I think, one of the formative experiences in my life. (p 9)

Then at Cambridge his intellectual admiration for the university was severely tempered by his belief that its cultural richness was not being shared with the local working population:

There was the other Cambridge. And the two cities exist today, and could be, and should be brought together more than they are, in terms of more access on the part of local population to the University, for example.... So I had a love/hate relationship, because at the same time as I was absorbing all the benefits of Cambridge, I knew there were others who were denied them, and those others, sometimes, were only a few streets away. And it was at the apex of the class system.... (p 18)

However, after leaving Cambridge and returning to London with Ruth, Peter was able to enjoy neighbouring relationships in London that came close to his ideals. In 1953 Peter and Ruth bought the tail end of a lease on a 'terraced cottage' in Hampstead that they later bought outright. They took a particular pleasure in:

—

... living in an area where it was literally true that there were people of wealth as well as professional class, but also manual labourers, and newly arrived immigrants from the Caribbean. This we luxuriated in, in a way. We knew we were lucky that we had around us, within very short distances, people of every class and age....

We were seized by it, but also endeavoured to respond.... There were a number of neighbours in each class who we got to know extraordinarily well, and as a consequence, were aroused by political ill-treatment. I mean, this arose with an old man, ... who lived in appalling circumstances, who we visited repeatedly, got his shopping, and to our dismay, was found dead with his ginger cat on his chest. And the way in which that had happened was like touching a raw nerve....

So there was a sense in which our ordinary domestic and neighbourhood life fuelled our interest in politics, but also was fuelled by politics itself, with events outside which impinged on their lives. And that was a fantastic asset....

It's almost like you were living out the ideal of the extended family and involvement with neighbours that you also saw in Bethnal Green.

I think that was partly conscious.... (pp 198-200)

Retrospectively Peter did reflect that because he became so 'enthusiastic about working-class culture, and certainly I was aware of the strengths which survive to this day', he was 'less sensitive to ... certain oppressive qualities about extended family existence, for example, certain oppressive factors about male domination, in terms of gender' (p 47). But before considering his crucial early research experience in Bethnal Green, we need to briefly touch on two other phases before he became a researcher.

The Army and Cambridge: the encounter with social anthropology

It was through Army education courses that Peter first became interested in philosophy, and this led to his first contact with Bertrand Russell. From the Army he went on to the University of Cambridge (1948–51) where he read Moral Sciences. Among the academics he heard, he was 'totally inspired' by the packed weekly lectures of Bertrand Russell, then 'in his Emeritus years', and met him personally (pp 21-2). But a more lasting influence was his first encounter with social anthropology. The Cambridge Professor of Anthropology at this time was Meyer Fortes, who, after fieldwork with the Tallensi in Ghana, had become a leading structural functionalist, emphasising especially the role of the descent group in the extended family. Peter became inspired by an anthropological approach to research.

> The anthropological method was so important. That idea that you didn't do things in an aloof way, you didn't send out teams of juniors to collect your data, and you sat at home in comfortable situations and looked through your microscope and wrote your reports, but you actually lived, you engaged with that society. There was a sense of you not being able to write anything decent about the societies you were trying to describe and understand, unless you at least spent part of the time there, and better, lived among them. (p 22)
>
> One excitement was feeling that Western society, our own society, deserved investigation and illumination, just as much as some of the poorer societies, which the social anthropologists had researched so industriously. That was certainly true.
>
> And it seemed to me, very exciting, in the early days, where we developed this at the Institute of Community Studies. Because this was directly inspired by social anthropology, that the extended family in Britain, [that] people have with a wider family than just parents and young children ... and are often driven by needs and duties, and obligations, which extend far wider than just

the two generations of young or middle-aged parents with young children. (pp 31-2)

Political and economic planning: starting to interview

Between leaving Cambridge and reaching Bethnal Green, Peter served a research apprenticeship in London at Political and Economic Planning (PEPP) (1952–54). This was an independent cross-party research bureau. 'My job, really, was to produce research pamphlets.... The very first pamphlet I did was called *Poverty: Ten years after Beveridge*, and that actually appeared in 1952' (p 27). Peter aroused considerable contention by showing how, despite Labour's welfare measures, significant poverty continued to exist.

He followed this by a second investigation, this time based on his own fieldwork, on the impact of the recession on the cotton industry in Lancashire, where he 'visited the various Employment Exchanges, as they were then called, to talk to people in the queues, waiting for Unemployment Benefit' (p 27). Peter describes this as 'a very deep and absorbing experience', staying in local pubs where he was woken in the small hours 'with the clatter of the clogs on the cobbled streets', which he felt 'symbolised the collectiveness of working-class life'.

It was in this project that Peter for the first time undertook his own interviews. It seems that he had been given no training of any kind in how to interview. With his acute interest in others, his willingness to listen and to observe, Peter was soon to become an outstanding interviewer. But even for him it was a struggle at the start. As he recollected in his essay for *Conviction* of his first interview:

> The first address I had chosen at random proved to be a dark, terraced house and I remember the whitened doorstep and the tall chimneys rising above the roofs in the distance. Twice my courage failed me and I walked past without knocking.... [Eventually] I knocked hesitantly and when the door opened explained myself rather abjectly to a woman in her early twenties. She was friendly.... Somehow she patiently coached me through my interview, tactfully answering the really

—

36

important questions which it had not occurred to me to ask. (Townsend, 1958, pp 93-120) (p 105)

Michael Young and the Institute of Community Studies

From this first fieldwork project at PEP, Peter went directly on to his first major independent research study, on old people and the extended family, working for three years at the Institute of Community Studies (1954–57) with Michael Young. Peter was initially optimistic about his collaboration with another researcher who was then even more politically involved than he was himself, but their joint work proved to be a more short-lived cooperation than he had first hoped.

> I met Michael Young during this period, and he had been, first of all, ... working with the Labour Party on its manifesto [which Young was then drafting]. But then finding that his interests were other than in politics, and more in creative ideas for new organisations. And one of those organisations he had the bright idea about was launching the Institute of Community Studies. I was involved in that in the very early days, when we were just drawing up applications for research money.... And we all got excited about investigating the extended family, and that was what I thought was the major purpose of the Institute of Community Studies.
>
> When it turned out, three years afterwards, that it wasn't the major purpose, as I understood it, I was less attracted to doing it. I was also less attracted, because Michael and I had different views about writing up a text, and what it should convey, and he did me the service of editing my first drafts of the old people, enormously, but ... I'm afraid, I didn't accept a lot of the, as I saw it, journalese that he was attempting to impose. (pp 43-4)

—

The family life of old people: mixed methods

The family life of old people, which was published in 1957, is the first of Peter's two classic early works, largely directly based on his own fieldwork. In both this project and subsequently in *The last refuge* (1962) he brought together three methodological strands: the interview survey method of sociology, the participant observation method of anthropology and a memory for telling individual detail, which was one of Peter's unusual skills. 'It's evident from the way I'm reacting, and the benefit I've gained from social anthropology, that one method cannot possibly give you all the answers' (p 37). In addition, Peter took many photographs of social life in Bethnal Green, which he was disappointed were rejected by Routledge for the book. He felt that they could bring important insights:

> For example, a common feature of ordinary street life at the time, was not only the way in which people stood outside their doors, leaning on their brushes, and women with aprons on, scrubbing their steps, or cleaning their windows, talking to each other in neighbouring terraced houses, but there were the "little mothers" wheeling the pram, the "little mother'" being the eldest daughter in a family of, say, 12, 13: and because there was still, then, many families of three, four, five, six in them, it was quite common for the eldest daughter, reaching her teens, to then be a kind of mother substitute in certain key activities.... (pp 39–40)

Peter also persuaded 10 of his interviewees to keep diaries, although, perhaps surprisingly, he did not keep an ethnographic diary himself.

Random sampling and observing families

Peter describes how he devised a special, and then novel, method of sampling in a study of old people; he quickly moves on to the 'extraordinary differences' within the local working class, and then illustrates this extraordinarily vividly, by describing his meetings with two Bethnal Green families, remembered from 40 years previously.

It's important to do a random social survey.... In all the work that we did, we found that, by sampling, and then by interviewing, we were able to contribute something quite fresh to British knowledge about family life.

Now, sampling could be done in different ways. One way of doing it is simply taking a list of household addresses, and going to visit, say, every 20th house, or address. Another way is – which I found I had to do, I wanted to get hold of old people, and, of course, if you just went to houses or flats, you'd have two-thirds or three-quarters of them would be pointless, because there'd be no old person living there, and it would cost a lot and waste a lot of time and energy. So the way we tried to do it ... we worked through general practitioners' lists. I went to, I think it was eight or nine, or ten general practitioners, requested, courteously, access to their medical cards, and just simply went through at an appropriate interval, every 30th card, or whatever. And that's how I collected a list of 200 old people to go and see in Bethnal Green and surrounding streets.

But in a representative sample of that kind, you do get extraordinary differences across the continuum from one person to another. It's not just in age, it's also in family living.

At one extreme was, I think I can say their name now, the Agombars, who, as I remember it, they had nine or ten surviving sons and daughters, all living in the surrounding streets, with their children. The Agombars, there were one or two grandchildren around, and a few great-grandchildren around too, and they lived in a house with an aviary in the back garden – like Club Row. They had birds in cages, and every time I went to that house, and I made it my business to go to the house quite often, because it was so intriguing, I never caught the Agombars alone. There was always two, three, four, five, six other people among the family there, and usually sitting around, when I was there, at least, and getting mugs of tea, with sterilised milk, I may say, which I wasn't too partial about! And slabs of bread pudding, given from the oven. And we'd sit around, and the interview, I could never conduct it in a kind of formal, officious way. It was like a joking relationship, that, you know, everybody was making – had great mocking fun of almost every question I asked! So, interpretation, even though many of the responses were rich in information, they were often also rich in humour and witticisms....

But it was like meeting a tribe, because they had, literally, something like 80, 90, 100 related people in the surrounding streets, who had different relationships among and with each other. And there were then ... pub outings, where the whole extended family would go. I got to collect photographs from those who'd emigrated to America, joining up with those who'd been left behind in East London....

But at the other extreme from that couple, ... was a single woman, who was the only daughter of an only child, and she lived in a fourth floor room, it was hardly a flat, in a set of industrial dwellings.... She lived in this single room, ... her mother had died 30 years previously, so she'd apparently lived on her own, she'd had nothing to do with her father.... She was a spinster, she seemed to have no relative. And the only person she appeared to have anything to do with, was a neighbour, three or four doors along, who, perhaps, once a fortnight, rather than even once a week, exchanged words with her on the landing, about whether one or the other would get the other a bit of shopping....

That was the only real contact. This woman went to the local library to look at the newspaper, it was a bit of a routine ... she had a single iron-frame bed, and she had a mandolin under the bed, which she occasionally took out, and once she took it out and demonstrated to me this was one way in which she filled her time, and entertained herself.

But it was an extraordinarily restricted life, not very much more than what we would regard as the experience of imprisonment. And I deliberately went back several times to try to get to know her, and she enjoyed those visits, I know. But, particularly, I'll never forget going to see her on one Christmas Eve, I think I took her a box of biscuits, and the only sign of Christmas was a piece of Woolworth's wrapping paper, Christmas wrapping paper, stuck up over the mantelpiece. (pp 32-4)

Listening and giving voice

One of the major advantages which Peter saw in participant observation was that it 'communicates some sense of order into the way in which you can describe society and its relationships.... You may disagree with all the people you meet, if they think the most important thing in life is money, for example, you may think, "Oh God, I don't agree with that, because they plainly act otherwise". And then you get very interested in the question of opinion being different from, or supportive of, behaviour.... So what I'm saying is, to get back to it, participative observation allows you to get the kind of sense of priorities as people regard them' (pp 36-7).

For this reason he used 'an open interview schedule' and did not 'attach as much importance to pre-coding as some other people have since, but knew that ... it was important to record some of the things people said, and then to code accordingly, on the basis of what they told you, rather than just ask them for one of three or four selected alternatives, in a language which they couldn't do anything about, because you gave it to them' (pp 37-8).

Despite this view, although he did carry out some tape-recorded interviews, Peter, like most researchers of the 1950s, preferred to record through his own memory rather than directly through his interviewees' words. He felt that with taped recordings, when 'you've done a hundred interviews, and you've got 500 hours of tape, or

300 hours of tape, the problem of selection is fantastic, without taking up the same amount of time looking for the things that you wanted' (p 40). Hence he used an alternative form of recording interviews, in which his own interpretative framework immediately shaped the outcome:

> [This] was to try and write out, or type up each interview as it was done. Because not only was I able to remember certain things which I didn't have time to record, but also to select and order it in a way which would easily be accessible afterwards. Everybody knows that if you just simply type up a recording, not only is it almost impossible to read, but it all happens in a somewhat haphazard order, and it's very difficult finding the key themes that you then want to analyse and write up subsequently. And therefore, as we did, we rearranged the interview into a certain order.... If you describe the interview, you can simply follow the order you want, so that you can find it accessible for writing up purposes later on.... I also cut out bits from the typescript copy, which I put in particular envelopes for recovery when I got to those chapters. And I found that that's time saving too.... (p 38)

He was all the same clear of the need for the voices of individual interviewees to come across strongly when presenting the research in a book:

> I was struck by the fact that when people gave quotations in books, from interviews, much turns on how you weigh the importance of that, in terms of who said it, and in what circumstances, and what kind of person they were. And so I adopted the technique of feeling that it would be better to have fewer quotations, instead of having two or three lines every so often, let's say, to have a longer passage, but to precede that with three or four lines, which made it absolutely crystal clear to the

—

reader, what kind of person was saying this, from the sample that you'd interviewed....

I often had criticisms, subsequently, of this method, because people said, "Oh well, he just picked out those things he wanted to illustrate, and, therefore, he got very biased". But then, frankly, that's true of almost every method that you adopt, because you still have to select. It's true of statistical stuff, and we all know that even collecting quantitative answers about behaviour, rather than even opinion, the way the question is framed, the way it's pre-classified, the way it's coded, what you do about "don't knows", what you've done about people who haven't answered the questions in the first place, these are all highly significant questions, in terms of how you interpret the statistical results that you're presented with. (p 41)

London School of Economics and Political Science (LSE)

By the time that *The family life of old people* was completed, Peter had decided to change his working base to the London School of Economics and Political Science (LSE) (1957–63), and it was from here that he launched his second major project, for *The last refuge* (1962).

> I felt I could learn more, at that stage, from association with Richard Titmuss. That was undoubtedly true, and my great friend, Brian Abel-Smith had already joined him.... I got the chance to go to LSE as Research Fellow cum Lecturer. And it was I who applied for money, to go to LSE, under the auspices of the Nuffield Foundation, to write *The Last Refuge*, which was the book on old people's homes. (p 44)

He had a mixed view of the academic context at LSE:

—

43

At that time, going back to the late fifties, LSE was, undoubtedly, as a Department of Sociology, in the vanguard.... [Nevertheless] the Department of Sociology at LSE, I discovered, was really rather set in a narrow mould, and was somewhat impervious to the ways in which policy, social policy in particular, acted as a cause of structural changes..., and it seemed to be that they'd accepted part of the American distinction between sociology and social work.... They talked of it as an applied science....

[On the other hand] the Department of Social Science and Administration was beginning to bubble, if that's the right word, intellectually.... [It] got a new lease of life when Richard Titmuss was appointed in 1950, ... as the Head of the Department. It was ... a place which inspired me, and I chose to go and work as a kind of apprentice with Richard Titmuss. (pp 50-1)

The last refuge

Peter threw himself into the fieldwork, analysis and writing of *The last refuge*, essentially using a very similar methodological approach. He developed a special sampling method to deal with the very varying numbers of residents in different types of homes.'We varied the number of interviews according to size of Home, but in a way which was still, that would still allow us to, with the weighting, we could get back to representativeness in the first place' (p 79). With this sample Peter and his research team visited some 180 institutions and homes for old people, ranging from tiny private homes with only four residents to enormous institutions with over a thousand 'inmates'.

Once again his detailed memory for the details of that fieldwork was very striking, reflecting the intense degree to which he was directly involved. He focused, as before, on contrasts, this time between different types of homes. At one extreme were the worst small private homes:

On the whole, the most sensitive behaviour from staff and the most comfortable experiences of residents were to be found in the voluntary Homes.... But at the other extreme, which was more common, were the disastrous private Homes for four, six, eight people, where the people were sometimes in a state almost of terror of the Matron, who ruled the roost, who decided how everything happened. She had only three or four staff and she made profits, and her object was really to run the most profitable establishment. And you got sometimes people being fed almost nothing: trays in their rooms, they were even more isolated, they didn't really have any contact with each other. They had single rooms, yes, but it was almost like a small prison. (pp 77-8)

A more 'average case' would be a medium-sized local authority home, typically in a converted large house, often quite 'pleasant', but run in a very negative manner which made it:

Extraordinarily difficult for residents to have any local life ... or even having visitors.... They were rationed in terms of their personal possessions, and what articles they could, let's say, decorate the room with. Extraordinarily limited ... how lacking they were in ordinary home facilities – furnishings and cushions and carpets, and the availability of hot water bottles, and all the rest of it. And that was the average experience....

It was rather carrying over the impression of how it would be convenient for the staff to run something close to an army barracks.... There was a very dependent relationship imposed upon the elderly, by virtue of the fact that the staff expected to do things, they didn't expect residents to do much for themselves, even when, as I found, a number of them were reasonably active.... People were discouraged from entertaining in their own bedrooms.... So the sociability was very restricted....

Much more shocking were the very large institutions, with 500 to 1,000 'inmates', which then still housed about a quarter of all the people in the entire country who were living in residential homes. Peter had first encountered an old people's institution of this type, Southern Grove in Stepney, when still working on *The family life of old people* in Bethnal Green, and the experience of this visit was especially important in making him want to carry out more research on older people's homes:

> It was a very daunting experience. It was really quite a shocking experience.... One went into this rather gaunt, vast place, busy – there were the noises of trolleys being pushed backwards and forwards, there were stone passages, stone slabs on the floors. There was little carpeting anywhere, there were mainly bare boards in the dormitories and the dining rooms. People were congregated in large numbers. You went into a day room, as they were called, and there might be twenty, thirty, forty, fifty people on Windsor chairs – wooden chairs usually with arms – arranged around the walls, sometimes with an old, I think it was then still black and white, television, at a distance where, of course, many people without good sight couldn't possibly see it beyond about ten or twenty feet. They were often just sitting rocking themselves, rocking to and fro, very little conversation....
>
> Between the staff and the residents there was almost a class situation, a polarised situation, where the staff, even when they got relatively modest salaries, because they did, were able to exercise a kind of control over very weak and infirm people....
>
> It meant that the power of whether certain monies could be conferred, even to get cigarettes or sweets, or a birthday card for a grandchild, all of that, people knew they had to do what the management suggested was the right and proper thing....
>
> For there was a kind of attitude of tending to exaggerate the infirmities of the people inside these institutions,

on the part of staff. As part of their work it was more convenient, frankly, to shepherd people in regular lines through the bathroom, one after the other, than to give up the much greater amount of time to just sitting with an elderly person who would prefer to do it on their own.... The result of that was to stunt people's activities, and to reduce them to virtually nothing. (pp 75-6)

In the research project itself, Peter went further than just visiting such institutions. After making his usual thorough tour of the ex-workhouse at Newholme in Manchester he seized the chance of taking a few days work as a bathing attendant. His account of this experience is one of the most poignant passages in Peter's entire interview, highlighting the combination of high research standards with the empathy and passion that drove his work forwards:

I did the usual thing of going round every part of it.... [But] I stayed on several more days and used the opportunity, like the good social anthropologist, of being around when I wasn't expected to be.... I think that's an extraordinarily important thing for any research done in such places, that you have to allow for the ordinary events going on in these places, and not at times chosen for what I've described as royal visits or the hour or two set aside by the management for some research worker or dignitary to come looking around, to be satisfied that all is well....

I became an attendant, looking after the bathing of the old men. And I think what forced itself upon my consciousness was a number of things.

One was the extraordinarily kind of – abject passivity of some of these elderly men. It was almost as if the process of institutionalisation had forced upon them how to behave, and how to be, as it were, preserve their integrity only within.... And some of them communicated this by talking a bit about their past and about what their feelings were for their loved ones. Mostly it was feelings

—

of being bereft and being abandoned. But it was also feelings of being neglected by staff, who didn't want to know, and didn't have any forms of communication....

That aspect of their demeanour and their behaviour, I think, was terribly important, and although this was only the one experience, it obviously then got related by me to all kinds of other interviews I'd had across the country, and helped to inform those interviews and the experiences other people touched upon.

But it was also physically the problem of seeing these very thin, many thin characters, how gentle one had to be to get them into the bath, how careful one had to be in using one's elbow to make sure the water wasn't too hot, how little they had in the way of personal belongings, how the underpants they had, the kind of combinations they were wearing, sometimes had six, seven, eight, ten laundry marks, or tabs attached, which almost underlined their loss of identity. They were just numbers in an institution where they didn't even possess underpants of their own....

Some of them had enormous resources in terms of personality, but they'd turned it inwards, in order to – oh, I don't know – make sure that they got another slice of toast at breakfast. It was conforming. They knew that conformity was the order of the day. And that was a terrible fact to learn in a place where we were supposed to be indulgent towards the physically infirm and disabled.

It was the old tradition of the workhouse to be strict and punitive towards the undeserving poor, but to be indulgent towards the deserving poor. And this tradition was supposed to be maintained. What I was discovering was that the tradition of being indulgent towards the deserving poor was not put into effect, because the other side of the workhouse story, the punitive discipline, was really ruling the roost, because you can't have staff behaving in a polarised or contradictory way with different groups of residents. And this is the ultimate story to learn, that an institution can't be both disciplinarian and, let's say, indulgent. (pp 87-8)

Poverty in the United Kingdom **and after**

The last refuge marks the culmination of Peter's earlier research and thus of the story of his 'making' as a major pioneering social researcher. The book was based on research in which he was directly involved and was written solely by himself. Peter observed, 'It was the most single thing that I did' (p 86). And indeed, from its publication onwards there is an important shift in Peter's research activity. This was due more to practicalities than to belief. Thus for his subsequent work Peter remained convinced of the need for an anthropological dimension, and he certainly approached his growing international work in this spirit. But for his major British projects it became more a matter of principle than practice. From his arrival at Essex in 1963 as founding Professor of Sociology, and as co-founder and mainstay of pressure groups like the Child Poverty Action Group (CPAG) (from 1965) and the Disability Alliance (from 1973), he could never again deeply immerse himself in in-depth fieldwork.

The first stage of this change was the research 'plan of campaign' for *Poverty in the United Kingdom*. The research was begun in 1964 and culminated with the book's publication in 1979. This time the in-depth research was confined to the first phase and split thematically between different members of the team: Dennis Marsden on mothers as lone parents, Adrian Sinfield on the unemployed, John Veit-Wilson on the disabled and Hilary Land on large families. Certainly Dennis Marsden's *Mothers alone* (1969) and Hilary Land's *Large families in London* (1969) are in their own right classic vindications of the value of combining sociological and anthropological approaches, and of Peter's overall design for the poverty research. But when the main national poverty survey took place in 1967–68, in contrast to Peter's own earlier work it was based instead on a 'very elaborate questionnaire' (p 102). This meant that his independent contribution in writing up was primarily in interpreting the statistics of the survey.

As a result, Peter's originality in his later work took a very different direction. He became increasingly concerned with measurement and statistical interpretation. In his interview he emphasised three dimensions of this. The first, which went back to his Bethnal Green days, was how to deal with the cases of people missing from a random sample:

> I think that, generally speaking, people engaged in research tend to fall into the conventional trap of finding that if they get ten per cent, or 20 per cent refusals from people they are supposed to interview, this doesn't matter too much because the great majority have answered....
>
> But I learned, to my cost, first of all, really, in the studies of the elderly, that you were missing, even among a small percentage of refusals or non-contacts, people who really mattered when it came to generalisation.... There were clearly ... people who were confused, or so severely disabled, or sick on the particular days, that it was impossible to arrange an interview.... It was quite clear to me that we were under-estimating the severely disabled, and the especially mentally disabled among them. And therefore I tried to counterbalance that to a certain extent....
>
> I then formed the idea that it was important, certainly in the case of the elderly, and especially the very old, to get proxy interviews. In other words, I'd noticed that during interviews, and this is very rarely reported, there are others present as well as the informant who is the particular subject of the interview....
>
> That led me to believe that when we carry out interviews and sampling, it's extremely valuable to obtain as much information about those who are not present when you call at an address, or those who refuse, or, more likely, people who refuse on their behalf. Because it's usually, in those cases, a husband or a wife, or a mother or a father, or another relative who deters you from

meeting the informant you want to address. So I began to develop this idea....

In the end, I formulated a mini-questionnaire for the interviewer to complete. This obviously covered straightforward issues like the type of house, and the ownership of the house ... [but also] items which were clearly not controversial or disputable, or in any sense confidential, but just how many people were there, what kind of age they were and who lived at that address, and ... even to the extent of an occupation.... (pp 114-16)

The second new strand, which began with *The last refuge*, was the development of agreed standard measures, in the first instance, for individual incapacity for self-care:

There were people who, though disabled in a minor way, were effectively being shunted out of their homes, either because a landlord had his eyes on possible profit, and this is a very important point to make, or because relatives were finding it increasingly difficult to visit, perhaps because they were coming from a long distance.... So, what I'm trying to say is that, for a variety of reasons, the infirmity of some of the people admitted to residential homes was exaggerated, as it is today....

We gave a score – we covered a range of activities, and it wasn't just whether people could get up and down stairs, and get in and out of bed and wash and dress themselves, which is reasonably obvious, but it was also whether they could communicate in speech and hearing and writing, and how far their mobility could lead them, whether they could engage in conversation, and did so. Now, that was very important at the time....

And that measure of incapacity for self-care, I'm pleased to say, was taken up in all sorts of places, overseas as well as in this country. It led eventually to ... an international classification of disability. (pp 80-1)

The third new strand was computing. When Peter began research in the 1950s there were no computers available for researchers, and calculations were made with primitive physical devices such as punched cards. This was still true in the late 1960s, when the research for *Poverty in the United Kingdom* began. But the situation changed very rapidly in the 1970s, not least at Essex that at the time had the largest computer memory capacity in the British university system. Peter was fortunate to work in these early years of research computing with Phil Holden, who was 'extremely patient with me'. From that pioneering experimental experience Peter advised other researchers:

> But what I'm trying to say is that not only should you proceed like that in dynamic interchange with the programmer, if you don't do the programming yourself, but that you need to remember that you've got a third stage of being really creative with statistics.... Part of the point about doing any research is to discover things you weren't quite aware of beforehand. And that will mean, sometimes, devising, putting groups together that you hadn't anticipated, to explore the results of doing that, and looking at gender, for example, in a new way ... The first stage is the initial outline, the second stage is the follow-up into sub-categories, which is easy to understand. The third stage is the really creative stage where you are checking your conclusions, and that is a very important way of using statistics creatively, and ... using your statistics to the hilt. (pp 109-10)

Thus the methodological issues which directly concerned Peter in the research programme for *Poverty in the United Kingdom*, and indeed subsequently in his later phases as a researcher in general, were very different from those in his classic phase in the 1950s and 1960s, when his emphasis was much more on the need to get behind the figures to the direct personal experiences which underlay them. But the programme as a whole was much broader, closer to the multi-method approach that he had previously advocated. Peter moreover believed that the best outcomes in social research came from a team which was 'collaborative rather than directional', giving new team members 'opportunities to develop some of their own ideas', rather than one 'determined and directed by some figure on high' (pp 118-20).

Yet while Peter held the reins of his team loosely during the fieldwork research phase in the 1960s, he saw the great book in which the project resulted as primarily his own task. Two out of 28 chapters were written in collaboration with Dennis Marsden and Alan Walker, but the remainder by Peter alone. It was thus 'predominantly a single-handed production' (p 86). Given all his other teaching, administrative and campaigning activities at this time, writing the book proved a marathon task. With time his aims for it grew too. 'I moved from realizing that a book on poverty need not only be valuable immediately after the event, in the sense of being a contribution to contemporary discussion and analysis, but more as a kind of summing up of where a nation had reached, two-thirds of the way into a century, and what major structural things needed to be done' (p 112). Through the later 1970s he was writing four chapters of the book a year, and he finally finished it in 1978. Very different from his earlier classics, *Poverty in the United Kingdom* (1979) is a massive and masterly social overview.

Bristol and the return to LSE

Scarcely months after his book was out, Peter met Jean Corston, who was to become his third wife and, in 1982, left Essex for Bristol. 'I didn't want to leave Essex. I left purely because I fell in love, to be absolutely honest' (p 171). At Bristol he was Head of the Department of Social Policy until 1993, and then Emeritus. In 1999 the Townsend Centre for International Poverty Research was created. In 1998 he returned to LSE, where he taught until shortly before his death. During that time he served as Director of the Centre for the Study of Human Rights.

While at Bristol, as well as continuing his focus on the scientific measurement of poverty nationally, Peter focused on its international dimension (see Chapter Thirteen, this volume); he also revisited his earlier interest in the field of health which had culminated in his co-authorship of the Black Report on *Inequalities in health* (1980)

—

(see Chapter Nine, this volume). That report presented a statistical analysis of existing data, and its crucial new contribution was to show the extent to which illnesses were linked not just to genes and to individual behaviour but also to social context and structure.

> We were clear that there were individual behavioural items which led to earlier death, like if you were a heavy smoker, if you ate too much fat, if you lay about and didn't take exercise at all.... But what we showed, and which was the really original feature, was that however you weighed that up, it was still quite evident that material deprivation accounted for more than half the difference between rich and poor in the inequalities of death, and there was no getting away from that.
>
> It was quite clear to us, that a lot more research ought to be done on this entire matter of which elements of deprivation were even more significant to certain forms of ill-health. And there hasn't been enough follow-up of that in my view.

During his Bristol years Peter also developed, especially with Peter Phillimore and David Gordon, a microscopic approach to the links between ill health and social deprivation, through contrasting wards across a number of cities: Bristol especially, but also northern cities including his own birthplace, Middlesbrough. The studies were essentially statistical, and led to the Townsend Index of Deprivation, but he argued that they should have been parallelled by qualitative research: 'indeed, a qualitative study is absolutely necessary, not just as a complement, but as a necessary part of the investigation'.

In his later years, Peter became increasingly involved in the international dimension of poverty. He did work for UNESCO in Kenya and India in the 1980s. His major work, *The international analysis of poverty*, was published in 1993. Child poverty internationally – within a human rights context – became his primary focus after returning to LSE. Again, Peter's approach in this late work is primarily quantitative. On the other hand, he was keen to record his own direct impressions when visiting other cultures, and his ethnographic impressions show what an acutely perceptive social eye he still had in new situations. To take one instance, his visit for the United Nations (UN) to Georgia in 1994:

> Georgia was a highly civilised country, an admirable society in many different ways. I discovered that it had more doctors per thousand people than anywhere in the world, including the United States.... It had more musicians, architects, sculptors, artists, opera performances, than is easy to acknowledge.... And it is not only a beautiful country, with a highly developed and appreciative history, which is a living history and culture, but ... it had the most generous social security system that I know anywhere in the world....
>
> But in some of these former Soviet Union territories, you have two kinds of Mafia.... One was the former Soviet bosses of the Defence Ministry, in particular, and the Army, who were lining their pockets by using fleets of military lorries, to deliver petrol from Turkmenistan to street corners in Tbilisi, in plastic cans, sold at the most exorbitant prices they could command, and this is a very sort of insidious form of corruption which was almost one of the throwbacks to Soviet authoritarianism.
>
> The other Mafia was the get-rich-quick from Western markets, those who were selling Marlboro cigarettes and Coca Cola, or delivering them to kiosks. Because a lot of the shops were largely empty, because people couldn't afford to buy anything, and as a consequence of that, there were kind of entrepreneurial kiosks, and sales of goods and clothing, almost like our car boot sales, along the sides of the streets. And this Mafia, you could see them, I saw them two or three times in Tbilisi, of young men with machine guns thrown around their shoulders, zooming around in BMWs. Very few cars on the streets, I may say, but those cars often were in the hands of such figures, and these were, you know, very influential in the control of Tbilisi....

—

So these observations were important, but they included one which is worth recounting. I suddenly observed, going around the streets, that occasionally I saw one woman with a hen in a sack, under her arm, and strangely enough, I then saw another and another.... But I saw this three or four times, and then asked what it was. And I found this a very vivid and seminal story, that this old woman told the interpreter. [She] was taking it from place to place, she lived in a block of flats, and the only way in which she could subsist, live, day by day, was to find places where the hen could peck, so that it could lay an egg the following day. And she was, literally, going around, routinely, every day, doing this, to find places where the hen, and she would look after, watch the hen, sit down and watch the hen for a few minutes, this place and that place, while the hen pecked around.

Now you have to kind of back this up by pointing out that because of inflation, pensions that might have, in our circumstances, let's say, would be equivalent to £50 a week, in UK comparisons, were now worth 50 pence per week, and pensioners were starving, and they had to grow something, or they had to sell something, or they had to depend on relatives out in the country growing something, in order to survive....

Now, anyone coming along, as I did, into that situation, was liable to say, "Hey, look, you've got enormous human assets and resources here. You have a framework of delivery. For God's sake, in the transition period, do what you can to prop it up. Pour in some minimal resources, in order to finance primary health care, in order to finance the elderly, to at least getting a tiny element of subsistence, and boost their pension amount, even if it's grants from abroad, which are rapidly going to diminish. Or see how urgent it is to introduce a new tax system, or what are the methods of getting hold of those who were exploiting the current conditions and lining their pockets. What could you do?"

These questions were not being addressed at all. The idea that was prevailing on the part of the IMF and World Bank delegations, and I met one delegation and had a stormy row with them, but their attitude was really that Communism had to be smashed, that nothing of the past was worth preserving. They adopted an extreme Friedmanite position of neo-monetary principles. Safety nets, even, had no part to play. And they had no ideas about the public sector, they only wanted to see more privatisation. And this was the story. (pp 147-9)

In conclusion, drawing on his own words, I have tried to pick out the main elements both in Peter Townsend's evolution as a pioneering researcher, and also in how his emphasis later changed. But the early and the later Peter Townsend have in common not only a prodigious research energy and prolific productivity, but also a continuing creativity in using research methods to the utmost in campaigning for a more equal, more caring and more just society.

Notes

[1] The page references given here refer to the full transcript of Peter Townsend's interview with Paul Thompson in the UK Data Archive at the University of Essex (for further details see note 2 below).

[2] The 'Pioneers of Social Research' interviewing programme was initiated in 1997 with Peter Townsend's interview with Paul Thompson, the first Director of Qualidata. The original intention was to record the life stories of researchers whose research data was being archived through Qualidata and the UK Data Archive, but the scope was later broadened to include other major British social researchers who at least partly used qualitative methods. Over 20 researchers have now been interviewed, and these include Michael Young and Dennis Marsden among those closely associated with Peter Townsend. A new wave of interviews is currently in progress with support from the British Academy.

The interviews are available to researchers either through Qualidata at the University of Essex or through the British Library Sound Archive.

—

References

Land, H. (1969) *Large families in London: A study of 86 families in London*, London: Bell.

Marsden, D. (1969) *Mothers alone: Poverty and the fatherless family*, London: Penguin Books.

Townsend, P. (1958) 'A society for people', in Norman Mackenzie (ed) *Conviction*, London: McGibbon & Kee, pp 98-120.

THREE

Peter Townsend, a man ahead of his time: re-reading *The family life of old people* and *The last refuge*

Hilary Land and Hilary Rose

In this chapter we explore two of Peter Townsend's pioneering studies: first, *The family life of old people* (1957), an ethnography of Bethnal Green, and second, *The last refuge* (1962), a nationwide study of old people living in residential homes. We suggest that these key texts laid the foundations of his entire opus.

The financial Dunkirk

Before describing these studies in more detail, and discussing their relevance for contemporary research and policy agendas, it is important to place them in context, opening with the immense challenge Britain faced in 1945. John Maynard Keynes had laid a paper before the Cabinet titled *The financial Dunkirk*, the title all too clearly setting out the scale of the problem (Toye, 2004). The national coffers were empty and an ill-fed, ill-clothed and ill-housed people believed that the hard-won victory would now bring prosperity or at least a job and a roof over their heads. Recovery, despite huge loans from the US, was desperately slow. David Kynaston calls the period from 1945 to 1951 *Austerity Britain* (2007). But while everyday life was indeed austere, his title underplays the achievement of the Attlee government in laying, however unevenly, the foundations of the welfare state. Its policy of redistribution of wealth and income was for Old Labour the beginning of the long march to a more just society.

Nonetheless the Labour government fell in 1951, punished for their failure to build enough council housing. When the Conservative manifesto pledged to build 300,000 homes a year, and achieved its target, Prime Minister Macmillan was able to declare triumphantly, 'You've never had it so good'. However, Labour's redistributive policies were sufficiently well entrenched and popular that the Conservative government could only begin to reverse this in the mid-1950s. Despite the struggle, with Peter among the leaders in the defence of the poor from the 1950s to his death in 2009, it has taken a combination of Conservative and New Labour governments to turn Britain into a massively unequal society in which the difference in expectation of life between the poor and the rich is now a full 10 years.

The 1950s: both young social sciences and social scientists

To return to the 1950s, the social sciences and most social scientists were both young and confident, committed to building a research-based knowledge of society to replace the armchair speculation so complacently in place among the upper reaches of the civil service. For many, the new social sciences would also make possible both the objective evaluation of social policy and proposals for evidence-based reforms (see Townsend, 1986, on Wootton, 1950). They would also document needs hitherto invisible. *The family life of old people* (henceforth *Family life*) and Peter Willmott and Michael Young's *Family and kinship in East London* (1957) were central texts of their twin project of advancing social science and social justice. Published in 1957 and conceived of as related studies, they became two of the classic texts produced by the small but prolific group of researchers based at the Institute of Community Studies in Bethnal Green.

They were not alone. In the light of his monumental study of social policy during the war years, modestly titled *Problems of social policy* (Titmuss, 1950), Richard Titmuss had been appointed to the first Chair in Social Administration at the London School of Economics and Political Science (LSE) in 1950. He was gathering an equally committed group of gifted social and economic researchers around him, among them the economist Brian Abel-Smith who was later to work so fruitfully with Peter on the hugely influential study *The poor and the poorest* (Abel-Smith and Townsend, 1965).

Sociology of the family: the challenge

The introduction to *Family life* makes it very clear that Peter understood the scale of the academic challenge. In the mid-1950s a researcher entering the sociology of the family in industrial society had a choice – either to embrace or to challenge the structural functionalist framework of Talcott Parsons whose theoretical stance dominated US sociology. Parsons (1943) argued that the family within urban industrial society shared in the helter-skelter of constantly changing new forms of solidarity, and was no longer able to provide the stable support of the traditional extended family. Instead he saw the structurally isolated conjugal family as functionally necessary to industrial society. This found pragmatic echo in the concerns of the UK senior civil servants who fretted about the family's inability to carry the 'burden' of care, not least that of the older generation. In Prime Minister Cameron's rhetoric of the 'broken society', we hear the longing for this 'burden' to be picked up by the family, or, as is clear from *Family life*, by women, above all grandmothers. In his book published just prior to joining Cameron's first Cabinet, Willetts (2010) documents the extensive care and support that the older generation, and grandmothers in particular, currently give the younger generations, but does not allow this to deflect from the book's main theme which portrays the older generation placing growing and unfair burdens on the young.

Titmuss agreed that industrialisation challenged the family. 'Its responsibilities have grown; it has been placed in more situations of divided loyalties and conflicting values; it has been forced to choose between kinship and economic progress; and it has been constantly subjected to the gales of creative instability' (Titmuss, 1958, p 117). Like the researchers at the Institute, Titmuss saw the role of social policy as supporting and enabling families in such turbulent times.

Within mainstream British sociology, relatively uninfluenced by Parsons, the sociology of the family was seen as 'a small, low status sub-field of sociology' (Davidoff et al, 1999). Elizabeth Bott's study of the conjugal roles of married couples (1957), although Parsonian, was treated as something of an exception. Townsend's challenge to Parsons stemmed from his training in anthropology where kin and generation are central: thus the family was to be tested through empirical research, not by its consistency within structural functionalist theory.

Quite exceptionally for sociological studies at this time, women were in the foreground of both his studies. Women outlived men on average; women respondents outnumbered men in *Family life* as well as among the very old residents in *The last refuge*. They also formed the vast majority of the staff of residential homes. In other words, it is difficult from the perspective of the early 21st century to grasp quite how exceptional and pioneering this book was.

The research focus on kin and generation was perhaps helped in that Peter, like Willmott and Young, came from a single-parent family, so had a sharper sense of the importance of the older generation, particularly grandmothers, in family life. It is therefore appropriate that *Family life* is dedicated to his mother and grandmother. Peter's mother was divorced, a singer, so constantly travelling; her mother lived with them taking care of Peter, so making her daughter's employment possible (see Chapter Two, this volume). As *Family life* constantly reminds us, shared care with a grandmother was, unless she had her child adopted, a common solution for lone mothers. Peter's closeness to his own grandmother, together with the uncertainties of the family income, meant that he knew precarious living from the inside, a huge asset to the man who was to become one of the most internationally famous poverty researchers.

In *Family life* we meet Peter as the ethnographer, at ease, whether sitting in a warm kitchen full of children, drinking tea or in a single dilapidated room, always listening or trying to listen over the commotion, watching and writing his notes. His meticulous descriptions of people's clothing, movements, facial expressions and gestures enrich the spoken word. In a review of *Family life* in the *New Statesman*, Richard Crossman, who a decade later was to become the first Secretary of State at the newly created Department of Health and Social Security in the Wilson government and was to clash bitterly with Peter over the government's failure to tackle poverty among pensioners, wrote: 'Superb study.... Here is a work of social science, which is also, in its way, a work of art. A novelist's eye for detail and power of description is nicely balanced by a passion for scientific analysis' (Crossman, 1958, p 340, cited on the back cover of the Pelican paperback edition of *Family life*, 1963).

There are events which tell us about the ethnographer as friend when he takes a tin of biscuits on Christmas Eve to a desolate elderly woman. With eyes made critical by feminism, we see both the ethnographer's friendship but also wonder about how his wife Ruth was managing the Christmas preparations, with Peter's grandmother sitting with a crocheted rug over her knees, the four boys under her feet, perhaps one sent round to take a cup of tea to their neighbour, old Percy.

Both *Family life* and *The last refuge* set out to challenge the view, still widely held, that older people are a 'burden' and therefore 'dependent'. Noting that older people 'not only receive all kinds of services, but perform many in return' (Townsend, 1962, p 3), Peter describes the reciprocal nature of care. His accounts of grandmothers in *Family life* who, even when severely disabled by problems of both health and age, are nonetheless still making dinner for employed sons and daughters, still bathing the baby, still minding the little ones, show both his precision and tenderness of observation. By making care in the family visible he, without the concept of gender, speaks of what was yet to become an issue, which second wave feminists took up again in the 1970s. Then lacking the crucial concept of gender, his work remains as providing rich ethnographic data. In his recognition of women, especially grandmothers, Peter was a pioneer and ahead of his time, but he was also a man of his time. For Peter, sharing and reproducing the ideology of the 1950s, care was what women 'naturally' did – as wives, daughters and mothers as well as granddaughters, sisters, aunts or nieces. However, it is a criticism of second wave feminism that we – especially those of us in social policy – failed to plunder his text for these meticulous descriptions of the gendered division of care and the gendered secrets of money.

The family life of old people

In *Family life* Peter is interested both in the distribution of caregiving within the family, which he speaks of as the 'family system of care', and also the 'home economy', namely how money came into the house and who spent it and on what. Thus while he, the 'breadwinner', was in work, she, the 'housewife', saw the money he gave her as 'her wage' and frequently shared with him the view that it was neither necessary nor right that she should know how much he earned. Conversely, money given to her by their children for their board, once they were at work, was similarly a matter for her, not him. Sons might give their mother money, but typically when their wife was not looking. Peter sensed and adapted his fieldwork to the micro politics of the family and its secrets around money, gathering much of the data by interviewing the older couple separately. Trusting Peter, each would separately share their secrets with him. Given that the concept of gender did not exist until the feminist movement, he is unable to problematise the secrets of the care system or the home economy in a way that would have sensitised subsequent researchers. Even today the government's Family Resources Survey is still unable to match his methodological sophistication.

Only the breadwinner was likely to have access to discretionary and personal money. Responsible for paying the rent and other regular household outgoings, the women had 'little scope for manoeuvre in their budgeting' (Townsend, 1957, p 69). After retirement some, particularly men, found part-time but less skilled and worse paid jobs. But for all, incomes drastically fell, managing became hard and the men missed the companionship of work and in leisure, the ability to stand a round of drinks. It was the loss of this that was one of the reasons that for men retirement and the resulting drop in income was 'a tragic event' (Townsend, 1957, p 137).

A few shared the loss of income shoulder to shoulder with their wives. However, as his pension arrived, the attitudes of husbands and wives to income subtly changed. As long as a man was of working age any social security benefit, including the additions for a dependent wife or a child, was paid to him when he was sick or unemployed. This is a reminder that the male breadwinner model was not only a way of sustaining a particular gender division of labour in the home, but that it also served a public purpose. The responsibility for the maintenance of a dependent wife and children was believed to be a way of sustaining male work incentives. As a leading female member of the Charity Organization Society and the Royal Commission on the Poor Laws wrote:

> Nothing but the combined rights and responsibilities of family life will ever rouse the average man to his full degree of efficiency, and to induce in him to continue working after he has earned sufficient to meet his own personal needs. (Bosanquet, 1906/1915, p 279)

Once a man was too old to work this was no longer necessary, and from the introduction of state old age pensions in 1908 husbands and wives were paid their pensions separately. This practice continued even when the wife's entitlement was based on her husband's National Insurance contributions. Peter describes how the couples capable of walking went to the Post Office, each with their own pension book, and collected their pension individually (Townsend, 1957, p 71). Although thereby demonstrating that having their own money was important to women, he does not reflect on the light this might throw on what he called the 'difficult and tangled subject' of the economic relationship between husbands and wives.

The family system of both care and the home economy was divided along gender lines: for the woman first obligations were to her husband, her children and her own parents, and yet she was called on to undertake her husband's obligations as well, simply because he had to be at work during the day. This did not change after his retirement. The care of children, disabled and frail elderly people, as well as of able-bodied husbands, remained the moral responsibility of women – as mothers and daughters and, above all, as wives. Further a wife was expected by her husband to give nearly all her attention to home and family. He looked indulgently on her gossiping but did not like her being in the homes of others. He also expected her undivided attention himself when he came home, and would rarely answer the door if any woman, whether wife, daughter or sister, was in the house. Unlike most social researchers Peter noted the differences between the attitudes and practices of husbands and wives towards each other, and also of sons and daughters towards their mothers and fathers. His conclusion was unambiguous:

—

While some men performed valuable domestic and
personal services for their families, this was usually when
female relatives were not available. Men, young as well as
old, rarely occupied a vital role in family care. The system
was chiefly organized around female relatives. At its focal
point stood the old woman. (Townsend, 1957, p 53)

Women's heavy involvement in providing care and domestic services
for their families did not prevent them from taking paid employment.
Indeed, to Peter's surprise, women who belonged to three-generation
localised families (as 58% did), found it easier to take part-time
employment than those with few or no relatives (Townsend, 1957,
p 149). This certainly did not match the stereotype. Altogether 58%
of his respondents in Bethnal Green had been in full-time or part-
time employment themselves in later life, with 39% retiring after the
age of 50 and nearly a quarter retiring between the ages of 61 and
74 (Townsend, 1957, p 148). Peter describes how, together with their
daughters, they managed childcare and the demands of employment:

A woman and her married daughters living nearby were
able to organise domestic work and the care of children
in such a way that each of them was able to maintain a
part-time job. The grandmother went off to work as an
office cleaner at six in the morning returning at 10am.
She then had the care of three grandchildren while two
married daughters went out to work, one as a waitress
and the other as a part-time newspaper wrapper. The
daughters did her shopping on the way home from
work.... (Townsend, 1957, pp 149-50)

The fact that the work the wife did 'was well within her capacities
because it resembled her work at home' (Townsend, 1957, p 150)
made it easier to undervalue it. Just as important, the personal
significance to husbands and wives of paid work was different:

Women thought of a job as largely a means of
supplementing their housekeeping money and meeting

other people and not, as men often did, as the main means
of securing enough money, prestige and associations to
justify life itself. (Townsend, 1957, p 150)

The development of part-time employment for married women
reinforced the prevailing ideology that women's earnings were 'pin-
money', therefore not essential for meeting the basic needs of the
household. Even Peter, having recorded the prodigious hours worked
by women, whether mothers or grandmothers, fails to compare the
total hours worked by the genders or to reflect on the significance
of the difference – a matter which second wave feminism was later
to raise angrily.

The family of official statistics

By contrast with Peter's work, the official statistics looking at families
through the lens of the nuclear family gave over-simplified pictures
both of family and work life. The 'nuclear family', namely a married
couple with children in which the husband was head of household,
dominated the pictures of family life, whether these were based on
official statistics or sociological studies. The definition of head of
household used by the Census, by giving precedence to full-time
over part-time, male over female, and older over younger workers,
ensured that the majority of recorded breadwinners were male. The
concept of the family used by the Census and other government
surveys stated that: 'In general families cannot span two generations,
that is grandparents and grandchildren cannot belong to the same
family' (OPCS, 1973, p 135).

Too often family was equated with household, thus ignoring the
ways in which families spill out of and across households. Peter
commented half a century ago: 'While necessary for much social
analysis, a working definition of "household" that is applied too
rigidly may cause part of the truth about people's home relationships
to be missed or misrepresented' (Townsend, 1957, p 24). He was
looking at older people, but it applied to younger generations too.
When the Finer Committee, appointed at the end of the 1960s to
examine the circumstances of lone parents, attempted to estimate

their number, they discovered that the 1966 Census figures had under-estimated their numbers by half. At this time most unmarried mothers lived with their parent(s) and were therefore 'hidden'. Their own mothers provided childcare so (like Peter's) they were able to take full-time paid employment. Fewer than one in five lone mothers were dependent on means-tested benefits in the 1950s. They did not even comprise a single category in the National Assistance Board's reports (Kiernan et al, 1998).

Changes in marriage and childbearing

The traditional nexus of marriage and childbearing flourished in 1950s Britain. Only 5% of births took place outside of marriage (compared with 9% in 1945); only 9% of women born in 1943 remained childless compared with 20% in previous decades. By 1961 the average age of marriage for both spinsters and bachelors had fallen by two years (to 23.3 and 25.6 years respectively) compared with the earlier decades of the 20th century. Children arrived soon after marriage – indeed by 1960 one in five brides was pregnant on their wedding day and among teenage brides the proportion was one in three (rising to two in five in the early 1960s).

From the perspective of the family care system, Peter noted that the generation gap had shrunk from 30 years in the late 19th century to 23 years in the 1950s. Grandparents were more youthful and in future 'it will be common for man and wife whose children have grown up (and are perhaps themselves parents) to argue about the care of *two* or even *three* or all *four* of their parents in their eighties' (Townsend, 1963 edn, p 251, original emphasis). The increasing popularity of marriage also meant that fewer single women were available to participate in full-time employment. This had particular consequences for residential institutions, discussed below.

The British postwar social security system was firmly based on the male breadwinner-dependent housewife model. The ideological grip of this model is revealed nowhere more clearly than in T.H. Marshall's classic 1950 essay, *Citizenship and social class* (Marshall, 1950). Here the theorist speaks of first civil citizenship, then electoral citizenship but then, as he sets out the great achievement of the mid-20th century of social citizenship, when he comes to women Marshall simply peters out. It was embarrassingly evident that women in the British welfare state in 1950 were not accorded full social citizenship. Men's rights to benefits were determined by their employment status, women's determined by their marital status. This did not change until the 1970s when women began to be treated as individuals in their own right, and government policies concerning families shifted from regulating marriage to regulating parenthood.

The growth of part-time work

Governments' employment policies in the 1950s were committed to a policy of male full employment. However, there was a labour shortage not least because the welfare state itself created tens of thousands of jobs in education, health and welfare services. These were seen as largely women's jobs but as noted earlier, most women were marrying and having children. The prevailing view, promulgated by the psychoanalyst John Bowlby, was that children's mental health was threatened if their mothers did not stay at home full time to look after them until they were in school (Bowlby, 1953). Only then could mothers work part time. Despite the trenchant criticism of Bowlby's thesis by Barbara Wootton (1962), a senior social scientist at Bedford College well known for its feminist tradition, attitude surveys during this period found that these views were widely shared by both men and women (Klein, 1960, p 77) and persisted for the next three decades.

Governments therefore developed policies to make part-time employment more attractive both to employers and to married women. At the same time they relied on Commonwealth migrant labour to work full time or unsocial hours in the health and welfare services and in jobs that white British males refused as too poorly paid (for example, working on the buses for London Transport). In the early postwar years part-time employment in the formal labour market was unusual and unmeasured. The 1951 Census found that among the seven million women in the working population there were 830,000 part-time workers. To these must be added the under-regulated cash in hand and undercounted shadow labour market. In the official statistics, four out of five of the counted women part-time workers were married.

Housing policies

For postwar Britain housing policies in the public sector, obtaining a council house depended on being a nuclear family, preferably intact and not too large (Land and Parker, 1978, p 354). Taking in lodgers or boarders was forbidden. Council housing allocation, bound as it was by the desire to achieve fairness through the application of the points system, did not and could not take into account the importance of proximity to wider kin that was, and still is, as important as co-residence. Only the charitable estates like Peabody, unfettered by the points system, were able to be more flexible. Nonetheless, Peter was critical of the assumption that 'if old people live alone, it is supposed, then they are isolated. Field studies of the family have not justified this interpretation' (Townsend, 1962, p 296). Rather the respondents in *Family life* reported 'they thought they best served their own interests and those of their children by living near them rather than with them' (Townsend, 1957, p 25). Of course such freedom had only been made possible by a universal pension system so that older people had less financial dependence on their children. Replicated in subsequent studies this was soon after summed up in the phrase 'intimacy but at a distance' (Rosenmayer and Kockeis, 1963).

And the residual social services

Childcare and social care remained residual services. Children were never seen as the shared responsibility of the parents and the state, as in the Scandinavian model. The objective of post-war health and social care policies was, and has remained, to reduce long-term institutional care and to keep people in the community as long as possible. Day nurseries and domiciliary services for older people were discretionary. The supports for family life ranged between the inadequate and the absent, both with an inexorable knock-on to the care work of women. Some 6% of older people received domiciliary services in Bethnal Green in the mid-1950s and even fewer nationally, some 3% (Townsend, 1963 edn, p 213 and n 2). These were disproportionately those without a spouse and/or no (surviving) children (Townsend, 1963 edn, p 214). Similarly those in residential care were also predominantly those without families or at least families nearby. Peter estimated that 'But for the care given by female relatives the number of old people seeking admission to hospitals and residential Homes would have been from three to five times greater' (Townsend, 1963 edn, p 229).

Institutional care: *The last refuge*

The last refuge was planned to study what happened when family and kin no longer offered refuge and companionship for many people of advanced age. The book is dedicated to Peter's first wife, Ruth, who had worked as one of the four principal researchers on the study.

The last refuge describes the staff as well as the residents of the homes: 'Many were unmarried or childless women, who to some extent found emotional fulfilment in their professional relationships with those dependent upon them. Individual energies normally divided between work and family could be concentrated on the former' (Townsend, 1962, p 130). Wootton, in *The social foundations of wage policy* (1955), noted that jobs and professions, which developed from unpaid work in the home or in the voluntary sector, were likely to be badly paid and heavily dependent on non-pecuniary rewards.

Soon after the publication of *The last refuge* an official committee was established to study employment conditions in residential care. The economist Gertrude Williams, a colleague of Barbara Wootton, chaired the committee. It found that two thirds of the staff in homes for children, people with disabilities and for old people were unmarried women. Most were over the age of 50 (Williams, 1967). The committee regretted the low value placed on care and caring. By contrast Peter assumes that women are naturally altruistic, an assumption we later questioned, asking whether altruism was only for some but not all (Land and Rose, 1986). Peter writes: 'those who gain from institutional and social services are not only the recipients of the service. Those who are employed in the services gain a great deal too, psychologically and socially' (Townsend, 1962, p 192).

—

Over half the proprietors of the private homes were women (Townsend, 1962, p 187). Many were without husbands. Some were widows with children living with them. Having lost a husband or another close relative, they 'felt an obligation to find other objects for their care and affection, besides the need to earn a professional living.... There was a useful job to be done and it could be rewardingly "vocational" in the best sense of the term' (Townsend, 1962, p 189). Others had adult children living nearby who were helping in the management of the home together with other female relatives: 'A daughter would work for a few hours a week, an aunt would do the washing up in part return for her keep' (Townsend, 1962, p 186). The widows running homes were seeking to maintain key aspects of their previous status as a married woman: 'Her skills as a wife cannot all be practised, but by caring for old men and women she can cook and run a household, she can manage illness, she can deal with intimate personal problems and she can find companionship. In short she can still lay claim to the title "housewife"' (Townsend, 1962, p 192).

This is a very good illustration of how at this time 'it was an expected aspect of femininity to like to as well as be able to undertake these tasks' (Davidoff et al, 1999, p 75). The models of care and service on which women were expected to draw were all familial wherever they took place. If they were badly paid this was not important because the activities and relationships of caring were intrinsically rewarding and essential to their femininity.

Providing institutional care faced the same challenges as other service industries in the 1950s – wage rates were low, and where there were other employment opportunities, the residential sector like public transport was facing recruitment difficulties. Married women found the hours, which might involve early mornings, evenings and weekends, unmanageable together with family commitments. 'The old reliables' as one of the wardens called them (Townsend, 1962, p 78) were the middle-aged and elderly staff who would soon be retiring. These problems were, as Peter noted, to be solved by recruiting staff from the former colonies including the Republic of Ireland and the West Indies.

Few staff had had any training, and from the evidence of this study, some were not doing a very good job. The treatment that the elderly residents were receiving in some of the homes was uncaring at best and cruel at worst. For example, routines and staffing levels meant that the residents were not given the time they needed:

> What the residents need is time to do things: not to be hustled when they are changing what they are doing at the moment to some other activity whether it is being got up to eat a meal or put to bed or into a bath. They seem to become more confused, more stupid and irresponsible when they are being hurried. (Townsend, 1962, p 273)

In other homes there was a more generalised uncaring atmosphere: 'To indulge in personal or social relationships with the residents was not a recognised part of their job' (Townsend, 1962, p 349). Those who currently talk of 15-minute 'packages of care' lack knowledge of this highly relevant research evidence. As Peter demonstrates again and again, good care flows from relationships based on trust and familiarity.

Reflecting on the confused systems and policies with which the staffs in some homes were trying to work, Peter asked how best to make a home homely: 'Do you behave like a hospital matron, a hotel manageress or a devoted daughter?' (Townsend, 1962, p 147). Taking for granted that care was women's work he did not see exploitation either in the home or workplace. Nevertheless he anticipated an important question with which we are still wrestling. As Norwegian sociologist Kari Waerness later wrote:

> There is a great need to find better models for organising caregiving work. To develop such models, it seems necessary to study not only the exploitative nature of women's traditional caregiving work, but also the positive qualities inherent in it, as well as why they seem to get lost when professionalised and socialised. (Waerness, 1987)

Peter's own answer to his question was not to have homes at all! Instead families – meaning daughters and wives – would care for frail elderly people at home: 'The first principle of policy must be to assist the family in carrying out its self-imposed duties to the old' (Townsend, 1962, pp 405-6). He therefore wanted services to provide respite care, attendance allowances for those needing constant attention so they could pay family members and sheltered housing. However, he also argued that: 'The first task of any comprehensive service is in effect, to provide normal family services for those who have no families' (Townsend, 1962, p 406).

Peter observed that the absence of familial care could often be explained by family histories that included desertion, remarriage and earlier breakdown of relationships, as, for example, Finch and Mason's studies later confirmed (Finch and Mason, 1993). For this reason Townsend regretted that he had not been 'more systematically on the look-out for family strains and tensions' (Townsend, 1963 edn, p 254), although he does record 'bundles' usually over money (Townsend, 1957, p 69). As the movement against male violence and its committed social researchers were to reveal, strains and tensions were but the tip of an iceberg. Violence, murder, psychological and sexual abuse were to be uncovered in every social class. The feminist movement and its professionals and academics have been crucial in revealing these massive social problems and working to end them. Retrospectively it is easier to see that what Townsend and his colleagues were doing was to normalise working-class families and to remove them from stereotypical condemnation simply because they were not middle class.

As a result of the rise of second wave feminism in the late 1960s, many disciplines have experienced significant change if not transformation as the concept of gender as relational has been adopted. Within social policy and sociology this has led to a huge literature acknowledging the concept of gender as a critical tool for social analysis. Care both inside the family and in the formal labour market has now been studied, analysed and theorised not only by sociologists but also by economists, philosophers, historians, political scientists and others much inspired by feminist perspectives (for example, Waerness, 1987; Held, 1993; Tronto, 1993; Sevenhuijsen, 1998; Daly and Lewis, 2000; Knijn and Komter, 2004).

These insights, however, are still too rarely fully used to inform policy debates and decisions. In the light of inadequate resources for social care, which have persisted to this day, social care services have continued to be concentrated on those without family care. Peter's conclusion, based on these two studies, rings all too true half a century later. He wrote:

> ... despite the government's emphasis for many years on the principle of caring for the elderly in their own homes, no evidence exists of the pronounced shift in priorities which would be necessary if this principle were to be applied in practice. A future historian may well select this as the most striking failure of social policy in the last decade. (Townsend, 1962, p 399)

Conclusion

Fifty years on it is clear that the demographic characteristics of the 1950s were unusual. Almost universal youthful marriage and childbearing were trends that did not continue. Even in 1961 nuclear families accounted for only half of all households, compared with just over a third today when greater proportions of older and younger people live alone. However, the nuclear family is still used as a benchmark against which to measure modern family lives in which nearly half of all children are born outside of marriage and a third of children may experience part of their childhood living with one parent or in a blended family.

The myth that family ties are weakening is still strong, despite estimates that without unpaid family care the volume of formal domiciliary and residential care services would have to increase five-fold (Lundsgaard, 2005). Women's care is still taken for granted. While the care mothers and fathers give to children is more visible in both everyday life and in policy debates, care exchanged within and between the older generations is less so. It is rarely acknowledged that addressing the problem of funding pensions by increasing the employment rates of older women may have consequences for the exchange of care between the generations. Care between heterosexual partners is becoming more important as mortality rates between men and women converge. Peter in the 1950s learned that husbands wanted their wives to provide bodily care, or what is now called 'personal' care. Wives, on the other hand, preferred such care from daughters (Townsend, 1957, p 57). Today there is a small but growing literature exploring how older men and women care for each other (see, for example, Rose and Bruce, 1995; Morgan, 2004). The emphasis in the debates about care on the goals of achieving 'independence' and 'control' reveal a failure to understand, as Peter did, that care takes place within relationships underpinned by notions of reciprocity. More important, at the societal level, by keeping the care given by the older generation in the shadows we continue to ignore Peter's warning that: 'We may be attaching too little weight to the contribution to society made by the aged and too much to their claims on it' (Townsend, 1957, p 50).

These two studies exemplify much more than Peter's considerable skills as a social researcher. His insistence on bringing into the light of day the lives of women and men, which the privileged and powerful would rather were not seen, never left him. He continued to use his data to challenge established theories in sociology but at the same time he remained committed to using this data to develop and press for the policies which would both bring about positive change in people's daily lives and move closer to a more just and less unequal society.

Note

[1] Here all references to *The family life of old people* and *The last refuge* are drawn from their first editions (1957 and 1962) except where indicated.

References

Abel-Smith, B. and Townsend, P. (1965) *The poor and the poorest*, London: Bell.

Bosanquet, H. (1906/1915) *The family*, London: Macmillan.

Bott, E. (1957) *Family and social network*, London: Tavistock.

Bowlby, J. (1953) *Child care and the growth of love*, Harmondsworth: Penguin.

Crossman, R. (1958) 'Two social scientists', *New Statesman*, 15 March, pp 339-40.

Daly, M. and Lewis, J. (2000) 'The concept of social care and the analysis of contemporary welfare states', *British Journal of Sociology*, vol 51, no 2, pp 281-98.

Davidoff, L., Doolittle, M., Fink, J. and Holden, K. (1999) *The family story: Blood, contract and intimacy, 1830-1960*, London: Longman.

Finch, J. and Mason, J. (1993) *Negotiating family responsibilities*, London: Routledge.

Held, V. (1993) *Feminist morality: Transforming culture, society and politics*, Chicago, IL: Chicago University Press.

Kiernan, K., Land, H. and Lewis, J. (1998) *Lone motherhood in twentieth century Britain*, Oxford: Oxford University Press.

Klein, V. (1960) *Working wives*, Occasional Paper No 5, London: Institute of Personnel Management.

Knijn, T. and Komter, A. (eds) (2004) *Solidarity between the sexes and the generations*, Cheltenham: Edward Elgar.

Kynaston, D. (2007) *Austerity Britain 1945–51*, London: Bloomsbury.

Land, H. and Parker, R. (1978) 'Family policy in Britain: the hidden dimensions', in A.J. Kahn and S. Kamerman (eds) *Family policy: Government and families in fourteen countries*, New York: Columbia University Press, pp 331-66.

Land, H. and Rose, H. (1985) 'Compulsory altruism for some or an altruistic society for all?', in P. Bean, J. Ferris and D. Whynes (eds) *In defence of welfare*, London: Tavistock, pp 74-96.

Lundsgaard, J. (2005) *Consumer direction and choice in long term care for older persons, including payments for older persons: How can it help improve care outcomes, employment and fiscal sustainability*, Health Working Paper No 20, Paris: Organisation for Economic Co-operation and Development.

Marshall, T.H. (1950) *Citizenship and social class*, London: Allen & Unwin.

Morgan, D. (2004) 'Men in families and households', in J. Scott, J. Treas and M. Richards (eds) *The Blackwell companion to the sociology of families*, Oxford: Blackwell, ch 22.

OPCS (Office of Population Censuses and Surveys) (1973) *General Household Survey*, London: HMSO.

Parsons, T. (1943) 'The kinship system of contemporary United States', *American Anthropologist*, vol 45, pp 22-38.

—

Rose, H. and Bruce, E. (1995) 'Mutual care but differential esteem: caring between old couples', in S. Arber and J. Ginn (eds) *Connecting gender and ageing: A sociological approach*, Buckingham: Open University Press, pp 114-28.

Rosenmayer, I. and Kockeis, C. (1963) 'Propositions for a sociological theory of ageing and the family', *International Social Services Journal*, vol 15, pp 410-26.

Sevenhuijsen, S. (1998) *Citizenship and the ethics of care*, London: Routledge.

Titmuss, R. (1950) *Problems of social policy*, London: HMSO and Longmans.

Titmuss, R. (1958) *Essays on 'The welfare state'*, London: Allen & Unwin.

Townsend, P. (1957) *The family life of old people*, London: Routledge and Kegan Paul [abridged edition with postscript published in 1963 by Pelican Books, Penguin].

Townsend, P. (1962) *The last refuge: A survey of residential institutions and homes for the aged in England and Wales*, London: Routledge and Kegan Paul [abridged edition published in 1964].

Townsend, P. (1986) 'Social planning: ideology and instruments', in P. Bean and D. Whynes (eds) *Barbara Wootton: Social science and public policy, Essays in her honour*, London: Tavistock, pp 19-39.

Toye, R. (2004) 'Churchill and Britain's "Financial Dunkirk"', *Twentieth century British history*, vol 15, issue 4, pp 329-60.

Tronto, J. (1993) *Moral boundaries. A political argument for an ethic of care*, London: Routledge.

Waerness, K. (1987) 'On the rationality of caring', in A. Showstack–Sassoon (ed) *Women and the state*, London: Hutchinson, pp 207-34.

Willetts, D. (2010) *The pinch: How the baby boomers took their children's future and how they can give it back*, London: Atlantic Books.

Williams, G. (1967) *Staffing in residential institutions*, London: Allen & Unwin.

Willmott, P. and Young, M. (1957) *Family and kinship in East London*, London: Routledge and Kegan Paul.

Wootton, B. (1950) *Testament for social science: An essay in the application of scientific method to human problems*, London: Allen & Unwin.

Wootton, B. (1955) *The social foundations of wage policy*, London: Allen & Unwin.

Wootton, B. (1962) *A social scientist's view of maternal deprivation and maternal care*, Public Health Report No 14, Geneva: World Health Organization.

FOUR

The case for universal child benefit

Anthony B. Atkinson

The story so far

Forty years ago, the Child Poverty Action Group (CPAG), led by Peter Townsend and Frank Field, was campaigning – as it had since its inception – for a substantial increase in family allowances. There were signs in 1970 that this campaign was bearing fruit. In its election manifesto, the Conservative Party had pledged to 'deal with family poverty', and its Treasury spokesman had talked about the need to raise family allowances. However, the incoming Conservative government decided instead to introduce Family Income Supplement (FIS), an income-tested benefit for low-paid working families with children. Under FIS, families where the head was in full-time work could claim payments equal to half the difference between their gross income and the prescribed amount.

Hopes for a substantial increase in family allowances having been dashed, in a special issue the next year on 'Poor people and the Conservative government', *Poverty* carried an article by Peter and myself on 'The advantages of universal family allowances' (Townsend and Atkinson, 1971) – the only joint article that we wrote. The article compared the new FIS with the CPAG proposals of raising family allowances and eliminating child tax allowances. The CPAG proposal would, in its more generous version, have raised the family allowance for all children (including the first child) to around 15% of mean gross income per person (gross income includes wage and salary income, income from self-employment, income from capital and state and private transfers). In the article, we argued that the CPAG route was the right one to follow in the long term and that it would 'lay the

—

79

foundation for equitable social and fiscal policies affecting families with children' (Townsend and Atkinson, 1971, p 21).

The CPAG campaign did bear fruit only four years later, with the introduction of Child Benefit by the Labour government elected in 1974. Child Benefit, a tax-free benefit paid for all children at the same rate, replaced Family Allowance and (from 1979) Child Tax Allowance. As it was put by Barbara Castle, then Secretary of State for Social Services, 'we shall have for the first time a single universal system of family support' (House of Commons debate, *Hansard*, 13 May 1975, col 334). The new benefit, set at £4 a week in 1979, represented some 9% of mean gross income per person in the UK (see Figure 4.1). This was below the 15% that had been proposed by CPAG, but the new scheme provided a potential springboard for movement upward to that target level and for the scaling back of the income-tested FIS.

Figure 4.1: Child benefit as % mean income per head in UK since 1979

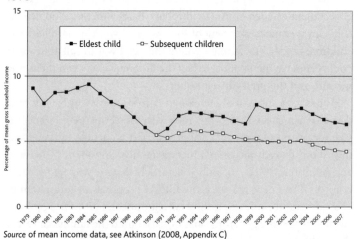

Source of mean income data, see Atkinson (2008, Appendix C)

This was, however, the high water mark. Rather than rising, Child Benefit fell as a proportion of mean income from 1984 until the end of the decade. There was a modest recovery in the John Major years, but by 1997 Child Benefit was less than 7% of mean income. The

—

rate for subsequent children in the family had fallen progressively behind the rate for the first child – see Figure 4.1 – and was little more than 5% of mean income. The number of families receiving means-tested family support rose from around 100,000 when FIS began, to some 600,000 families receiving Family Credit (which replaced FIS in 1988) in the mid-1990s.

One of the early acts of the Labour government elected in 1997 was to raise Child Benefit significantly: a rise of a quarter for the first child in 1999. This caused a jump in the series – see Figure 4.1 – but the momentum was not sustained. Ten years after the Blair government was elected, the benefit for the first child was no higher than in 1997, and Child Benefit for subsequent children had fallen from 5% to 4%. Expressed as a percentage of average earnings (DWP, 2008, Table 5.6), Child Benefit for a one-child family was 3.3% in April 2008, whereas it had been 3.0% in April 1997. For subsequent children, Child Benefit in April 2008 was below the percentage it had been in 1997. In contrast, income-tested tax credits have been greatly expanded: Working Families' Tax Credit from 1999, replaced by Child Tax Credit and Working Tax Credit from 2003. In December 2009, more than four million families with an adult in work were receiving the Child Tax Credit.

The Child Benefit story is part of a wider picture. Growth of social spending over the first part of the postwar period was dominated by contributory benefits, but since the 1970s these have levelled off as a proportion of national income. The growth since the 1970s has been in means-tested benefits (and now tax credits) (see, for example, Hills, 2004, Figure 6.7). This increased spending has undoubtedly contributed to the reduction of income poverty. From this perspective, the tax credit expansion is better than if nothing had been enacted. But I am not persuaded that means testing provides a long-term strategy for the support of families with children – for reasons that are the subject of the rest of this chapter.

The economist's analysis of income testing

Why did Peter and I oppose income testing in the 1970s? Why did we believe that tax credits were the wrong way for the 1997–2010 Labour government to go? After all, to most of my fellow economists, income testing appeared then, and appears today, to be a sensible use of 'targeting'. Brewer, Saez and Shephard (2010) have recently proposed an Integrated Family Support (IFS) scheme targeted towards low-income families, with the possibility of this being financed by cutting Child Benefit. Their study was prepared for a review chaired by Sir James Mirrlees, and their analysis draws on his highly influential article on the optimal design of income taxation and income maintenance. This article (Mirrlees, 1971), which won a Nobel Prize for its author, illustrates well the strengths of the model-building approach of economists, and provides my starting point here.

A simple model of individual work behaviour, with its predictions about responses to taxation, was used by Mirrlees to provide new insights, particularly regarding the role of *marginal* tax rates (how much extra tax you pay on an extra £1 of gross income). For many years, high marginal tax rates on high incomes were seen as a hallmark of a progressive tax policy. However, the mathematical analysis brought out that, if policy makers are concerned with the distribution of after-tax income, then the purpose of high marginal tax rates is to raise the *average* tax rate paid by people on higher incomes. The amount of tax paid by the rich depends not on the marginal tax rate they face but on the marginal tax rates lower down the scale. To make this concrete, consider the question whether the 50% top Income Tax rate in Britain should start at £100,000 or £150,000. Starting at £100,000 would indeed mean that those in the range from £100,000 to £150,000 would face a higher marginal tax rate, but the important point is that the average tax rate would rise for all those above £100,000. People with incomes above £150,000 would pay an extra £5,000 a year in tax.

How far is this analysis relevant to the debate about Child Benefit and tax credits? In one important respect it is not directly relevant, since no distinction is made between people with and without children. One of the major purposes of Child Benefit financed out of

—

82

general taxation is to redistribute away from those without children towards those with children. I come back to this in the next section. But in another respect the Mirrlees analysis *is* relevant. Income testing is equivalent to raising the marginal Income Tax rate, since earning an extra £1 means that a person loses some part of the family benefit. Under FIS as introduced in 1971, the marginal tax rate was 50% plus Income Tax plus National Insurance contributions. The combined marginal tax rate faced by poor families was higher than that faced by many top earners. As Tony Lynes famously remarked, it was possible to pay surtax while living on the breadline (Lynes, 1971). The income-testing strategy may therefore be seen as offering help to low earners but then 'taxing' this away through a high rate of withdrawal. The implicit marginal tax rate has been reduced but is still substantial: a person paying Income Tax and National Insurance contributions faces a marginal tax rate of 70% or more.

In this way, the cost is contained and the working poor can be helped without the need for substantially higher taxes on the better off. The strategy is the mirror image of that at the top: *reducing* the average tax rate (typically negative in fact) on the poor, while maintaining that in the middle. In contrast, the alternative strategy that I continue to espouse is to pay more generous universal benefits to families with children but to tax these with a fully graduated set of Income Tax rates. If these Income Tax rates were to rise in 10% steps from 20% to 60%, the net Child Benefit to a rich family would be half that to a family paying the lowest marginal rate. One key difference between the two strategies lies in where marginal tax rates are highest. With income testing, marginal tax rates are highest on those with low incomes; with the alternative strategy, the marginal tax rates are raised on those with middle and upper incomes. (Again it is important to remember that a higher marginal rate does not imply a higher average rate, so that many of the people in the middle-income group would be better off.)

Seen in this way, the case for and against income testing appears to be a largely technical one. The Mirrlees formula for an optimal tax scheme indicates that marginal rates should be high *either* where there are relatively few people *or* where people are relatively unresponsive to the magnitude of the marginal tax rate. Whether this favours one

—

strategy over the other depends largely on empirical matters. However, the economic analysis sketched above is only a partial one, and, as already indicated, fails to capture all of the relevant considerations. It ignores the key difference between the two approaches which is that the Child Benefit strategy would continue to make transfers to families with children at all income levels.

Social welfare and family size

The standard optimal tax analysis does not allow for differences in the number of children. This is necessary, however, in order to investigate the case for paying Child Benefit to families at all income levels. Should the optimal policy mean, as would be implied by the income-tested child transfer, that above a certain income level families with children receive the same net income as families without children? Or should the UK Prime Minister, as a family man, have a higher net income than a childless counterpart with the same salary?

In one of the few analyses of the optimal tax implications of differing family size, Mirrlees (1972) concentrates, not on the differential treatment of rich and poor, but on the fertility decision, which I leave to one side here. I also leave to one side the tax/benefit treatment of couples: I examine the treatment of independent adults with and without children. I assume that the distribution of earning power is the same for both groups. In other respects, the analytical framework is the same as that employed by Brewer et al (2010), who assume that labour supply is affected only by marginal tax rates and not by the level of income. I consider the case where there is a single rate of Income Tax, and where the income-tested child transfer (referred to as IFS) is withdrawn at a single specified rate. The government's freedom of action is to choose the level of the maximum family support (incorporating Child Benefit) under IFS, the level of the Child Benefit paid to all other families with children, and the tax threshold for everyone (treated as a tax credit).

Where there can be no increase in the overall tax rate, there is an evident logic to the argument that reducing the universal child benefit would allow a larger transfer through the income-tested scheme to families who are poorer. The social marginal valuation of income to the recipients is on average greater than that of income to those who would lose. However, there are two further considerations that need to be taken into account. The first is the efficiency cost associated with the marginal rate of withdrawal of the IFS. The IFS means that there is a wage level such that people earning less cut back their labour supply. A reduction in Child Benefit to pay a larger IFS maximum causes more people to cut back their work effort, leading both to higher IFS payments and to lower Income Tax receipts.

The second consideration is that, even where the efficiency costs are deemed acceptable, there is an alternative source of funding the increased IFS, and that is by lowering the Income Tax threshold for everyone. This means that we have to examine the way in which families with and without children enter our social evaluation – an issue not discussed in the standard optimal tax analysis. Suppose that we consider two people with incomes above the cut-off for the income-tested Family Benefit. Should we attach a higher marginal social value to £1 received by the person with a child than to a person with no children? Some people would say 'no'. They would say that having children today is a 'lifestyle choice' and that the parent should be treated no differently than if he or she made a different consumption choice. With such a judgement, the withdrawal of Child Benefit would indeed be the distributionally preferred policy, since income would be taken from those who on average were better off. Given the assumption that the distributions of earning power are the same for those with and without children, then lowering the tax threshold would hit all income levels, whereas withdrawing Child Benefit would exempt those with lower incomes on IFS.

Such a 'lifestyle choice' view, however, attaches no weight to the welfare of the child and would run counter to the widely adopted practice in distributional analyses (such as those conducted by the Institute for Fiscal Studies) of adjusting household income for differences in family composition. With the modified Organisation for Economic Co-operation and Development (OECD) scale, for example, a child is allocated 30% of the needs of an adult, so that income is divided by 1.3 where the person has one child. We are then comparing a childless person with income X and a person and a child with equivalent income X/1.3. There is then a question of weighting. The person and the child should certainly count 1.3 times. Where the social marginal valuation of income is a strictly declining function of income, this then implies that an extra £1 to the person with a child is given a higher valuation at all income levels. It could be argued, moreover, that the person and a child should have a weight of 2 (people). This is indeed the standard practice in distributional analyses: we count people, not equivalent people. In that case, the social marginal valuation of income is higher by a further factor of 2/1.3 or approximately 50%.

The choice between reducing the tax threshold and reducing Child Benefit depends therefore on whether the higher social marginal valuation of income for families with children offsets the fact that Child Benefit recipients are better off. That the right policy choice should depend on our social values regarding children would hardly come as a surprise to non-economists. Indeed, those approaching the issue from a different disciplinary perspective may well feel that there are other respects in which the economic analysis is too narrow. This is the subject of the rest of this chapter.

Perception of income transfers

The optimal tax treatment of the policy choice focuses on the tax and benefit formulae without regard to how these are perceived and interpreted. The analysis treats the receipt of income-tested benefits as simply the negative of tax payments, but individuals do not necessarily make this equation. More generally, we cannot assume that people treat all components of the household budget as equivalent; they may feel differently about different sources of income. Different types of transfer may be more or less effective in helping families.

A particular concern is the incomplete take-up of certain benefits. Unlike the close-to-complete take-up of Child Benefit, a significant minority of those entitled have failed to claim FIS and its successors. This was one of the important findings of *The poor and the poorest* (Abel-Smith and Townsend, 1965), confirming earlier research on older people by Dorothy Wedderburn (Cole and Utting, 1962) and Peter (Townsend and Wedderburn, 1965). Take-up has improved since the early days of FIS, when it was around 50%, but the latest official

—

estimates still show significant non-take-up: the central estimate is 19% for Child Tax Credit and 43% for Working Tax Credit (HM Revenue and Customs Analysis Team, 2010, Table 1). Non-claiming continues despite the intense efforts at national and local level, which must have gone a long way to make information available about the benefits. Nor is it a purely UK problem. At a European level, the report on *The social situation in the European Union 2008* concluded that 'non-take-up of benefits appears to be widespread' (European Commission, 2009, p 45), citing evidence from Austria, Denmark, Finland, France, Germany, Greece and Portugal.

The persistence of non-claiming in Britain – 50 years after the problem was clearly identified – should surely therefore raise questions about the reliance on income-tested schemes. Failure to claim may be explicable as a rational response to the time and trouble required to make a claim. Compliance costs are discussed by Bennett, Brewer and Shaw (2009), who classify them under the headings 'time', 'money' and 'psychological'. The last of these includes 'stress and worry', 'intrusion into privacy' and 'stigma/shame'. When asked in 1824 by the Select Committee on Labourers' Wages whether he had ever applied for an addition to his wages, Thomas Smart replied 'No, I never did. I always try to do without' (quoted in Rose, 1971, pp 63-4). We live in very different times, but it remains the case that the capacity of a transfer scheme to provide effective income support depends on how it is viewed by the potential beneficiaries. How do people feel about relying on tax credits to supplement their wages? Are they part of the family's planned life course or an unfortunate sign of failure as a breadwinner? Are such benefits to be avoided if possible? Do families effectively apply a 'discount factor' to transfers paid under a means test?

The existence of such a discount, coupled with a fixed cost of claiming, could explain incomplete take-up. It would also mean that the net benefit to families would be less than the cash amount received, thus diminishing the effectiveness of the income-tested transfer in reducing child poverty. This is missing from the analysis described in the previous section, and adds to the case for Child Benefit. (Equally missing are the compliance costs for employers of operating tax credits.)

—

Broader concepts of equity

The optimal tax analysis embodies the equity/efficiency trade-off within the maximisation of a social welfare function. The social welfare function provides a valuable framework, but it is not all-encompassing.

First, marginal tax rates are not just a matter of incentives: the change in take-home pay as a consequence of an increase in earnings is also judged in terms of its intrinsic fairness. Fairness involves a perceptible link between effort and reward: people deserve to keep at least a reasonable proportion of what they earn through increased hours or taking increased responsibility or doing a second job. The objections to the 'poverty trap' are not only that it discourages work (and savings) but also that it raises questions about fairness where people keep very little out of their extra earnings. If this is the case, then considerations of fairness and justice may apply to marginal as well as to average tax rates. The high marginal rates are now playing a different role in our moral calculus. In practical terms, if the policy objective is to limit the extent of variation in marginal rates, then this points to a flat tax (with a constant marginal rate) funding a universal child benefit and universal basic income.

The second example concerns gender equity. One of the latent – and sometimes manifest – functions of social transfers is to offset the labour market disadvantage faced by many women. In the case of Child Benefit in the UK, an express intention of the legislation was to aid women by making the benefit payable to the mother in the first instance. Child Benefit guarantees an independent source of income for the mother in a way that cannot be reproduced by an income-tested benefit payable on the basis of a couple's joint circumstances, requiring that the partner furnish income and other information. There are good reasons for concern about the possible loss of one of the few mechanisms by which the government can influence the within-family distribution of income.

Conclusion

The case of Child Benefit, like most cases, is not open and shut. It is not simply a matter of determining an optimum in a fully specified model. There are always elements not captured by the model; social objectives are not completely represented by a single welfare function. Rather it is a matter of judgement, weighing different considerations. My own judgement remains, as 40 years ago, that universal child benefit should be a major plank in UK social policy. In part, this judgement is based on the failure of income-tested transfers to reach all of those entitled, a problem that the attempts of successive governments have not succeeded in eradicating. In part, this judgement is based on a concern about the 'unfairness' of 70+ per cent marginal tax rates, where this applies as much to those on low incomes as to those at the top of the scale. But above all this judgement is based on a wider view of social justice, concerned to redistribute towards families with children and with gender equity. A renewed commitment to Child Benefit by a future government would be a fitting testament to Peter.

References

Abel-Smith, B. and Townsend, P. (1965) *The poor and the poorest*, London: Bell.

Atkinson, A.B. (2008) 'The distribution of top incomes in the United Kingdom 1908-2000' in A.B. Atkinson and T. Piketty (eds) *Top incomes over the twentieth century*, Oxford: Oxford University Press, pp 82-140.

Bennett, F., Brewer, M. and Shaw, J. (2009) *Understanding the compliance costs of benefits and tax credits*, London: Institute for Fiscal Studies.

Brewer, M., Saez, E. and Shephard, A. (2010) 'Means-testing and tax rates on earnings', in J.A. Mirrlees (ed) *Dimensions of tax design*, Oxford: Oxford University Press, pp 90-173.

Cole, D. with Utting, J. (1962) *The economic circumstances of old people*, Occasional Papers on Social Administration, no 4, Welwyn: Codicote Press.

DWP (Department for Work and Pensions) (2008) *Abstract of statistics 2008*, London: DWP.

European Commission (2009) *The social situation in the European Union 2008*, Luxembourg: Office for Official Publications of the European Communities.

Hills, J. (2004) *Inequality and the state*, Oxford: Oxford University Press.

HM Revenue and Customs Analysis Team (2010) *Child Benefit, Child Tax Credit and Working Tax Credit take-up rates*, London: HM Revenue and Customs.

Lynes, T. (1971) *How to pay surtax while living on the breadline*, CES Working Note 256, London: Centre for Environmental Studies.

Mirrlees, J.A. (1971) 'An exploration in the theory of optimal income taxation', *Review of Economic Studies*, vol 38, pp 175-208.

Mirrlees, J.A. (1972) 'Population policy and the taxation of family size', *Journal of Public Economics*, vol 1, pp 169-98.

Rose, M.E. (1971) *The English Poor Law*, Newton Abbot: David and Charles.

Townsend, P. and Atkinson, A.B. (1971) 'The advantages of universal family allowances', *Poverty*, no 16/17, pp 18-21.

Townsend, P. and Wedderburn, D. (1965) *The aged in the welfare state*, Occasional Papers on Social Administration, no 14, London: Bell.

FIVE

Poverty

Jonathan Bradshaw

In the 10 years between the mid-1950s and the mid-1960s Peter Townsend published three of the most outstanding social policy studies ever produced in this country. In 1957 he published his superb interview and observational study, *The family life of old people*. Then in 1962 he published *The last refuge*, a survey of residential institutions for the aged. Even today no one can fail to be transfixed by this combination of empirical research, passionate, beautiful writing and outrage at the conditions of old people in Poor Law institutions. Reading it at university decided me to switch to social policy. His studies of older people were followed by *The aged in the welfare state* (with Dorothy Wedderburn, 1965) and the mammoth *Old people in three industrial societies* (Shanas et al, 1968). However, before these great works, he published what is arguably his major contribution to social science. In the 1950s, when he was only in his 20s, he began to produce the work that eventually transformed how we think about poverty, especially in a Political and Economic Planning (PEP) report (1952) and a seminal article in the *British Journal of Sociology* on 'Measuring poverty' (1954). He followed this up with another *British Journal of Sociology* article on 'The meaning of poverty' in 1962 and *The poor and the poorest* (with Brian Abel-Smith) in 1965, which he had worked on between 1961 and 1963. The latter can claim to be the book that rediscovered poverty in postwar Britain.

It is quite extraordinary that Peter produced so much work in those 10 years between the mid-1950s and the mid-1960s – enormous, original, brilliant research. Remember that as late as 1970 we did our data analysis pushing knitting needles through holes in cards, shaking them and counting the cards that fell out, and then building tables by hand!

Townsend's great work on poverty, *Poverty in the United Kingdom*, was not published until 1979, 1,216 pages, 10 years after the survey on which it is based (for reasons that he explains in the preface and which still make me wince to read – they recruited their own field force, the London School of Economics and Political Science [LSE] and Essex computers were incompatible and so they had to enter the data twice). It is amazing that it was ever completed. It is a Great Work, the place poverty researchers should start from.

I am going to mention just three elements of this work: the concept, resources and groups.

The concept

We can certainly claim that he was the first to conceptualise poverty as relative. Others, notably Gary Runciman (1966), had written about relative deprivation, but Peter did it earlier, mainly in his criticisms of the absolutist biological understandings of Rowntree and Beveridge. It must have been hard reasoning at the time, but it was an idea which was nothing less than scintillating, a genuine shift in the paradigm and, by golly, it was well argued and evidenced. As he pointed out, understanding poverty as relative to a time and place was the only way in which we could reconcile talking about poverty in the 19th and 20th centuries, and the only way to reconcile poverty in Ethiopia and Luxembourg.

This reconceptualisation was enormously influential. It was more or less immediately operationalised in the UK in the government series Low Income Statistics and then more fully after 1980 in the Households Below Average Income series. Today we monitor the poverty strategy with regard to relative poverty – equivalised income less than 60% of the conventional average. So does the European Union (EU), so does the Luxembourg Income Study, so does the Organisation for Economic Co-operation and Development (OECD), so does UNICEF. The US government still holds out against defining poverty as relative. Although its poverty line was relative when Molly Orshansky first developed it in 1961 (Fisher, 1997), it has been more or less frozen in real terms since then.

—

The World Bank is the only international body still giving official credence to an absolute poverty threshold. Their US$1 a day poverty line was established for the 1990 *World Development Report* based on background research by Ravallion and colleagues. It became the basis of the first Millennium Development Goal – to abolish US$1 a day poverty by 2015.

> The explicit aim was to set a global poverty line such that poverty in the developing world as a whole was assessed by the standards of what 'poverty' means in the world's poorest countries, recognising that richer countries naturally have higher standards. This (intentionally frugal basis for measuring global poverty) gives the '$1-a-day' line a salience in focussing international attention on the world's poorest – a salience that a higher line would not have. (Ravallion et al, 2008)

Thus, far from being an absolute poverty threshold in a scientific sense, it was a marketing tool, a heuristic device, to provide an acceptable focus for world efforts to tackle poverty. In practice it became more than that – The World Bank used it in household consumption surveys undertaken for poverty assessments as a 'food poverty line' and then advocated that (conditional) social assistance schemes were needed only to meet that target, or something very little above it.

The US$1 a day concept actually came from an exercise of collecting together the standards used by 15 of the world's poorest countries. It has been much criticised (Pogge and Reddy, 2005; Reddy and Minoiu, 2007; Pogge, 2008; Reddy, 2008) on the following main grounds:

- A calorific-based poverty line is not enough – there are other basic material needs that need to be taken into account such as housing, clothing and heating. In particular UNICEF (Hoelscher, 2008) has argued that a calorific poverty line cannot cover the right of a child to a standard of living adequate for the child's mental, spiritual, moral and social development (Convention on the Rights of the Child, Article 27, paras 1 and 3).

- The US$1 a day is arbitrary. In the revision in 2008 published by Ravillion et al (2008) it should have been US$1.45 a day but, because that would have included too many people, they fixed it at US$1.24 a day. Again it was an assumption about the acceptability of the threshold that determined it.
- The use of purchasing power parities (PPPs) to translate a US$ into a national currency amount is unsatisfactory. PPPs are based on average consumption patterns and not on the consumption patterns of the poor.
- The choice of the base year for the calculations makes a big difference to the results for countries that have experienced sharp changes in their living standards.

I return to these issues further below.

Meanwhile the international consensus that poverty is relative is really quite extraordinary. With the exception of John Moore (he was very briefly Margaret Thatcher's Secretary of State for Social Services), who declared 'the end of the road for poverty' and expunged the 'p' word from official reports, no thinking politician has sought to deny the relative concept of poverty (1989). There was the debate with Amartya Sen (1983) over whether there was an absolutist core to poverty, but Sen's capabilities have never been operationalised satisfactorily while Townsend's relative deprivation has been.

This definition in the first paragraph of *Poverty in the UK* says it all. It demonstrates the extraordinary prescience of Peter Townsend:

> Individuals, families and groups in the population can be said to be in poverty when they lack the resources to obtain the types of diet, participate in the activities and have the living conditions which are customary, or at least widely encouraged or approved, in societies to which they belong. Their resources are so seriously below those commanded by the average family or individual that they are in effect excluded from ordinary living patterns, customs and activities. (Townsend, 1979)

Peter invented social exclusion long before the French and the EU, and the Social Exclusion Unit leant heavily on his work (without acknowledging it) when they described social exclusion as:

> ... a combination of linked problems such as unemployment, low skills, poor housing, family breakdown, high crime rates that lead people or places to be excluded from the mainstream. (ODPM, 2004)

Resources

Townsend's second contribution in the field of poverty was to get us to think about resources. It was a social insight that we should take into account a variety of resources. Poverty had been understood economically as a lack of income (or spending power), but Townsend argued it was concerned with much more – working conditions, the quality of the local environment, capacity to participate in social activities, access to assets 'widely encouraged and approved' and socially determined, and the availability of services and capital. It was for this reason that he pioneered the use of social indicators to measure poverty, counting the number of deprivation items that were lacking. For this he was much criticised. Some of the criticisms were dealt with by Mack and Lansley (1985) in the first *Breadline Britain* survey, and Townsend was an enthusiastic participant in the second and third surveys (Gordon and Pantazis, 1997; Gordon et al, 2000; Pantazis et al, 2006) that led eventually to the government complementing its income-based poverty measures with an index based on a lack of socially perceived necessities. He was looking forward to participating in the fourth survey, starting in 2010, when he died.

The other controversy that arose out of *Poverty in the UK* concerned whether there was a point on the income distribution where the lack of necessities increased – whether there was a threshold. David Piachaud (1987) said he could not find it. Megnad Desai (1986) said that he could. I have never understood why it was important. Why should there be a threshold? Lacking socially perceived necessities has its own independent value; it does not need to be validated by

—

income. Indeed we have argued that income and deprivation measures should be used in combination – in 'overlaps analysis' (Bradshaw and Finch, 2003).

Groups

The third element in Peter's poverty work to draw attention to is the way he classified groups. He was not alone in this – Seebohm Rowntree had also classified groups in poverty, but Peter took it to another level. Not initially in *The poor and the poorest,* but in *Poverty in the UK* he actually organised his research assistants around groups! Hilary Land did large families, John Veit-Wilson disabled people, Adrian Sinfield unemployed people and Dennis Marsden lone-parent families. Thanks to Peter we no longer talk about the poor as a single class, but as human beings with certain (structural) characteristics we can identify and overcome. It sounds so obvious and simple but it was one of Peter's great contributions. Of course he wrote about the circumstances of each of these types of people with great sensitivity and authority and campaigned on behalf of them, especially in his years of service to the Child Poverty Action Group (CPAG) and the Disability Alliance, and in his work with Barbara Castle on pensions reform.

Looking forward

In these chapters we are supposed to look forward. Needless to say there are many challenges and much work to be done. Thanks to Peter and the way his work has now been incorporated into official and independent research we are much better equipped with data on poverty in Britain and comparatively.

I have three thoughts about looking forward.

Minimum income standards

We still need minimum income standards to guide policy. The income poverty threshold and a socially perceived necessities index are fine for research and analysis, but they do not provide a basis for policy decisions. The Chancellor announces the uprating of benefits and tax allowances each year on the basis of a bizarre set of rules that have no regard to the needs of people in different circumstances, and which are now resulting in outrageous inequities – for example, in 2010 a single person aged 59 received £65.45 per week in Employment Support Allowance. In contrast, a single pensioner aged 60 received £132.60 in Pension Credit. This difference is simply unjustifiable and unsustainable.

Peter probably never approved of our work on budget standards (Bradshaw, 1993). He may have felt it was a reversion to Rowntree's physical necessities that he had been so critical of. But the work on minimum income standards (Bradshaw et al, 2008) is important and is still going on at the University of Loughborough, supported by the Joseph Rowntree Foundation (see www.minimumincomestandard. org/). Minimum income standards can provide a basis for assessing the adequacy of benefit levels and depicting the kind of consumption that can be afforded at income poverty thresholds. They have been used to inform judgements in the courts about the level of fines that are affordable, assessing the adequacy of foster care allowances and, most excitingly recently, the campaigns for a living wage in London and other cities have been underpinned by evidence from budget standards.

Subjective well-being and poverty

My second challenge is that although we know how to measure the lack of material resources and we also know a good deal about the effects of the lack of material resources on, for example, health and educational attainment, we do not know much about the relationship between poverty and subjective well-being. At its heart relative deprivation and indeed inequality are important because they have an impact on well-being or happiness. Those are psychological states. Peter was the first person to distinguish between isolation and loneliness in his research on older people. I think we now need to understand more about the association between poverty and psychological stress, happiness and well-being. We have been exploring this issue in national (Rees et al, 2010) and comparative research (Bradshaw and Richardson, 2008) on child well-being and, although there is no doubt an association at both levels between material poverty and the subjective well-being of children, it is not the same thing. More work is needed on this relationship – not just for children but other population groups as well.

The World Bank

My third challenge is The World Bank. I shall deal with this at greater length, starting with a story and then presenting some data.

On behalf of UNICEF I recently wrote a chapter on child poverty for a World Bank poverty assessment of Georgia. After many drafts The World Bank dropped the UNICEF chapter because it used a relative poverty threshold, used more than expenditure as an indicator of resources and demonstrated that the targeted social assistance scheme that had been imposed on Georgia by The World Bank was considerably less effective than the old age pension scheme or a universal child benefit would have been in reducing child poverty. None of this was acceptable to The World Bank. Since then the neocon Georgian government has started and lost a war, and so it was all water under the bridge. I shared this experience with Peter and discovered he had worked in Georgia in the early days of transition (see Chapter Two, this volume). He sent me a paper he had written in which he sought to defend the good elements of the old Soviet welfare state. He was equally unsuccessful.

In his 70s he started to teach a course at LSE on human rights and social policy and began to publish work articulating the case for social security in developing countries. This stream of his work on poverty is very important and deserves more attention than it has received. It is also, to an extent, unfinished. The day before he died he completed a paper on the need for (universal) child benefits in developing countries that has now been published in a collection he edited for the International Labour Organization (ILO) (Townsend, 2009). The week after he died he was coming to the annual Foundation for International Studies in Social Security conference in Sigtuna, Sweden, to give the opening plenary on this theme.

—

Child poverty and social protection in the Central and Eastern Europe (CEE)/Commonwealth of Independent States (CIS) region

In the last three years I have been working with UNICEF Regional Office for the CEE/CIS countries. It can be argued that children have been the real victims of the transition process in the CEE/CIS (The World Bank, 2005; UNICEF, 2006). The general picture is that the collapse of the Soviet Union resulted in a sharp fall in parental employment. As well as unemployment, many parents sought work abroad, leaving children with one parent or no parent, to be cared for by relatives and strangers. The transition process destroyed the benefits and services that had supported families with children in the Soviet era – family benefits, insurance benefits, clinics, nurseries, even schools were swept away – with much suffering.

Eventually transition countries began to recover and economies began to grow, but inequality grew as well, and there is evidence that the benefits of growth have not trickled down to children, especially poor children, as much as to other groups in these countries. One reason why the benefits of growth did not trickle down is that the transfer mechanisms that were adopted in place of the Soviet system, usually on the advice and financial support of The World Bank, have proven ineffective.

Recently the region has faced the consequences of a hike in food and energy prices and then the economic crisis. Child poverty rates are very high in the region. The global economic crisis is threatening the limited progress that has been made since 1998. There is already evidence that it has had an impact on trade, investment, remittances and growth. Unemployment has increased, particularly youth unemployment that is already very high in the region.

Arising from a concern about the impact of economic crisis the UNICEF Regional Office launched a project to investigate its impact. There were a number of elements in this package of work, including a comparative analysis of the social protection schemes I undertook with Emese Mayhew. This was based on the so-called 'model family' method, comparing social protection schemes. The Organisation for Economic Co-operation and Development (OECD) has used this method for many years to compare social protection packages in its

Benefits and Wages series. We have also undertaken a series of studies since 1980 using the method to compare child benefit packages, social assistance, child support and policies for lone parents (most recently see Bradshaw, 2006 and 2009). This is the first time the method has been used in CEE/CIS countries.

National informants (in this case social policy officers in UNICEF country offices) provided information on the tax/benefit system in their own countries. In order to compare like with like, they estimate what a set of standard model families would receive, at a specified set of earnings levels, in the way of a specified set of taxes and benefits that make up the social protection package for families with children. The information is entered into a set of data matrices and these are used to explore the level and structure of the child benefit package, converted to a common currency (US$ PPPs) or expressed as a proportion of average earnings.

We found that there are really no countries in the CEE/CIS region that are providing minimum social protection that can be described as satisfactory. For low wage earning families, the Ukraine, Bulgaria, Belarus, Turkmenistan and Serbia are the best of the bunch. Turkmenistan is an oil and gas exporting country making an effort, but there are no real exemplars, nothing of real merit. Figure 5.1 compares the value of the child benefit package for a low-paid working family in 2009. The UK has been included as an example of a EU country and South Africa a middle-income country pursuing a different model – not one influenced by The World Bank. In South Africa there is a constitutional obligation to tackle poverty. One important measure that does this is the Child Support Grant (CSG) paid to caregivers with children up to the age of 15. It is means tested but 80% of households are eligible. There is evidence that the CSG increases school enrolment rates from a high base by 50%; it reduces hunger and improves nutrition, height for age and therefore future earnings; and it increases labour participation (Delany et al, 2008). It is distributed very efficiently from payment points using fingerprint recognition technology. A recent review recommends it become universal on the grounds that rich Whites would not bother to claim it and, anyway if they did, it could be recouped through taxation (Lund et al, 2009).

Only the Ukraine approaches the level of child support provided in the UK, and the majority do much less for children than South Africa. There are some of the richer countries in the region where the effort to support low-paid families is nothing short of hopeless – Russia, Romania, Kazakhstan, Turkey and Macedonia could all be doing much more given their gross domestic product (GDP) per capita.

Figure 5.1: The child benefit package for a couple plus 2 children (2 years 11 months, and 7 years) as a proportion of net income of childless couple with one earner on half average earnings, June 2009

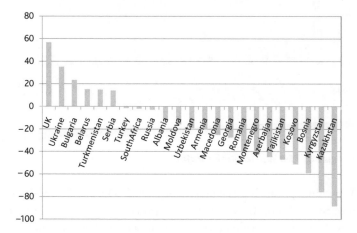

Figure 5.2 also includes the UK and South Africa and is a comparison of the level of social assistance package paid as the minimum income for households with no other financial resources. No country in the region has a social assistance package anywhere near the UK's.

None of these countries is devoting enough of their national resources to poor children. The OECD analysis of family spending shows that on average countries in the OECD spent 2.4% of GDP on families with children in 2005 in cash benefits, services and tax breaks (see www.oecd.org/dataoecd/55/58/38968865.xls). Turkey, the only country included in that analysis from this region, was bottom of the league table, spending 0.024% of GDP. There is no similar consistent series for CEE/CIS countries but the latest Innocenti Social Monitor has produced a table (3.4) that includes nine countries from the region, showing that they were all spending less than 1% of GDP on family allowances in 2004–06. The little they are devoting is wiped out by charges for health and education services that should be free.

Figure 5.2: Level of income on social assistance by family type in 2007, $US PPPs

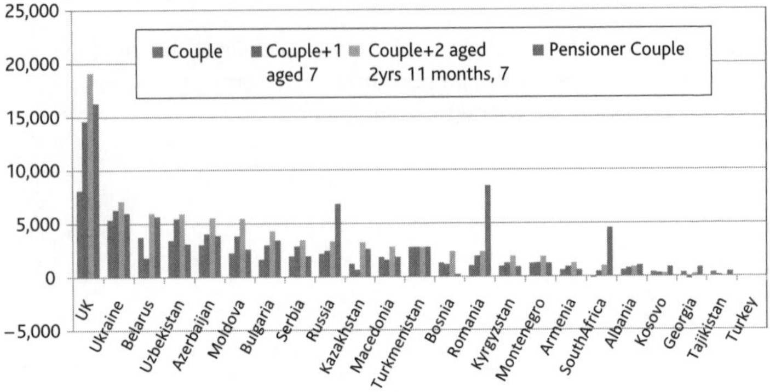

Failure of The World Bank model

Why is this – why is social protection so bad? During the transition process The World Bank has been the major influence on countries rebuilding their social protection systems. Their advice and funding has typically led to the development of social assistance schemes targeted at the very poor using a quasi-means test. The quasi-means test is designed to target resources in countries with large rural sectors, substantial informal economies and minorities dependent on remittances. Typically the processes are horrendously complicated, with much discretion leading to administrative corruption. The behavioural consequences of the schemes are likely to be dire. They help to undermine family support, gifts, living together, work and earnings, and home production. The level of payment in most of these regimes is so low that no one can be expected to live on it. Yet the rules are designed to ensure that only those without any other resources receive the benefit. Large proportions of applicants are refused help. Survey evidence suggests that large proportions of recipients are not poor – at least using the very low thresholds used by The World Bank. Substantial proportions of the poor do not apply or get help.

In response to criticisms, The World Bank and national governments have produced two arguments:

1. They claim that they are actively seeking to improve the quasi-means test, to improve the targeting of the schemes. This is often accompanied by the introduction of conditions on the payments.
2. There is no fiscal space for anything else.

There is in fact no way that these schemes can be effective – tightening the rules is not going to improve targeting because the whole conception is mistaken. Conditions do not work (Freeland, 2007; Barnes, 2008; Gabel and Kamerman, 2008; Villatoro, 2008; Carmona, 2009).

The tax base is certainly a problem in many of these countries. But, if the issue is the amount of national resources spent, there is evidence that none of these countries is spending enough on social protection and their investment in children is so low as to present dire consequences for their future development.

These schemes are pure window dressing. The model has succeeded in providing an image of concern for the poor, while neoliberal economic policies are pursued. The benefit levels are generally very low, designed to relieve absolute poverty (food poverty and food poverty plus) at minimal cost. They are more or less completely ineffective.

We have some hard-won evidence to support this claim. The World Bank dominates poverty research in the region, paying for much of it, providing technical advice and imposing their own thresholds on national statistical offices. A typical World Bank report will employ a very low US$1 a day poverty threshold and seek to demonstrate that economic growth and targeted social assistance are reducing poverty.

UNICEF and their national offices have helped us obtain micro data sets for six countries over the last three years. We have submitted these to secondary analysis using the child as the unit of analysis. One focus of this work was to evaluate the effectiveness of the existing transfer systems.

Figure 5.3 shows that pensions for old people are quite an effective anti-child poverty measure – without pensions contributing to family income, many more children would be poor.

Figure 5.3: Impact of pensions on child poverty rates (2* food poverty except Bosnia and Herzegovina, and Serbia 4* food poverty)

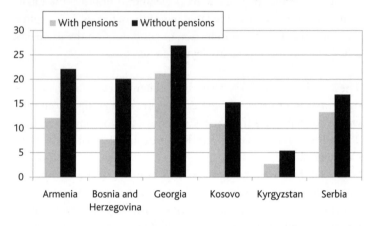

Figure 5.4 shows that in comparison Targeted Social Assistance (TSA) benefits are comparatively ineffective in reducing child poverty.

Figure 5.4: Impact of TSA on child poverty rates (2* food poverty except Bosnia and Herzegovina, and Serbia 4* food poverty)

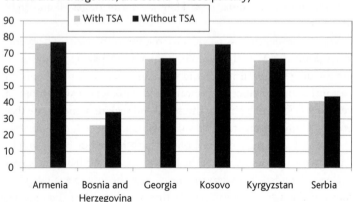

These results are highly challenging. The World Bank is an organisation committed to Washington consensus understandings, driven by neoliberal economic ideas. Its staff, the many consultants it employs, the staff of national statistical offices and sadly most of the governments in this region have a very heavy investment in these policies. They are absolutely infuriated by these criticisms, and UNICEF, UNIFEM, the International Labour Organization (ILO) and a few academics engaged with them are subject to constant vilification for expressing them.

Yet many of the countries in this region are candidate or potential candidate countries of the EU. The EU has ambassadors in every country. Yet the European social project is hardly understood in the region. Governments in the region will look wide-eyed and askance when it is suggested that they should spend at European levels, that universal child benefits, universal services, social insurance and residual rights-based social assistance are the main vehicle used in EU countries for supporting families with children. No one, including the EU ambassadors, has ever suggested this before.

Frankly The World Bank has a terrible record in the region. The international community that supports The Bank should be ashamed. Effectively World Bank poverty policies have been pure window dressing. Using their huge resources they have funded both the production of the evidence and the response to the evidence and manipulated the truth. The Washington neoliberal consensus has failed the region and with the recession these schemes have come under increasing strain.

The region needs to invest in a decent social protection system along European lines. There are no inspiring models in the region – thanks to the influence of The World Bank – and this is a great pity. But the EU model needs to be asserted and actually there are visions from middle-income countries to aspire to – the South African CSG, the Basic Income experiment being trialled in Namibia (see www.bignam.org/Publications/BIG_Assessment_report_08a.pdf), and, partly in response to Townsend's advocacy, Argentina has just implemented a child benefit system for those excluded from the existing system for formal employees.

Conclusion

Peter Townsend had reconceptualised poverty as relative before he
was 30. He had rediscovered poverty (with Brian Abel-Smith) before
he was 40 (at the same time as he was doing his wonderful research
on older people). His great work on poverty – *Poverty in the United
Kingdom* – was eventually published in 1979 when he was 50, after
many vicissitudes and long after the research that underpinned it had
been completed; by then he was working on health inequalities. He
achieved all this without ever receiving a grant from the Economic
and Social Research Council (ESRC) or the government. *Poverty
in the United Kingdom* was supported by the Joseph Rowntree
Foundation – with extreme patience on their part. It was the best
thing they have ever done.

Peter helped to create and led CPAG. The glorious outcome was
Child Benefit (see Chapters Seven and Fourteen, this volume). They
are an obvious target for the new Coalition intent on reducing
the deficit. Before the election the Institute of Directors and the
TaxPayers' Alliance had already singled them out for abolition. In
the Coalition's first budget they were frozen for three years. We all
need to defend them resolutely.

But in his 70s Peter turned his attention to developing countries.
His last book articulated the case for social security in developing
countries. He argued that poor countries should be following the
example of rich countries and developing universal child benefits. He
believed that international institutions and transnational corporations
have an obligation to fund these benefits. He advocated that the
sources of finance should include a Tobin tax on currency flows. I
hope that at least some of us can find the time and energy to focus on
sustaining Peter's last campaign – for child benefits in poor countries.

References

Abel-Smith, B. and Townsend, P. (1965) *The poor and the poorest*, London:
Bell.

Barnes, H. (2008) *Links between matriculation, poverty and the Child Support
Grant: A review of the evidence*, Working Paper 7, Oxford: Centre for the
Analysis of South African Social Policy, University of Oxford.

Bradshaw, J. (ed) (1993) *Budget standards for the United Kingdom*, Aldershot: Avebury.

Bradshaw, J. (2006) 'Child benefit packages in 15 countries in 2004', in J. Lewis (ed) *Children, changing families and the welfare state*, Cheltenham: Edward Elgar, pp 69-89.

Bradshaw, J. (2009) 'An international perspective on child benefit packages', in S. Kamerman, S. Phipps and A. Ben-Arieh (eds) *From child welfare to child well-being: An international perspective on knowledge in the service of policy making*, Dordrecht: Springer, pp 293-308.

Bradshaw, J. and Finch, N. (2003) 'Overlaps in dimensions of poverty', *Journal of Social Policy*, vol 32, no 4, pp 513-25.

Bradshaw, J. and Richardson, D. (2008) 'Does child income poverty measure child well-being internationally?', *Social Policy and Society*, vol 7, issue 4, October, pp 521-36.

Bradshaw, J., Middleton, S., Davis, A., Oldfield, N., Smith, N., Cusworth, L. and Williams, J. (2008) *A minimum income standard for Britain: What people think*, York: Joseph Rowntree Foundation (www.minimumincomestandard. org/).

Carmona, M.S. (2009) *Promotion and protection of all human rights, civil, political, economic, social and cultural rights, including the right to development*, Report of the Independent Expert on the Question of Human Rights and Extreme Poverty, Geneva: UN General Assembly, Human Rights Council.

Delany, A., Ismail, Z., Graham, L. and Ramkisson, Y. (2008) *Review of the Child Support Grant: Uses, implementation and obstacles*, Johannesburg: UNICEF.

Desai, M. (1986) 'Drawing the poverty line: on defining the poverty threshold', in P. Golding (ed) *Excluding the poor*, London: Child Poverty Action Group, pp 1-20.

Fisher, G. (1997) 'The development and history of the US poverty thresholds – a brief overview', *GSS/SSS Newsletter* (Newsletter of the Government Statistics Section and the Social Statistics Section of the American Statistical Association), winter (http://aspe.hhs.gov/poverty/papers/hptgssiv.htm).

Freeland, N. (2007) 'Superfluous, pernicious, atrocious and abominable? The case against conditional cash transfers' *IDS Bulletin*, vol 28, no 3, pp 75-8.

Gabel, S.G. and Kamerman, S.B. (2008) 'Do conditional cash transfers work? The experience of the US and developing countries', in *The future of social citizenship: Politics, institutions and outcomes*, Stockholm: RC19 Conference.

Gordon, D. and Pantazis, C. (1997) *Breadline Britain in the 1990s*, Aldershot: Ashgate.

Gordon, D., Adelman, A., Ashworth, K., Bradshaw, J., Levitas, R., Middleton, S., Pantazis, C., Patsios, D., Payne, S., Townsend, P. and Williams, J. (2000) *Poverty and social exclusion in Britain*, York: Joseph Rowntree Foundation.

Hoelscher, P. (2008) *The new World Bank £1.25 a day: A global poverty line for children?*, Geneva: UNICEF RO CEE/CIS.

Lund, F., Noble, M., Barnes, H. and Wright, G. (2009) 'Is there a rationale for conditional cash transfers for children in South Africa?', *Transformation*, no 70, pp 70-91.

Mack, J. and Lansley, S. (1985) *Poor Britain*, London: Allen and Unwin.

Moore, J. (1989) 'The end of the line for poverty', Speech to the Conservative Political Centre, London, 11 May.

ODPM (Office of the Deputy Prime Minister) (2004) *The Social Exclusion Unit*, London: ODPM.

Pantazis, C., Gordon, D. and Levitas, R. (eds) (2006) *Poverty and social exclusion in Britain*, Bristol: The Policy Press.

Piachaud, D. (1987) 'Problems in the definition and measurement of poverty', *Journal of Social Policy*, vol 16, no 2, pp 147-64.

Pogge, T. (2008) *A consistent measure of real poverty: A reply to Ravallion*, One pager No 54, Brasilia: International Poverty Centre (www.ipc-undp.org/pub/IPCOnePager54.pdf).

Pogge, T. and Reddy, S. (2005) *How not to count the poor* (http://ssrn.com/abstract=893159).

Ravallion, M., Chen, S. and Sangruala, P. (2008) *A dollar a day revisited*, Washington: The World Bank.

Reddy, S. (2008) *Are estimates of poverty in Latin America reliable?*, One pager No 52, Brasilia: International Poverty Centre (www.ipc-undp.org/pub/IPCOnePager52.pdf).

Reddy, S. and Minoiu, C. (2007) *Has world poverty really fallen?* (http://ssrn.com/abstract=921153).

Rees, G., Bradshaw, J., Goswami, H. and Keung, A. (2010) *Understanding children's well-being: A national survey of young people's well-being*, London: The Children's Society.

Runciman, W.G. (1966) *Relative deprivation and social justice*, Harmondsworth: Penguin.

Sen, A. (1983) 'Poor relatively speaking', *Oxford Economic Papers*, vol 35, no 1.

Shanas, E. et al (1968) *Old people in three industrial societies*, London: Routledge and Kegan Paul.

Townsend, P. (1952) 'Poverty – ten years after Beveridge', *Planning,* no 344, London: Political and Economic Planning.

Townsend, P. (1954) 'Measuring poverty', *British Journal of Sociology*, June, pp 130-7.

Townsend, P. (1957) *The family life of old people*, London: Routledge and Kegan Paul.

Townsend, P. (1962a) *The last refuge: A survey of residential institutions and homes for the aged in England and Wales*, London: Routledge and Kegan Paul.

Townsend, P. (1962b) 'The meaning of poverty', *British Journal of Sociology*, vol 13, no 3, pp 210-27.

Townsend, P. (1979) *Poverty in the United Kingdom: A survey of household resources and standards of living*, London: Penguin.

Townsend, P. (ed) (2009) *Building decent societies: Rethinking the role of social security in state building*, Geneva: International Labour Organization/ Palgrave Macmillan.

Townsend, P. and Wedderburn, D. (1965) *The aged in the welfare state*, London: Bell.

UNICEF (2006) *Innocenti Social Monitor 2006: Understanding child poverty in South Eastern Europe and the commonwealth of independent states*, Florence: UNICEF Innocenti Research Centre.

Villatoro, P.S. (2008) 'CCTs in Latin America: human capital accumulation and poverty reduction', *Poverty in Focus*, no 15, pp 14-15.

World Bank, The (2005) *Growth, poverty and inequality: Eastern Europe and the former Soviet Union*, Washington, DC: The World Bank.

SIX

Social justice for children: investigating and eradicating child poverty

Ruth Lister

Peter Townsend was a towering figure in the anti-child poverty cause. It is difficult to exaggerate the impact he had both on the study of child poverty and on the campaign to eradicate it. Yet, surprisingly, the concept of 'child poverty' does not figure prominently in his writings about poverty in the UK. Of course, this is not to say that Townsend downplayed the significance of child poverty in the UK. He was, after all, a prominent campaigner against it. Rather, he did not separate it out from the wider issues of poverty and privilege as a discrete problem, which could be solved without addressing the underlying structures of inequality that maintain social injustice. In the Foreword to a history of the Child Poverty Action Group (CPAG), with which he was closely associated, he wrote: 'More attention must be given to the exposure of excessive and unnecessary privilege, as much as excessive and unnecessary power. It is impossible to raise the poor without simultaneously diminishing the rich' (1986). This means, therefore, that any assessment of his work on child poverty and its impact cannot be easily divorced from his work on poverty and inequality more generally. The first part of this chapter considers Townsend's contribution both as a social scientist and as a campaigner within this wider context. The second part discusses how we might build on Townsend's legacy with regard to both the investigation into and the eradication of child poverty.

The contribution: social scientist and campaigner extraordinaire

Townsend's contribution to the anti-child poverty cause is particularly notable for his powerful structural analysis of poverty, his conceptualisation of poverty as relative, his contribution to the 'rediscovery' of child poverty and his role as an engaged academic who also campaigned against child poverty.

A structural analysis

Underlying Townsend's contribution as a social scientist and campaigner was a clear structural analysis of poverty and its causes. This was firmly articulated in *Poverty in the United Kingdom*:

> The theoretical approach developed in this book is one rooted in class relations. Some account has to be given to allocative principles and mechanisms and developments in the pattern of social life and consumption. In all societies, there is a crucial relationship between the production, distribution and redistribution of resources on the one hand and the creation or sponsorship of style of living on the other. One governs the resources which come to be in the control of individuals and families. The other governs the 'ordinary' conditions and expectations attaching to membership of society, the denial or lack of which represents deprivation. The two are in constant interaction and explain at any given moment historically both the level and extent of poverty. (Townsend, 1979, p 917)

He also underlined that 'many people, and overwhelmingly married women and children, are not in poverty by virtue of any *personal* characteristics so much as indirectly by virtue of the labour market, wage or social security characteristics of the principal income recipient of the family unit' (1979, p 899, original emphasis). While we might want to place more emphasis today on the wages and social security benefits received by married women in their own right, the key message lies in the secondary role attributed to personal characteristics.

The relative conceptualisation of poverty

Townsend's structural explanation underpinned his conceptualisation of poverty as relative and multi-faceted (discussed in more detail in Chapter Five, this volume). He was not the first to conceptualise poverty as relative to contemporary 'ordinary living patterns, customs and activities' (1979, p 31) in the society in which an individual or family lives. Nevertheless, it was Townsend who put the relative nature of poverty at the core of his conceptualisation and who was responsible for its most detailed and sophisticated exposition. The particular importance of such a conceptualisation for children has been demonstrated in subsequent research with children themselves (notably Middleton and colleagues, 1994, and Ridge, 2002). For children, the inability to 'join in' and 'fit in' (Ridge, 2002) can be especially hurtful and damaging at a time when their identities are emerging and their peers can be most cruel.

Townsend's relative conceptualisation of poverty frames most subsequent social scientific work on the topic, even if the original distinction between absolute and relative poverty is now questioned (Lister, 2004). It has also strongly influenced social democratic thinking. However, its most extensive exposition in *Poverty in the UK* was published in 1979, the year that Margaret Thatcher came to power. This meant that its political impact in the late 20th century was more muted than it might otherwise have been. Indeed, a decade after its publication, John Moore (1989) infamously declared the 'end of the line for poverty', and dismissed the idea of relative poverty as simply inequality, espoused as a concept by the Left in order to condemn capitalism. It is, however, one of the marks of Cameron's Conservatives that they have embraced the idea of relative poverty and explicitly rejected Moore's claim. One of the consequences is that the Conservatives have signed up to the objective of eradicating child poverty (although see Lister and Bennett, 2010, for a critique of the Conservative position).

Townsend's conceptualisation of poverty has thus had a considerable impact on both academic and political definitions and measures of child poverty. The same is not really true, however, of more popular understandings. According to the British Social Attitudes survey, in 2006, only just over a fifth (22%) of the population subscribed to a relative definition of poverty as 'lack of sufficient income to "buy the things most people take for granted"' (Taylor-Gooby and Martin, 2008, p 241). At no time since 1986 has the proportion exceeded 28% (in 1994). Relative poverty is all too often regarded as not being 'real' poverty, including by some practitioners and service providers (Cameron et al, 2008).

Particularly challenging is the evidence of how some people in poverty themselves subscribe to more absolutist understandings. Jan Flaherty's insightful study of how people with experience of poverty talk about it throws some light on this. While participants were willing to talk about the deprivations and hardships they experienced, hardly any of them accepted that they were 'poor'. She writes that 'for respondents in the study talk about "poverty" was to discuss a phenomenon that was seen as having more to do with Comic Relief and famine news-reports than with their day-to-day life....The few respondents who stated that they were in poverty did so within a stringent definition of necessities and barely acceptable quality of life' (2008, p 216). It is difficult to be sure how far the refusal to identify with the label of poverty reflected a desire to distance themselves from the stigmatising label, but there was certainly no acceptance of a relative notion of poverty among the participants in her study.

These issues are hinted at in Townsend's discussion about the relationship between 'objective' and 'subjective' deprivation in *Poverty in the UK*. Here, he acknowledges 'a genuine problem ... of people with extremely low resources who deny feelings of deprivation' (1979, p 426). And he notes that 'about half of those living in poverty said, in answer to one question, that they never felt poor', even if they 'recognized in other ways that they were worse off than people with high or middle incomes' (1979, p 431).

More recently, Townsend developed a human rights perspective on poverty (see Chapter Twelve, this volume). Although this was primarily in an international development context, it is consistent with his more general structural analysis of poverty. And his observations are as apposite when applied to child poverty in the UK: 'The language of rights ... shifts the focus of debate from the personal failures of the "poor" to the failures to resolve poverty of macro-economic structures and policies of nation-states and international bodies. [Child poverty then has to be seen as a] "violation of rights" that nation-states, and international agencies, groups of governments and TNCs [transnational corporations] have a legal and institutional obligation to remedy' (Townsend, 2010a, p 115). Even though human rights did not figure explicitly in Townsend's writing about child poverty in the UK, his work was always infused with the essence of a human rights perspective, namely respect for the fundamental dignity of each human being. As far back as 1958, he envisaged 'a society where respect for people is valued most of all. For that brings real equality' (2009, p 158).

The 'rediscovery' of child poverty

I have argued that Townsend did not separate out child poverty as a discrete category in his social scientific work on domestic poverty. Nevertheless, it was the research he conducted with Brian Abel-Smith that led to the public 'rediscovery' of child (and family) poverty in 1965. It is difficult to think of any other single piece of research that has had more political impact than that which was published as *The poor and the poorest* (1965).

This report exemplified how Townsend combined social science – 'the cool test of evidence' (2009, p 149) – and political action. Grouping Townsend and Abel-Smith with Richard Titmuss, Keith Banting explains that 'their research was explicitly political: they were setting out to reshape policy-makers' interpretation of their environment' (1979, pp 69-70). One of the reasons that this research had such an impact was that it provided the basis for the first major campaign of the newly formed CPAG in the early years of Harold Wilson's Labour government. According to Banting, CPAG 'were creating a new issue and entrenched images of society were shifting' (1979, p 73). The significance is spelt out more fully by Whiteley and Winyard:

> It was highly successful and had an immediate effect
> on politicians and civil servants.... Academic research
> and the CPAG campaign had done more than simply
> prick the conscience of the Labour party. It had put
> the issue of poverty back on the political agenda and
> stimulated a public debate. This was a crucial catalyst in
> the development of the new poverty lobby. (1987, p 53)

Townsend was to play a pivotal role in 'the development of the new poverty lobby'. He was among the founding members of CPAG. The group's original name – the Family Poverty Group – was quickly forsaken, largely under the influence of probably its key founding member, Dr Harriett Wilson. She argued that children stood to be affected most by poverty and that 'even the most bigoted person will usually agree that the needs of children should be viewed in a different way from those of their parents' (quoted in McCarthy, 1986, p 63). The concept of child poverty thereby entered the political lexicon, to be picked up again by the New Labour government with its commitment to the eradication of child poverty.

Campaigning against child poverty

Townsend became Chair of CPAG soon after Frank Field took over as Director in 1969. According to Michael McCarthy, 'their partnership in forging a new style and role for CPAG, a determined switch from the defensive to the offensive, was crucial not only to the Group's regeneration but to its survival in the political arena' (1986, p 106). While much of this offensive was directed at politicians, from the outset Townsend appreciated the wider role that groups such as CPAG could and should play as 'agencies of popular education' (2010b, p 544). Although he was to play a less central and active part in later years, Townsend continued as a guiding light in his capacity as CPAG's Chair until 1989 when he became the group's Life President. In that role, according to Kate Green, CPAG's Chief Executive at the time of his death, he could 'still be relied on to inspire and exhort us to take a tougher line' (quoted in Clark, 2008).

One issue, in particular, on which he could always be counted on to take a 'tough' line was that of universal versus means-tested benefits (see Chapter Seven, this volume). *Poverty in the United Kingdom* devoted a chapter to 'the failure of means-tested benefits'. 'On all the evidence', he later wrote, with fellow authors of the Black Report on health inequality, 'means tested benefits are poor in coverage, costly to administer, do not encourage savings, and are generally inadequate in meeting needs, as well as being unpopular' (Black et al, 2010, p 400). Universal benefits and services, in contrast, represent 'an efficient, economical and socially integrative mechanism' to prevent poverty (Townsend, 2010c, pp 639-40). Not only was Townsend an indefatigable defender of universal family allowances/child benefits in the UK context, but he also, more recently, made the case at a global level (see Chapter Four, this volume).

Building on the legacy

We turn now to consider how we can best build on Townsend's legacy with regard to both the investigation and eradication of child poverty. First, however, in the face of a resurgence of more individualistic and cultural explanations of poverty, there is an urgent need to reassert the kind of structural analysis in which his contribution as both a social scientist and a campaigner was rooted.

Reasserting a structural analysis

John Welshman (2007) details how Townsend led the critique of the 'cycle of deprivation' thesis, popularised by leading Conservative politician Sir Keith Joseph, in the 1970s. This thesis attributed poverty to behavioural and cultural causes. Paraphrasing Townsend (1970), Welshman writes:

> The elimination of poverty required not the reform, education, or rehabilitation of the individual, or even the creation of more opportunities for upward mobility, but the reconstruction of the national and regional systems by which resources were distributed, or the introduction

of additional systems that were universal and egalitarian.
(Welshman, 2007, p 194)

The significance today of Townsend's intervention in the 1970s is
demonstrated by Welshman's work. He reveals the strong continuities
between Joseph's cycle of deprivation thesis and New Labour's social
exclusion agenda. He argues that the key elements of this agenda:

> ... the belief in the paradox of the persistence of
> deprivation in the midst of rising living standards and
> developing welfare services; the focus on intergenerational
> continuities; the enumeration of problem individuals and
> groups; the significance attached to early intervention;
> and the claim that these are supported by evidence and
> academic research – were all there in Joseph's speech of
> 34 years earlier. (Welshman, 2007, p 258)

Welshman compares Tony Blair's major social exclusion speech,
delivered to the Joseph Rowntree Foundation (JRF) in September
2006, with Joseph's: 'If the texts of the two speeches are placed
alongside each other, it is very difficult to tell which was Joseph, and
which is Blair' (2007, p 258). The relative weakness of New Labour's
structural analysis is also reflected in its 'what works' problem-solving
approach, which presented poverty and social exclusion as a series of
discrete social problems rather than as systemic (Lister, 2001). This
is reinforced by its discursive construction of poverty as in part a
problem of 'welfare dependency' and a 'dependency culture' (Lister,
2010a, Chapter 5).

This construction, reinforced by the return of the concept of the
'underclass', is even more central to contemporary Conservative
accounts of poverty (see Lister and Bennett, 2010). The Party's analysis
relies heavily on that developed by Iain Duncan Smith's Centre for
Social Justice. It is framed by a discourse of 'broken Britain/society'
and 'big government versus big society'. Key tenets are that the state
is part of the problem rather than the solution, and that the causes
of poverty are behavioural and cultural rather than structural, and

lie in families and communities and in 'wrong personal choices' (Cameron, 2010).

While social scientists increasingly acknowledge the importance of recognising the agency of people living in poverty and that culture can shape behaviour, typically they are also clear that this agency is exercised within severe structural constraints (Lister, 2004). There is a need today for the kind of incisive critique mounted by Townsend in the 1970s in order to demonstrate the continued power of these structural constraints and the limitations of a diagnosis and prescription, which focus on 'the reform, education, or rehabilitation of the individual, or even the creation of more opportunities for upward mobility' (Welshman, 2007, p 194, paraphrasing Townsend).

Investigating child poverty

An important development over the past decade or so in researching child poverty has been a focus in some studies on how children themselves experience poverty. Previously it was implicitly assumed that it was sufficient to aggregate children with other household members in order to measure poverty and deprivation and to interview parents or other responsible adults in order to gain a picture of the effects of poverty. Townsend was involved in the major 1999 Poverty and Social Exclusion (PSE) survey. This added 'a new dimension to the exploration of children's experience of poverty and social exclusion by directly measuring their access within households to necessities of life, both items and activities, rather than focusing primarily on the household level' (Lloyd, 2006, p 315).

The PSE survey has been complemented by a growing number of qualitative studies. Two literature reviews, by Gerry Redmond (2008) and Tess Ridge (2009), demonstrate their valuable contribution. Redmond emphasises the importance of 'children's standpoints ... for understanding poverty as it affects children and their families, and the effectiveness of policies to support them' (2008, p 12). One of the key messages emerging from the studies reviewed by Ridge is that 'the experience of poverty in childhood can be profoundly disturbing and disruptive. However, children are not passive victims of their circumstances; the evidence shows that they try to mediate and make sense of their experiences and are often engaged in negotiating a complex mix of everyday challenges and disadvantages' (2009, p 22; see also Redmond, 2008, 2009). In another review of children's perspectives on poverty, Ridge and Saunders welcome a growing body of international research, 'informed in part by the new sociology of childhood, which posits children as competent social actors, and by the growth of children's rights and the new politics of participation' (2009, p 500). They believe that it 'has the potential to bring children's voices and experiences to the very centre of the political stage', which in turn can lead to better informed policy (Ridge and Saunders, 2009, p 500).

Potentially valuable also is the sustainable livelihoods approach, which has been piloted in the UK by Oxfam and Church Action on Poverty, drawing on experience in a development context where it originated. They conclude from their piloting work 'that the approach is as relevant within a rich (yet unequal) Northern country as it is in poorer Southern countries' (May et al, 2009, p 5). The basic premise is that 'everyone has assets in their life, both financial and non-financial; these assets are combined to create a livelihood....The ways in which people combine their assets to support themselves and their families, and the decisions and choices that they make within the context in which they live, is what makes up their livelihood strategy' (May et al, 2009, p 9). As this quotation implies, not surprisingly, livelihoods analysis is currently typically used with adults. However, suitably adapted, it might also throw a penetrating light on children's 'strategies of survival' as they draw in particular on social and meagre material resources (Ridge, 2009, p 92).

Both Redmond and Ridge identify gaps in our knowledge about child poverty and some of the difficulties involved in qualitative research with children. Ridge underlines the need for 'more rigour' in such studies, although makes clear that 'this does not mean a withdrawal from the development of innovative studies like peer research and participatory projects' (2009, p 94). There may be scope for further developing participatory poverty research with children as well as with adults.

Ridge and Redmond also emphasise the importance of recognising the heterogeneity of children and their circumstances. 'Of importance in this respect are likely to be age, gender, family type, ethnicity, indigenous status, disability and location' (Redmond, 2008, p 12). Ridge points to the 'relative dearth of evidence about the experiences of poverty from different ethnic minority groups' and 'the need to understand the ways in which poverty might impact on different minority families and the men, women and children within them, across all areas of their lives' (2009, p 93). Analysis of quantitative data reveals that, despite considerable differences between minority ethnic groups, 'all minority groups have higher rates of child poverty than the majority' and 'minority groups were at greater risk of deprivation even among the income poor' (Platt, 2009, pp 1, 5). Lucinda Platt (2009) observes that the evidence base regarding ethnicity and child poverty 'remains partial', and she suggests where additional research is needed. The racialised nature of poverty was under-developed in Townsend's own work and, as Platt and Ridge indicate, still needs more attention.

Ridge also exposes the marginalisation within poverty research of highly marginalised groups:

> Children and families who are on the margins of society and highly vulnerable to poverty and exclusion are also poorly represented in research, particularly in relation to the experience of poverty across their lives rather than the focus of research on their difference.... As a result, there is very little research that engages with gypsy and traveller children, refugees or asylum seeking children that looks explicitly at how poverty affects their lives. (2009, p 93)

These are groups who are not identified in the official poverty statistics and therefore our knowledge of the incidence of poverty among them as well as their experience of poverty is very limited. They are largely invisible in the poverty literature (Preston, 2005). The National Equality Panel (2010) has called for better data collection to improve our knowledge of these groups who are at high risk of poverty and disadvantage. On the basis of the evidence that is available, it describes the position of the Gypsy and Traveller community as being 'of great concern' (2010, p 397). Similarly, various investigations have identified extreme poverty and even destitution among some asylum seekers. Pamela Fitzpatrick criticises the treatment of asylum-seeking children as different: 'Asylum seeker children are not treated as children in the general population and their needs are not determined in the same way as other children. Instead they are viewed first and foremost through their immigration status' (2005, p 106). It is important that researchers do not reinforce the marginalised status of these groups.

Redmond emphasises the importance of family context to understanding how children cope with poverty and the need for more 'evidence, from the children's own perspectives, of what happens when family relations are under strain' (2008, p 12). One example of such strain is domestic violence (see, for instance, Hooper et al, 2007), which reminds us of the importance of applying a gendered lens to the study of child poverty and also policies for its eradication (Women's Budget Group, 2005; Lister, 2010b). Townsend recognised that gender is 'a prime determinant of the construction of society and hence of unequal privilege and the unequal distribution of income and other resources in society. The reverberations are fundamental' (1993, p 106; see also Chapter Three, this volume). As the managers of poverty, women bear much of the strain and often act as shock absorbers, shielding children from the full impact. It is not surprising, therefore, that much research into family poverty, including in two-parent families, tends to involve mothers. Without losing sight of the burden that women often carry, Ridge suggests that the perspective of low-income fathers is now 'an important area for further exploration' (2009, p 93).

Redmond argues also that there is 'a need to better understand the influence of structural and cultural factors that facilitate or inhibit the use of different types of agency by children' (Redmond, 2008, p 9). This serves as a reminder of the dangers of pointing the research microscope exclusively at the powerless so that the agency of the powerful and the structures that underpin their power and privilege remain hidden. Townsend was keenly aware of this danger: 'Hundreds, if not thousands, of research reports dealing with the bottom end of the distribution but only a tiny handful dealing with the top end have been issued during the 1990s. Yet the form and depth of the entire social hierarchy is conditioned by the decisions made and the conventions asserted at the top end of the hierarchy' (1997, p 267).

One of the few pieces of research into those at 'the top end of the hierarchy' led to the conclusion that their ignorance about the income distribution and their position within it 'should disqualify the wealthy from pontificating about taxation or redistribution' (Toynbee and Walker, 2008, p 26). These rich City bankers and lawyers 'considered themselves normal, when they were anything but' (2008, pp 24-5). We need more research into how the rich and powerful use their income and wealth and how they exercise their agency to preserve their privileges and pass them down to their children. Privilege at one end of the hierarchy and deprivation and exclusion at the other are perpetuated in part by a culture that legitimates the hierarchy itself and that serves to 'other' those at the bottom. Interdisciplinary research, drawing on social psychology as well as social policy and sociology, could help to deepen understanding of the processes of 'othering' and the social relations of poverty and inequality.

Eradicating child poverty

This is not the place to outline a detailed blueprint for the eradication of child poverty. Instead, it is worth reflecting on the principles that Townsend advocated, as these help set a radical social policy agenda. Broadly these are the principles of equality and redistribution, universalism and human rights.

Townsend was always clear that policies to eradicate child poverty have to be part of a wider egalitarian, redistributive strategy, embracing the distribution of original incomes as well as the state's reallocation of resources through taxation, benefits and public services. Indeed, in an essay written shortly before New Labour came to power in 1997, he argued that redistribution represented the 'only convincing alternative to achieve success', for it denotes 'the direction of the structural change which must be engineered to address social polarisation and related concerns' (1997, p 266). He argued that the inclusion of original earnings within the meaning of redistribution 'would lead to more informed recognition of the contributions made to overall production and services by many people in the lower ranks of earnings' (1997, p 267). This is especially important from a gendered perspective, given that women's contributions are typically undervalued.

Townsend called for a transformation in 'the nature of our strategic thinking' and gave as an example: 'Giving effect to equality of opportunity makes no sense if the structure of existing inequalities ... and the forces determining inequality of outcomes are not addressed' (1997, p 267). The Fabian Commission on Life Chances and Child Poverty (of which he and I were members) took a similar stance (2006, p 27):

> ... there is something fundamentally unfair about the distribution of rewards attached to particular positions in UK society today. For this reason, the life chances framework is necessarily broader than that of social mobility: we are concerned with the chances of everyone living a full and flourishing life, irrespective of how they come to occupy different positions.... We need to confront the complacent view that a steep hierarchy in social positions is inescapable.

As well as a list of specific policies designed to equalise children's life chances, the report recommended that the government should 'adopt the objective of reducing income and wealth inequalities over time, in recognition of their impact on life chances' (2006, p 197).

The Commission also argued for a rebalancing of financial support for children through an improvement in the real value of Child Benefit. As noted earlier, Townsend was a passionate advocate of universalism. In the 1980s, CPAG brought together a wide range of organisations under the Save Child Benefit campaign in the face of a threat to the universal nature of Child Benefit. A similar threat faces us again, as Child Benefit will no longer benefit families containing a higher-rate taxpayer and rates will be frozen for three years. Furthermore, the erosion of contributory benefits continues.

A more recent Fabian Society report on building 'the solidarity society' provides a robust defence of the universalist approach to which Townsend was committed. The insight that 'welfare systems which are focused on addressing "poverty" do worse in poverty outcomes than broadly-based systems which aim to reflect a shared sense of citizenship across society ... underpins the new welfare settlement' it advocates (Horton and Gregory, 2009, p xix). One piece of evidence, from which this insight is gleaned, is a cross-national study, which found that 'when states spend more of their financial resources on citizen welfare, poverty is reduced', with universal child and family allowances emerging as a 'particularly effective anti-poverty instrument' (Moller et al, 2003, p 45).

Another 'key lesson' emphasised in the Fabian report in support of universal benefits and services 'is that institutions for successful poverty prevention must attend very closely to the way in which they affect and structure the social relations between individuals and groups in society' (Horton and Gregory, 2009, p xvi). At stake here, argue Horton and Gregory, is the quality of citizenship. Their argument can also be used in support of a human rights approach to poverty.

It has been suggested that 'to date, there has been little integration of human rights and anti-poverty work in the UK, either in public policy or among communities experiencing poverty and their allies' (Donald and Mottershaw, 2009a, p 9). This is beginning to change, at least among some anti-poverty organisations (BIHR et al, 2008), building on the work of organisations such as ATD Fourth World. International experience, including in the US, suggests that the language of human rights can help to reframe the poverty debate and provide an empowering mobilising banner for people experiencing poverty. It also provides a language through which asylum seekers can seek justice.

With regard to policy, a human rights approach has implications for both process and outcome. Attention to process is crystallised in demands for respectful treatment by public services and for participation in policy making. A range of studies demonstrates that the key to how parents who are living in poverty feel about services is whether they treat them with respect. All too often service providers betray a lack of understanding of what life is like on a low income, talk down to parents and treat them with disrespect, and fail to listen to what they have to say because their own knowledge and understanding, born of experience, is not valued. In contrast, where parents are treated as equals, listened to and given the opportunity to offer their own views, they are more likely to respond positively to the services provided. The same principles apply to children, although we know less about how they experience services. At the same time, demands for participation in policy making are becoming more vocal among poverty activists. 'The right to participation is woven through the fabric of international human rights law' (Donald and Mottershaw, 2009a, p 14). The traditional marginalisation of both people living in poverty and children in policy making thus represents a major challenge (Lister, 2007).

A vital outcome from a human rights perspective is the right to an adequate income, sufficient to enable people to live decently and with their human dignity respected. The minimum income standard, developed by JRF, represents what 'ordinary people, through group discussion define [as] the minimum ... [including] having sufficient resources to participate in society and to maintain human dignity, consuming those goods and services regarded as essential in Britain today' (Bradshaw et al, 2008, p 3). For those below pension age, the safety-net benefit of Income Support/income-based Jobseeker's Allowance provides an income well short of the minimum income standard (Hirsch et al, 2009). While there has been a significant real increase in the value of safety-net benefits paid for children under New Labour, the benefits paid to adults, with or without children, have for the most part stagnated, which means that their value has fallen further and further behind average incomes (Sutherland et al, 2008; Kenway, 2009). From a slightly different perspective, the Marmot review of health inequalities endorsed the case for 'a minimum income for healthy living', arguing that 'it would ensure that all would receive an appropriate income for their stage in the life course, and would reduce overall levels of poverty as well as child poverty' (Marmot, 2010, p 120).

International research into the use of human rights in anti-poverty strategies and politics points to the 'potential for using human rights to reframe public debate about poverty in the UK.... Polling and qualitative research shows that most people in the UK support the existence of human rights legislation and respond positively to the human rights values of dignity, respect and fairness and to the idea of legally-enforceable socio-economic rights' (Donald and Mottershaw, 2009b, p 4).

The JRF Public Interest in Poverty Issues programme, of which the study was a part, was motivated by a belief in the importance of public attitudes towards poverty (emphasised too in the Fabian report on the solidarity society; see Horton and Gregory, 2009). An overview of the programme concludes that 'a long-term programme involving government, civil society, media and private sector organisations is needed for sustained attitude change and to build public awareness that solutions to poverty need a society-wide response' (Hanley, 2009, p 1). It makes clear that as well as 'building awareness of poverty', such a programme should also be 'about changing the terms of the debate, using frameworks and narratives that move the debate beyond individuals and their needs to broader explanations of causes and solutions to poverty' (Hanley, 2009, p 11). This not only echoes Townsend's repeated call for a structural analysis of poverty but also the emphasis he placed on the importance of public education as part of the role of anti-poverty organisations.

Conclusion

David Gordon has criticised the scant attention paid to children by the philosophical and economic literature on social justice and its failure to recognise children as 'citizens with human rights that are independent and co-equal to the adults with whom they live' (2008, p 174). Children may be largely invisible to philosophers and economists, yet child poverty continues to represent one of the most fundamental violations of social justice. Children in poverty are victims of an unjust distribution of society's resources. Their rights as children are undermined and both their childhood and their life chances are constrained. Peter Townsend provided us with many of the tools needed to investigate child poverty and thereby expose its damaging effects. His memory serves as inspiration to continue fighting for its eradication.

Acknowledgement

Thanks to Adrian Sinfield for his helpful comments on the first draft of this chapter.

References

Abel-Smith, B. and Townsend, P. (1965) *The poor and the poorest*, London: Bell.

Banting, K.G. (1979) *Poverty, politics and policy*, London and Basingstoke: Macmillan.

BIHR (British Institute of Human Rights), Joseph Rowntree Foundation, Amnesty International and Oxfam (2008) *Human rights and tackling UK poverty: Report of roundtable meeting, 17 January 2008*, London: BIHR.

Black, D., Morris, J.N., Smith, C. and Townsend, P. (2010) 'Better benefits for health', in A. Walker, D. Gordon, R. Levitas, P. Phillimore, C. Phillipson, M.E. Salomon and N. Yeates (eds) *The Peter Townsend reader*, Bristol: The Policy Press, pp 395-403 [originally published in 1999].

Bradshaw, J., Middleton, S., Davis, A., Oldfield, N., Smith, N., Cusworth, L. and Williams, J. (2008) *A minimum income standard for Britain*, York: Joseph Rowntree Foundation.

Cameron, D. (2010) 'Supporting parents', Speech to Demos, London, 11 January.

Cameron, D., Fryer-Smith, E., Harvey, P. and Wallace, E. (2008) *Practitioners' perspectives on child poverty*, London: Department for Children, Schools and Families.

Clark, T. (2008) 'Making poverty history', *Society Guardian*, 2 April.

Donald, A. and Mottershaw, E. (2009a) *Poverty, inequality and human rights: Do human rights make a difference?*, York: Joseph Rowntree Foundation.

Donald, A. and Mottershaw, E. (2009b) *Poverty, inequality and human rights; Findings*, York: Joseph Rowntree Foundation.

Fabian Commission on Life Chances and Child Poverty (2006) *Narrowing the gap*, London: Fabian Society.

Fitzpatrick, P. (2005) 'Asylum seeker families', in G. Preston (ed) *At greatest risk*, London: Child Poverty Action Group, pp 92-108.

Flaherty, J. (2008) '"I mean we're not the richest but we're not poor": discourses of poverty and social exclusion', Unpublished PhD thesis, Loughborough University.

Gordon, D. (2008) 'Children, policy and social justice', in G. Craig, T. Burchardt and D. Gordon (eds) *Social justice and public policy*, Bristol: The Policy Press, pp 157-79.

Hanley, T. (2009) *Engaging public support for eradicating UK poverty*, York: Joseph Rowntree Foundation.

Hirsch, D., Davis, A. and Smith, N. (2009) *A minimum income standard for Britain in 2009*, Findings, York: Joseph Rowntree Foundation.

Hooper, C., Gorin, S., Cabral, C. and Dyson, C. (2007) *Living with hardship 24/7*, London: The Frank Buttle Trust.

Horton, T. and Gregory, J. (2009) *The solidarity society*, London: Fabian Society.

Kenway, P. (2009) *Should adult benefit for unemployment now be raised?*, York: Joseph Rowntree Foundation.

Lister, R. (2001) 'New Labour: a study in ambiguity from a position of ambivalence', *Critical Social Policy*, vol 21, no 4, pp 425-47.

Lister, R. (2004) *Poverty*, Cambridge: Polity Press.

Lister, R. (2007) 'From object to subject: including marginalised citizens in policy-making', *Policy & Politics*, vol 35, no 3, pp 437-55.

Lister, R. (2010a) *Understanding theories and concepts in social policy*, Bristol: The Policy Press.

Lister, R. (2010b) 'Linking women's and children's poverty', in S. Chant (ed) *The international handbook of gender and poverty*, Cheltenham: Edward Elgar.

Lister, R. and Bennett, F. (2010) 'The new "champion of progressive ideals"? Cameron's Conservative Party: poverty, family policy and welfare reform', *Renewal*, vol 18, no 1-2, pp 84-109.

Lloyd, E. (2006) 'Children, poverty and social exclusion', in C. Pantazis, D. Gordon and R. Levitas (eds) *Poverty and social exclusion in Britain*, Bristol: The Policy Press, pp 315-46.

McCarthy, M. (1986) *Campaigning for the poor: CPAG and the politics of welfare*, London: Croom Helm.

Marmot, M. (2010) *Fair society, healthy lives: Strategic review of health inequalities in England post-2010*, London: UCL.

May, C., Brown, G., Cooper, N. and Brill, L. (2009) *The sustainable livelihoods handbook: An asset based approach to poverty*, Manchester: Church Action on Poverty and Oxfam.

Middleton, S., Ashworth, K. and Walker, R. (1994) *Family fortunes*, London: Child Poverty Action Group.

Moller, S., Huber, E., Stephens, J.D., Bradley, D. and Nielson, F. (2003) 'Determinants of relative poverty in advanced capitalist democracies', *American Sociological Review*, vol 68, February, pp 22-51.

Moore, J. (1989) 'The end of the line for poverty', Speech to the Conservative Political Centre, London, 11 May.

National Equality Panel (2010) *An anatomy of economic inequality in the UK*, London: Government Equalities Office and Centre for the Analysis of Social Exclusion, London School of Economics and Political Science.

Platt, L. (2009) *Ethnicity and child poverty*, London: Department for Work and Pensions.

Preston, G. (ed) (2005) *At greatest risk*, London: Child Poverty Action Group.

Redmond, G. (2008) *Children's perspectives on economic adversity: A review of the literature*, Innocenti Discussion Paper No IDP 2008-0, Florence: UNICEF Innocenti Research Centre.

Redmond, G. (2009) 'Children as actors: how does the child perspectives literature treat agency in the context of poverty?', *Social Policy and Society*, vol 18, no 4, pp 541-50.

Ridge, T. (2002) *Childhood poverty and social exclusion*, Bristol: The Policy Press.

Ridge, T. (2009) *Living with poverty*, London: Department for Work and Pensions.

Ridge, T. and Saunders, P. (2009) 'Introduction: Themed section on children's perspectives on poverty and disadvantage in rich and developing countries', *Social Policy and Society*, vol 8, no 4, pp 499-502.

Sutherland, H., Evans, M., Hancock, R., Hills, J. and Zantomio, F. (2008) *The impact of benefit and tax uprating on incomes and poverty*, Findings, York: Joseph Rowntree Foundation.

Taylor-Gooby, P. and Martin, R. (2008) 'Trends in sympathy for the poor', in A. Park, J. Curtice, K. Thomson, M. Phillips, M. Johnson and E. Clery (eds) *British Social Attitudes: The 24th report*, London: Sage Publications, pp 229-57.

Townsend, P. (1970) *The concept of poverty: Working papers on methods of investigation and life-styles of the poor in different countries*, London: Heinemann.

Townsend, P. (1979) *Poverty in the United Kingdom*, London: Penguin Books and Allen Lane.

Townsend, P. (1986) 'Foreword. "Democracy for the poor"', in M. McCarthy, *Campaigning for the poor: CPAG and the politics of welfare*, London: Croom Helm.

Townsend, P. (1993) *The international analysis of poverty*, Hemel Hempstead: Harvester Wheatsheaf.

Townsend, P. (1997) 'Redistribution: the strategic alternative to privatisation', in A. Walker and C. Walker (eds) *Britain divided*, London: Child Poverty Action Group, pp 263-78.

Townsend, P. (2009) 'A society for people', *Social Policy and Society*, vol 8, no 2, pp 147-58 [originally published in 1958].

Townsend, P. (2010a) 'Investment in social security: a possible UN model for child benefit?', in A. Walker, D. Gordon, R. Levitas, P. Phillimore, C. Phillipson, M.E. Salomon and N. Yeates (eds) *The Peter Townsend reader*, Bristol: The Policy Press, pp 111-27 [originally published in 2009].

Townsend, P. (2010b) 'The disabled need help', in A. Walker, D. Gordon, R. Levitas, P. Phillimore, C. Phillipson, M.E. Salomon and N. Yeates (eds) *The Peter Townsend reader*, Bristol: The Policy Press, pp 539-44 [originally published in 1967].

Townsend, P. (2010c) 'We have got a fair way to go', in A. Walker, D. Gordon, R. Levitas, P. Phillimore, C. Phillipson, M.E. Salomon and N. Yeates (eds) *The Peter Townsend reader*, Bristol: The Policy Press, pp 635-40 [originally published in 1994].

Toynbee, P. and Walker, D. (2008) *Unjust rewards*, London: Granta.

Welshman, J. (2007) *From transmitted deprivation to social exclusion*, Bristol: The Policy Press.

Whiteley, P.F. and Winyard, S.J. (1987) *Pressure for the poor: The poverty lobby and policy making*, London and New York: Methuen.

Women's Budget Group (2005) *Women's and children's poverty: Making the links*, London: Women's Budget Group.

SEVEN

For universalism and against the means test

Carol Walker

Throughout his career, Peter sought not only to reveal the true extent of poverty and its impact on people's lives but also to campaign for new policies to prevent and alleviate it. At the heart of this struggle was a commitment to fair, just and effective social security provision. Social security was at the heart of the human rights approach which he explored in his later work but which, in his final book, *Building decent societies: The role of social security in development* (Townsend, 2009), he reminds us is not new: social security was incorporated into the Universal Declaration of Human Rights (Article 25) in 1948; in the International Covenant on Economic, Social and Cultural Rights; and was reaffirmed in the European Social Charter (Article 12) and the Amsterdam Treaty of 2002 (Articles 136 and 137). Nevertheless 'over half the world's population lacks access to any type of social security protection and only one in five people have adequate social security coverage' (Committee on Economic, Social and Cultural Rights, 2006, p 3, cited in Townsend, 2009, p 2).

At the heart of his argument for adequate social security provision, both as an academic and as a campaigner, was the need for an approach based on universal principles. This applied especially to Child Benefit (see Chapter Four, this volume). He was a vehement opponent of the alternative strategy of selectivity and the failings of the means test, both as a principle and in practice, was a powerful and consistent theme throughout his work (see Chapter Six, this volume). First, his critical gaze fell on British social assistance benefits, and especially the precursors to Income Support (National Assistance and Supplementary Benefit) as well as the plethora of other, smaller, means-tested benefits that gradually accumulated in the postwar period. Later he became an outspoken critic of the growing prevalence of means testing in international systems of social security (see Chapter Five, this volume): most notably The World Bank's insistence on the inappropriate use of minimal, residual systems of social security in developing economies (Townsend, 2009).

This chapter looks at Peter's arguments for universalism and against selectivity in social security provision, first, in the UK context and briefly with regard to international development. It considers the inexorable growth both in the number of means-tested benefits and the number of people dependent on them despite their failure to reach all those for whom they are intended and their socially divisive impact. Finally, it considers whether the holy grail of adequate universal benefits is achievable, and whether we can once again build on a spirit of solidarity and support of people at vulnerable periods in their life or whether it is inevitable that they will continue to be disparaged and excluded.

Goodbye to the means test: long live the means test

Today the assertion that means-tested provision is superior to universal benefits is widely accepted. The 1979–97 Conservative governments' emphasis on concentrating benefits on those 'in greatest need' or 'genuine need' (Walker, 1993), the 1997–2010 New Labour governments' emphasis on the expansion of means-tested tax credits to reward 'hardworking families' and the 2010 Coalition government's caricature of 'poorer working families paying taxes to provide benefits for the better off' are all sentiments which, at first glance, appear hard to refute and indeed they seldom are in public debate. However, such populist arguments wilfully neglect the proven success of universal benefits in preventing poverty and the failure of means-tested systems to adequately alleviate it. Peter was well aware of both. Today it is even more important that policy makers, researchers and students are aware that the triumph of the means test over universalism not only impoverishes the poor but also creates social divisions in society as a whole.

How did we get here? From universalism to means testing

The British social security system was built largely on the broad foundation provided by the Beveridge Report (1942): first, and most importantly, a comprehensive *social insurance* system intended to provide incomes for the majority, which were sufficient both 'in amount and in duration'; second, a *universal children's allowance*; and third, means-tested *social assistance* intended as a 'minor but integral part' of income maintenance provision, dependence on which would fall as the National Insurance (NI) fund built up (Beveridge, 1942, para 369). Beveridge argued that contributory benefits engendered a sense of responsibility in both recipient and the government but, equally, he was responding to the 'the strength of popular objection to any kind of means test' (Beveridge, 1942, para 21). Because of its savings and income rules the means test also penalises both thrift and work.

Unlike in other European welfare systems, British NI benefits were never paid at an adequate level to prevent poverty or, for the unemployed and later the sick, for as long as the need lasted. From the outset a significant proportion of social assistance payments were made in supplementation of inadequate NI entitlement and the various postwar British schemes of social assistance (National Assistance, Supplementary Benefit and Income Support) have expanded exponentially ever since. The demise of NI began as the result of omission, neglect and the failure to counter the long legacy of stigmatising Poor Laws; later it was the result of a policy of attrition (Deacon and Bradshaw, 1983; Walker, 1993). The universal element of children's allowances did survive many rumoured/threatened changes until the Coalition government proposals to deny it to households containing a higher-rate taxpayer. The 2010 Coalition government is also the first since the Second World War to propose replacing the existing multiplicity of benefits – contributory, universal, means-tested and tax credits – which now exist with one 'universal' means-tested credit (discussed later).

Peter blamed the demise of universalism on three factors: the subordination of social to economic objectives and strategies; the shift away from social equality as a national objective; and the replacement of large-scale planning by piecemeal improvisation (Townsend, 1976, pp 122-3). Elements of all three explanations can be found in the growth of means testing in Britain over the last half-century (Hill, 1972). First, governments have normally taken the cheaper option of extending selective provision rather than improving universal or NI benefits. In a period of modest welfare expansion in the early 1970s, they represented a compromise between meeting need and containing costs. A number of new such benefits were introduced: to cover rent (Rent Rebates/Housing Benefit); local taxes (Rent Rebates/Council Tax Benefit); low wages (Family Income Supplement/Family Tax Credit); and health costs (help with prescriptions/dental costs/eye tests). Between 1979 and 1997 the Conservative administrations oversaw a rapid increase in unemployment, including long-term unemployment, and accompanying cuts in benefits. As a result more people needed social assistance either as a top-up to inadequate NI entitlement or as a replacement for it. Policies which led to rents in both the private and public sector increasing also led to a huge increase in the Housing Benefit budget, despite a series of cuts to reduce the bill.

The contribution of the New Labour governments (1997–2010) to the expansion of means testing was a wide-ranging tax credits system as the centrepiece of an anti-poverty strategy, although the introduction of a minimum wage and above-inflation increases in Child Benefit were two universal approaches to poverty reduction. Tax credits, which boosted the incomes of both working and non-working families, cost a total of £30 billion per year when Labour lost power in 2010. Over six million families received Child Tax Credit and Working Tax Credit, and around 2.8 million people over the age of 60 received Pension Credit (ONS, 2009). Although in a new guise and with a different label and different administrative arrangements (covered by Her Majesty's Revenue and Customs [HMRC] – the 'tax office' – not the Department for Work and Pensions, which is responsible for other benefits), tax credits are means tested. They brought an additional problem because they are based on predicted annual income. Over the years, this has led to both substantial over- and substantial under-payments (around £1.7 billion and £0.5 billion respectively in 2008), both of which present serious problems for households living on low wages. However, the tax credits system is not loaded with the same range of conditionalities, discussed below, which apply to means tests in the social security system.

When the Conservatives came to power in 1979, means-tested benefits accounted for less than 16% of the benefits bill; this had doubled to 32% by the time they lost power in 1997 and rose further to 36% by 2007–08 (these figures do not include tax credits) (Levell et al, 2009). This underestimates the actual rise because the earlier figure includes Family Credit but the later figure does not include its current equivalent in tax credits.

Means-tested benefits enable governments to exercise greater control of levels of benefit and access to them (Clasen and Clegg, 2007). Access can be restricted by changing (up or down) any of the many needs or income components that determine entitlement: the treatment of savings and earnings; acceptable levels of rent; the inclusion or exclusion of specific needs; or variation in the component rates for adults and children of different ages. Access can also be restricted by changing the rules of eligibility (for example, the exclusion of 16- to 17-year-olds in 1988) or by extending conditionality (for example, in relation to availability for work or requiring lone parents to register for work when their children are younger). While the tightening of conditionality tests not only affects means-tested benefits, as the application of ever more rigorous rules to long-term Incapacity Benefit and Employment and Support Allowance demonstrate (see below), they do offer greater scope for more frequent, low-profile changes which, cumulatively, have a significant impact on the coverage of the system but attract little public attention. Contrast this with changes to universal benefits, which are very clear-cut. Thus, the restriction of Child Benefit to standard-rate taxpayers announced by the Coalition government in 2010 was highly controversial. The benefits cap, which only affects those on means-tested benefits, announced at the same time attracted less attention and considerably more support. Encouraged by a hostile media and, especially in a febrile political climate, when governments are seeking ways of cutting the overall social security budget, there is little public support for protecting benefits for the poor.

The case against means tests

The case against means testing in social security was cogently made in *Poverty in the UK* (Townsend, 1979): one chapter was devoted to the operation of the then social assistance scheme, Supplementary Benefit, and another to the multiplicity of other means-tested benefits (45 in 1972) which had been added to Beveridge's simple three-pronged framework for social security. At the time Peter wrote, the Supplementary Benefits scheme was straining at the edges and under review. The problems he raised then, however, became even more glaring as dependence on particularly Income Support (and its successors) and Housing Benefit expanded. Peter criticised means tests because, first, they are inefficient and impractical and, second, 'the fatal objection' that they are socially divisive because they misconceive 'the nature of poverty and [reinforce] the condition [they are] supposed to alleviate' (Townsend, 1976, p 126).

The reasons why means tests are inefficient and impractical were spelt out in *Poverty in the UK* (Townsend, 1979, pp 823-4): in particular, the inevitable consequence that they fail to reach all those who are eligible. First, assessment is complicated because people's circumstances are complicated. Consequently, very detailed information on many aspects of applicants' lives is required. For example, the application form for Pension Credit, one of the simpler means-tested benefits, is 23 pages long. Claims have to be recalculated whenever there is a relevant change of circumstances within the household, for example if someone moves in or out of the home, or if part-time earnings change; some, for example tax credits, have to be reclaimed every year. The complexity of the system leads to a second set of criticisms that it is not only extremely expensive to administer but also leads to poor quality administration with high error rates (CPAG, 2009). Third, there is an in-built deterrent to potential recipients who are intimidated by the process of claiming. Fourth, further barriers to claiming highlighted by Peter ranged from people not wishing to acknowledge their own poverty to others (especially when there is uncertainty as to whether they will get help or not), to not wishing to be subject to the level of intrusion into their personal finances and living arrangements which is required, to the stigma felt by potential recipients towards means tests which has survived across the generations from the Poor Law onwards, despite some genuine attempts, especially in the 1940s and 1960s, to implement means-tested systems which would overcome this inherent flaw (Atkinson, 1970; Walker, 1993).

Explanation of non-take-up of benefits generally focuses on the individual explanations for why people do not claim, discussed earlier. While Peter acknowledged these, in *Poverty in the UK* he also argued that the more important inherent structural weakness lay in the means-tested principle itself:

> How can both the failure to apply for means-tested benefits and the variation in take-up be explained?... In public discussion, references have been made for generations to pride, the shame of pleading poverty, ignorance of entitlement, lack of clear information and difficulty of making claims in explaining failure to come forward for benefit. While each of these deserves examination, they are expressed in such an unconnected way that attention is diverted to the shortcomings of clients from the organisation and functions of means-tested schemes in society. Explanations have generally been unhelpful, becoming fragmented and individual-centred.... Implicitly or explicitly, their lack of education and intelligence is treated as paramount. So the policy solution is restricted in the short term to improving methods of communication, simplifying the presentation of rules and exhorting the poor to apply.... *Yet is there not something self-defeating about a scheme which can be understood or managed only by the well-educated*, or which is based on rules which rigidly assume that incomes and social conditions are stable and that the opportunities to obtain paid employment are uniform? (Townsend, 1979, pp 879-80, emphasis added)

Attempts to make means tests more 'palatable' (Townsend, 1958, p 523) have proved futile. A simple and accessible means test is a contradiction in terms. Thus despite endless restructuring and some, albeit rare, take-up campaigns by national and local government and major pressure groups, incomplete take-up has been a feature of all the British social assistance schemes (from the Poor Law through National Assistance, Supplementary Benefit and Income Support), as well as the many other means-tested benefits, large (for example, Housing Benefit) and small (for example, free school meals).

In 2006–07 means-tested benefits to the value of £10.5 billion and £6.2 billion in tax credits were not claimed (www.dwp.gov.uk/docs/ifd250609benefits.pdf; www.hmrc.gov.uk/stats/personal-tax-credits/cwtc-take-up2006-07.pdf). As a result, four out of five low-paid workers without children (1.2 million households) did not receive tax credits worth £38 per week; half of all working households did not claim the Housing Benefit to which they were entitled (worth an average of £37.60 per week); three million households did not get Council Tax Benefit at an average of £13 per week; 1.7 million retirement pensioners did not claim an average of £31 per week in Pension Credit (Citizens' Advice Bureau, February/March 2010, press release). Overall, take-up of Income Support and Employment and Support Allowance ranges between 78% and 90%, according to category of claimant, and Pension Credit between 62% and 73% (http://research.dwp.gov.uk/asd/income_analysis/jun_2010/0809_Summary.pdf). The level of take-up by pensioners has remained almost static over the past 40 years regardless of which variation of means-tested benefit has been devised for them. Recent research on the take-up of Pension Credit found that there were three familiar barriers to older people claiming: first, and least significant, was a lack of awareness of the benefit; the second was the fear that receipt of this benefit would compromise entitlement to another benefit; the third, and most significant, was a belief that they were not eligible. A reluctance to disclose financial information together with concerns about making a mistake in completing a complicated application form 'dissuaded older people from making "speculative" applications but most admitted they would go through it if they KNEW they were eligible' (Blunt et al, 2006).

The Labour government's commitment to its flagship programme of Child Tax Credit (which differs from familiar selective social security benefits in that it is available to families considerably above the median income) and Working Tax Credit was not deterred by yet another failure of the means test to reach all those eligible. The caseload take-up rates for Child Tax Credit and Working Tax Credit were 81% and 51% respectively in 2007–08; the expenditure take-up rates were 89% and 76%. While take-up fell in line with income, 20% of people earning less than £20,000 per year failed to claim their entitlement. These figures contrast with a 97% take-up for Child Benefit (HMRC Analysis Team, 2010).

Most attempts to reform social assistance have been aimed primarily to reduce their inherently high administration costs, not to address the problem of take-up. After many false starts – including the replacement of discretion by regulations in Supplementary Benefit in 1980 – the Conservative government finally managed to get social assistance out of the headlines with the introduction of Income Support and the creation of the Social Fund in 1986. This move resolved many of the financial and administrative headaches of managing the complexities of a means-tested system which endeavoured to be responsive to individual circumstances on a mass scale. However, the price of so doing was 'rough justice', with rather more losers than winners (DHSS, 1978; Walker, 1993). A system of weekly additions to meet special needs (for example, for extra heating, special diets) was replaced by premiums for some categories of claimant (families, people with disabilities) leading to those with the greatest level of needs (for example, those with the most severe disabilities) losing most. The system of lump sum payments to meet large unplanned expenses (broken washing machine, clothing) was replaced by a capped Social Fund, which provided much more limited assistance generally in the form of loans. The regulatory changes brought into the Supplementary Benefits system in 1980 and then the introduction of Income Support illustrate very vividly that simplification of a means-tested system inevitably comes at a price – either to the Exchequer or, more likely as happened in these cases, at the expense of the poor. It provides a salutary lesson to the Coalition government as it considers the introduction of one single benefit – a so-called 'universal credit' – to replace all working-age benefits and tax credits. Peter would have been among the first to challenge the misuse of the term 'universal' to a benefit which is universal only in its coverage. It is in fact selective, based on a single 'super-means-test' (DWP, 2010).

The continued failure of many people to claim their entitlement is an inevitable and intended consequence of all means-tested systems (see Chapter Four, this volume). The design and administration of benefits has prioritised the goal of not paying benefits to those who are not entitled over that of ensuring that benefits are paid to all those who are. It would also explain the extremely high profile given to the problem of fraud and abuse in the benefits system – an emphasis not similarly applied to tax evasion and avoidance. Instead the well-rehearsed problems associated with means testing, not just in the UK (see Chapter Four, this volume), have never been resolved and indeed have been compounded by the introduction of greater controls and conditions and the growing climate of hostility towards those dependent on benefits.

Social consequences of means tests

The second aspect of Peter's criticism of selectivity relates to its social divisiveness and is the 'fatal objection' made in *Sociology and social policy*:

> ... (selectivity) misconceives the nature of poverty and reinforces the condition it is supposed to alleviate. The policy assumes that poverty is an absolute condition, a lack of minimum subsistence cash income, which requires little more than the diversion of a minute proportion of national income in an efficient manner to alleviate it. It fosters hierarchical relationships of superiority and inferiority in society, diminishes rather than enhances the status of the poor, and has the effect of widening social inequalities ... it lumps the unemployed, sick, widowed, aged and others into one undifferentiated and inevitably stigmatized category. (Townsend, 1976, p 126)

This theme is picked up even more forcefully in *Poverty in the UK*:

> ... means-tested services ... are essentially devices which
> ration and control ... very important is the fact that
> the rules framing eligibility themselves reflect values
> approved by society.... (Townsend, 1979, p 880)

It is this application of 'values' to individual behaviour which presents the greatest challenge to social solidarity and the achievement of a social security system which protects all vulnerable people from the cradle to the grave, as Beveridge intended. It inevitably leads, both in policy and in the way claimants are treated by frontline staff (Hill, 1969) and then amplified by the media, to judgements being made about the deservingness of individuals and 'suspicion of clients' claims' (Rothstein, 1998) being inevitable.

> *May not the shame of pleading poverty for substantial sections*
> *of the population have something to do with administrative*
> *treatment of claimants or the attitudes adopted by the media*
> *and public towards them?* And may not the pride which
> prevents (people applying) ... be a necessary product, not
> only of the conduct expected of individual members of
> British society as a whole but of the structure and values
> of means-tested schemes themselves? (Townsend, 1979,
> p 880, emphasis added)

Peter believed that universal benefits were based on the principle of employing 'one standard of value' throughout society: they recognise diversity (the differential needs of different groups) without 'ordering people in superior and inferior social ranks' (Townsend, 1973, p 125). By contrast, means-tested benefits create a hierarchy and a 'division of the population into first-class and second-class citizens' (Townsend, 1958, p 523): between the 'deserving' and the 'undeserving', between different categories of claimants and between claimants and taxpayers (notwithstanding that they are sometimes the same people!). It is these divisions which are embedded in the modern British social security system that have contributed to the contemporary discourse on the so-called 'dependency culture' or 'welfare culture'.

> ... all such (means-tested) schemes tend to acquire characteristics which are different from those which allocate benefits according to some other criterion ... Although, in principle, benefits are dependent primarily on test of means, in practice they have to be governed by other considerations as well, whether someone is genuinely sick or seeking work, whether a woman is genuinely supporting children on her own and whether an elderly person is or is not the householder ... In different ways, benefits under means-tested schemes have to be conditional on behaviour and upon the readiness of potential recipients to submit themselves to test. The function of the schemes is as much to control behaviour as to meet need. (Townsend, 1979, p 823)

Over the past 20 years the extension of conditionality associated with means tests, which has stemmed from successive governments' negative and pessimistic expectations of claimants, has spread across other aspects of the benefits system in response to the over-arching objective of cutting benefits expenditure. During periods of economic constraint and/or rising unemployment, in the 1930s, 1980s and 2010s, politicians and the media concentrate on the perceived failings of the poor rather than the reasons for their poverty (Deacon, 1976; Golding and Middleton, 1982; Walker, 1993; Cameron, 2010). As Clasen and Clegg (2007, p 13) point out:

> ... past activities – the status and origins of claimants (contributions, employment status) – have all but become irrelevant. Instead, the new British conditionality logic is both wider (beyond unemployment) and more focused on work tests and employability criteria than previously.

Higher levels of proof that one is 'genuine' are applied to the category of claimant rather than to the type of benefit s/he is claiming. Thus, applicants for both contributory and income-based Jobseeker's Allowance have to meet stringent rules regarding their attempts to find work and their willingness to take it. For the past 30 years, eligibility for benefits for long-term sick and disabled claimants (mainly insurance-based) have been subject to increasingly stricter testing introduced by all governments, and this remains a top priority for the Coalition government. Peter foresaw the possibility for group discrimination:

> At one stage in history, the application of a label to a particular group in the population seems to assist the allocation to them of resources; yet, at a later stage, the label may be a hindrance or a positive handicap, because of the stigmatising connotations which it has in the meantime acquired. It is perhaps in this sense that the minimum rights for the many, as it is applied in policy, has to be watched most carefully. (Townsend, 1979, p 924)

Means tests inevitably foster fears that people who *could* work, do not. There is an in-built disincentive within their structure because the more is earned, the lower the benefit is. Claimants can face high marginal tax rates, sometimes over 100%, as increases in earnings exceed the loss of total means-tested entitlement. This unavoidable shortcoming contributed to its rejection by Beveridge. Government responses to this have concentrated on ever more rigorous seeking-work tests and monitoring of unemployed claimants. It also provides the overall narrative in which benefit levels are measured – that people should not be better off out of work than in work. The New Labour government's response was to extend means-tested in-work benefits and to stress total disposable income in-work (from benefits, credits and earnings) rather than just earnings. The Coalition government's proposal for a 'universal credit' is also justified by the goal of 'making work pay' by reducing the impact of the earnings taper and unifying several means-tested benefits and tax credits into one system (DWP, 2010). All such solutions merely respond to an inherent weakness in the means test itself, that it creates a disincentive to work and save, which is not addressed.

Social control

The concentration of both government and media on the benefit recipient as at best undeserving and at worst flagrantly dishonest, rather than as an individual in need, has been the backdrop against which governments of all parties have explicitly sought to reduce both the scope and the value of benefits for more than 30 years. This inherently cynical view of the poor was one which Peter despised but which is increasingly common today. The Thatcher administrations introduced a 'shop a cheat hotline'. This was continued by the New Labour governments, which ran several high-profile anti-fraud campaigns in the media focusing on 'benefit thieves'. The demand for draconian cuts in benefits sought by the Coalition government – including the use of a less favourable inflation index, radically scaling back entitlement to Housing Benefit, enforcing ever stricter medical tests – was accompanied by the Prime Minister launching, in July 2010, yet another clampdown on the estimated '£1.5 billion of hard earned taxpayers' money … being stolen from the taxpayer' (Cameron, 2010). Such emotive language ensured that the subsequent media coverage focused on the losses through fraud not the larger losses due to administrative error. The strategy is a very familiar one: cuts in benefit are more easily made when recipients of those benefits are seen to be dishonest, undeserving or doing as well as, if not better than, those in work.

The use of the benefits system to control behaviour is now reaching beyond the application of greater conditionality attached to eligibility for benefit. The Welfare Reform Bill 2009 linked criminal behaviour with welfare sanctions: benefit recipients found guilty of some crimes or anti-social behaviour would be at risk of losing their benefit in addition to the normal legal punishment (Deacon, 2004; Barker and Lamble, 2009). The proposal of a benefit cap announced in October 2010, which will impact on those with high rents and/ or large families, generated an unresolved debate on the morality of people with many children being supported by the state.

International social security and the role of means testing

Peter sustained his commitment to social security as 'the principal weapon in the continuing fight against world poverty' throughout his life, and his argument is strongly expressed in his last book for the International Labour Organization (ILO), *Building decent societies* (Townsend, 2009, p xvii). In the final phase of his career Peter focused on a human rights approach to poverty not because it marked any major shift in his thinking but as a pragmatic approach to his continuing attempt to keep both national and international poverty on the agenda. However, much of the emphasis of his later work did turn to the international agenda and, in particular, the failure of the international agencies to tackle world poverty effectively. He was a great critic of the omission of social security from the structural adjustment policies of the 1980s and 1990s and to the residual approach to social protection then promoted by The World Bank and the International Monetary Fund (IMF).

Building decent societies highlights the 'divergent historical experience in "developed" and "developing" countries of putting into practice the fundamental rights to social security, including social insurance, and an "adequate" standard of living' (Townsend, 2009, p 4). Peter contrasts the universal human rights approach which marked the emergence of the social security systems in developed countries with the residual schemes being imposed on developing countries today. While, he argued, universal benefits and comprehensive contributory-based systems, with a small targeted component, typified the social security programmes of the new welfare systems of much of Western Europe in the postwar period (Townsend, 2009, p 5), the embryonic systems in developing countries are not given this head start. Instead The World Bank and IMF have promoted the residual model of social protection targeted on the few on the basis of a means test, a model which presents even greater challenges in developing countries and emerging democracies than the well-rehearsed ones in established welfare states.

While universal benefits can contribute to unity and stability within nations, the alternative, means-tested systems can exacerbate social divisions between the 'deserving' and 'non-deserving' poor; they are more likely to retain the support of those who, although they contribute, are not poor enough to qualify; and they are less likely to be undermined by a lack of capacity in the administration and monitoring of conditionality or by corruption which is a feature of many young democracies (de Neubourg, 2009).

For example in Mongolia, which adopted a proxy means-testing method to simplify the selection of beneficiaries and transfer allocation, 'more than one-third of the target group did not receive a benefit (exclusion error) while two-thirds of the non-targeted group received a transfer (inclusion error)' (de Neubourg, 2009, p 70). The complexity of means-tested schemes, compared with social insurance schemes, also makes them more exposed to corruption. As de Neubourg (2002) argues, 'the simpler the scheme, the less corruption will be the result'.

Under the prevailing neoliberal ethos of the international agencies, generous social security provision is often vetoed on the grounds of cost. However, Peter powerfully promoted the opposite argument of a 'virtuous circle between social protection and growth in a development context' (Townsend, 2009, p 331):

> Countries which have been the most successful in achieving long-term sustainable growth and poverty reduction have achieved this ... by putting in place extensive systems of social security.... In reality ... evidence suggests that growth and social security have been mutually interdependent and have together contributed to the long-term success of these countries. There is no doubt that OECD countries have made the conscious decision to invest heavily in social security – often at more than 15% of GDP – as part of their long-term growth and poverty reduction strategies. (Behrendt et al, 2009, p 325)

Challenges for future policy

The principle of selectivity is now deeply entrenched both in the UK social security system and in the models of social development imposed by The World Bank. Their very dominance means that it is harder for the arguments in favour of universalism to be heard (Rothstein, 1998). The rise of means tests is both the cause and the result of the triumph of individualism over collectivism. The end of universal Child Benefit, with its withdrawal from higher-rate taxpayers, could be seen as the final nail in the coffin of universal benefits in the UK. Or, it could be the rallying call that has been missing as successive governments, of all political parties, supported the inexorable rise in means testing.

Universal benefits are more than just a better alternative to means-tested benefits. They do, of course, overcome the problems spelt out in this chapter not least of poor take-up, the separation of the poor as different from the rest of society, and the high marginal 'tax' rates as earned income begins to replace benefits. But the principle of universalism in social security must be defended in its own right or other non-means-tested benefits such as the Retirement Pension will be threatened, as will other parts of the welfare state. It does not take a very great leap of imagination to move from questioning why the rich should get Child Benefit to why the rich should get free healthcare. Peter (Townsend, 2010) argued that universal benefits were 'an efficient, economical and socially integrative mechanism' to prevent poverty. It would also 'have as its by-products certain advantages, such as the reduction of social conflict, the greater integration of certain social minorities, and a strengthening of the earning incentives of low-income households, quite apart from any strengthening of social morals as a basis for a more productive economy' (Townsend, 1972, p 29).

The arguments in favour of universalism must be reiterated. Current generations, brought up in an era when individualism is paramount, need to be taught and older generations be reminded of its significance, both for the relief of poverty and for social cohesion:

- Universal benefits offer the most effective way of tackling poverty. They are the only benefits that are capable of reaching all those who are eligible.
- Universal benefits are the basis of social justice. They allow redistribution vertically and horizontally.

- Universal benefits show solidarity between the rich and the poor; between the sick and the well; between the old and the young; between families with children and those without.
- Because universal benefits are received by the affluent as well as the poor, they are less likely to be poor quality.
- For those who do not wish to see universal benefits 'squandered' on the rich (Townsend, 1972, p 31), they can be recouped by a more equitable tax system. The outcry accompanying Child Benefit for rich families has not been repeated in relation to the many tax advantages they receive.

The challenge to provide a fair, just and effective social security system is greater than ever. The entrenchment of the means-tested philosophy in practice and in the public's mind makes the defence of universalism even harder but more important. However, as Peter reminds us: 'What is at stake is not just the most technically efficient or cheapest means of reaching an agreed end. It is the kind and quality of the society we wish to achieve in Britain' (Townsend, 1968, p 121).

References

Atkinson, A.B. (1989) *Poverty and social security*, London: Harvester Wheatsheaf.

Barker, N. and Lamble, S. (2009) 'From social security to individual responsibility: sanctions, conditionality and punitiveness in the Welfare Reform Bill', *Journal of Social Welfare and Family Law*, vol 31, no 3, pp 321-32.

Behrendt, C., Cichon, M., Hagemejer, K., Kidd, S., Krech, R. and Townsend, P. (2009) 'Rethinking the role of social security in development', in P. Townsend (ed) *Building decent societies: Rethinking the role of social security in state building*, Geneva: International Labour Organization/Palgrave Macmillan, pp 325-37.

Beveridge, Sir W. (1942) *Social insurance and allied services (Beveridge Report)*, London: HMSO.

Blunt, K., Adam, L. and Leo, C. (2006) *Barriers to the uptake of Pension Credit: Understanding the barriers and triggers to claiming Pension Credit*, Research Report 36, London: Department for Work and Pensions (www.dwp.gov. uk/asd/asd5/rrs-index.asp).

Cameron, D. (2010) 'Cameron launches "uncompromising" crackdown on fraud', *Manchester Evening News*, 10 August.

Clasen, J. and Clegg, D. (2007) 'Levels and levers of conditionality – measuring change in mature welfare states', in J. Clasen and N.A. Siegel (eds) *Investigating welfare state change: The 'dependent variable problem' in comparative analysis*, Cheltenham: Edward Elgar, pp 166-97.

Committee on Economic, Cultural and Social Rights (2006) *General Comment No 20: The Rights to Social Security, Article 9*, Geneva.

CPAG (Child Poverty Action Group) (2009) *Ending child poverty: A manifesto for success*, London: CPAG (www.cpag.org.uk/manifesto/manifesto_2009. htm).

de Neubourg, C. (2002) *Institutional design and institutional incentives in social safety nets*, Social Protection Discussion Paper No 0226, Washington, DC: The World Bank.

de Neubourg, C. (2009) 'Social protection and nation-building: an essay on why and how universalist social policy contributes to stable nation-states', in P. Townsend (ed) *Building decent societies: Rethinking the role of social security in development*, Basingstoke: Palgrave Macmillan.

Deacon, A. (1976) *In search of the scrounger*, London: Bell.

Deacon, A. (2004) 'Justifying conditionality: the case of anti-social tenants', *Housing Studies*, vol 19, no 6, pp 911-26.

Deacon, A. and Bradshaw, J. (1983) *Reserved for the poor*, Oxford: Basil Blackwell and Martin Robertson.

DHSS (Department of Health and Social Security) (1979) *Social assistance: A review of the Supplementary Benefits scheme in Great Britain*, London: DHSS.

DSS (Department of Social Security) (1998) *New ambitions for our country: A new contract for welfare*, Cm 3805, London: The Stationery Office.

DWP (Department for Work and Pensions) (2010) *21st century welfare*, DWP Benefits Reform Division, Cm 7913, London: DWP (www.dwp. gov.uk/21st-century-welfare).

Golding, P. and Middleton, S. (1982) *Images of welfare*, Oxford: Martin Robertson.

Hill, M. (1969) 'The exercise of discretion in the National Assistance Board', *Public Administration*, vol 47, no 1, pp 75-90.

Hill, M. (1972) 'Selectivity for the poor', in P. Townsend and N. Bosanquet, *Labour and inequality*, London: Fabian Society, pp 335-45.

HMRC (Her Majesty's Revenue and Customs) Analysis Team (2010) *Child Benefit, Child Tax Credit and Working Tax Credit: Take-up rates 2007–08*, London: HMRC (www.hmrc.gov.uk/stats/personal-tax-credits/cwtc-take-up2007-08.pdf).

Levell, P., May, R., O'Dea, C. and Phillips, D. (2009) *A survey of the UK benefits system 2009*, London: Institute for Fiscal Studies (www.ifs.org.uk/bns/bn13.pdf).

ONS (Office for National Statistics) (2009) 'State pensions', *Pensions Trends*, June, Chapter 5 (www.statistics.gov.uk/pensiontrends/).

Rothstein, B. (1998) *Just institutions matter: The moral and political logic of the universal welfare state*, Cambridge: Cambridge University Press.

Townsend, P. (1968) 'Selectivity: a nation divided', in *Social services for all?*, London: Fabian Society [reprinted in 1976].

Townsend, P. (1972) *The scope and limitations of means-tested social services in Britain*, Manchester: Manchester Statistical Society.

Townsend, P. (1973) *The social minority*, London: Allen Lane.

Townsend, P. (1976) *Sociology and social policy*, Harmondsworth: Penguin.

Townsend, P. (ed) (2009) *Building decent societies: Rethinking the role of social security in development*, Basingstoke: Palgrave Macmillan.

Townsend, P. (2010) 'We have got a fair way to go', in A. Walker, D. Gordon, R. Levitas, P. Phillimore, C. Phillipson, M.E. Salomon and N. Yeates (eds) *The Peter Townsend reader*, Bristol: The Policy Press, pp 635-40 [originally published in 1994].

Townsend, P. and Bosanquet, N. (1972) *Labour and inequality*, London: Fabian Society.

Walker, C. (1993) *Managing poverty: The limits of social assistance*, London: Routledge.

EIGHT

Underclass, overclass, ruling class, supernova class[1]

Danny Dorling

Introduction

One man in his mid-thirties hoped that his six-figure income would grow rapidly, and admitted that his assets would be valued at nearly a million pounds. He held strong views about poverty. 'There is no poverty. Now you can get money from the state. People don't even have to go to work. You don't have to put up with working in an unrewarding situation.' He strongly disagreed with the propositions that the gap between rich and poor was too wide and that the rich should be more highly taxed. He strongly opposed the idea of putting limits on 'some people's expensive way of living' to reduce poverty and disagreed with the statement that a lot of people entitled to claim benefits do not claim them. Finally, he strongly agreed that cuts in public services like health and education could be made without increasing the number of people in poverty and that, if there was any poverty, it was more likely to be reduced by increasing Britain's wealth than by making incomes more equal. (Peter Townsend, describing the views of one of the new overclass of London, recorded in 1985-86; see Townsend, 1993, p 109)

By 2010 one in ten of all Londoners had the wealth of the man who Peter had described some 25 years earlier as being part of a tiny elite (see Hills et al, 2010). The Hills inquiry into inequality revealed that one in ten Londoners now have wealth of nearly a million pounds, some 273 times the wealth of the poorest tenth of today's Londoners. *The Sunday Times* Rich List of spring 2010 reported that the wealth of the richest 1,000 people in Britain had risen by 30% in just one year. And this was not any old year, but the first full year after the economic crash of 2008. Above the overclass, above the ruling class, the wealth of a new supernova class was exploding in size.

As the pound fell against other currencies, property values in Kensington and Chelsea, the richest borough in the world, escalated, while housing prices almost everywhere else in Britain fell, or rose only slightly. In that same Royal borough, life expectancies rose by more than one year in the same year, a rate only sustainable if the inhabitants there became immortal. We are witnessing the final crescendo of a 37-year escalation (it began in 1974) of wealth and income inequalities in Britain (Dorling, 2010). But this trend will end because it has to. What matters is how the end will come: with a bang, a whimper, or something in between? What matters is who is going to suffer, who will benefit and what new groups are formed. If our future is at all like our past, the end to this escalation in wealth for a minority will happen, but will only occur when recent certainties that the super-rich will always be with us melt away. What will emerge when the dust settles will largely depend on how well we are able to fight poverty, inequality and injustice. The rich may always be with us, but they need not be as rich as they are today. Neither need the poor be so poor.

What Peter Townsend revealed on wealth

Peter spotted the trend towards increased selfishness (more and more wealth for the richest minority) first and repeatedly warned against it. He did not just write about it in what could have become obscure book chapters, leaflets or pamphlets, but he published his findings in outlets of the elite, such as the *British Medical Journal* (Townsend, 1994). In writing to medical doctors, the readers of the *British Medical Journal* (wealthy people themselves), Peter explained: 'To the privileges of a wealthy home are added the privileges of increasingly segregated wealthy schools, clubs, and transport and health services and the discriminatory barriers to entry. When the punitive attitude is in the ascendant – as witnessed in Reagan's United States and Thatcher's Britain – the material divide between the rich and the poor and the numbers living in abject poverty both grow' (Townsend, 1994, p 1674).

In any assessment of Peter's work on the rich it is clear that he contributed to the understanding, achieved with the election of the New Labour government in 1997, that enough was enough, and times had to change. This new government came to power largely due to the work of people like Peter helping to expose how unjust the old Conservative regime had been. What Peter did not foresee, however, was just how endemic the thinking that inequality is good had become. He worked at a time when sociologists were writing about class interests as if different classes consisted of groups who met and planned what they might do. It is unlikely Peter had ever seen Conway's 1968 'Game of Life' flicker on a computer screen – if he had watched a simple computer model that shows how shapes can take form with no guiding hand to control them, how patterns and behaviour emerge that are self-replicating, how simple behaviour can reproduce complex ideas both far more powerful for good and far more dangerous (if bad) than people consciously colluding, how ideas can have lives of their own, then he may have realised that there was more to fight against than just the class interests of the very rich. Social scientists of the 1970s and 1980s perhaps ascribe too much agency to the wealthy. But some did use the great power their money gave them to great ill effect.

Peter understood that the rich were the problem, not the poor. His impact was in making that understanding mainstream. Where his impact was strongest was in redefining the notion of poverty worldwide, and where his impact may have been weakest was in unravelling the mechanisms that perpetuate poverty. He talked of dominant classes and overclasses because this was the way many of his contemporaries talked. His work uncovered what looked far more like a fractal pattern to affluence. He produced detailed figures where, for the first time, it was possible to see that if you removed the wealthiest small proportion of the population in a country like

Britain, the shape of the overall curve of wealth did not alter; its gradient remained the same. He compiled tables of such revelations and drew countless histograms of these tables, but he did not suggest why such a pattern was emerging. He had many other things to explain and to counteract.

Much of Peter's work involved uncovering and explaining truths which we now take for granted, such as that 'conventional measures of cash incomes are becoming more and more misleading of the real distribution of living standards, because [of] employer indirect welfare, or "fringe" benefits, and the acquisition of substantial forms of wealth' (Townsend, 1993, p 94). Peter was also engaged in arguments of how class (and especially what was becoming called the 'underclass') was defined and these arguments, although necessary, were a distraction, leading to a concentration on description over explanation (Townsend, 1993, pp 102, 103).

Updating Peter Townsend's estimates of wealth inequality

Peter had carried out much of his early work at a time when the rich were becoming less expensive (or, in conventional terminology, when the rich were becoming less wealthy). He charted how, across the UK, the most wealthy 1% of the population appeared to see its share of wealth fall from 21% of all personal wealth in the UK in 1976 to 17% in 1988 (Townsend, 1991, p 33), but after this time the trend reversed, the curve began to steepen again, and what were to become the super-rich began to re-emerge at its steepest end. Peter was writing, counting and campaigning as the social ground he was surveying was changing under his feet, as one progressive era was coming to an end and a repressive one, in terms of wealth distribution, was emerging. When the ground under your feet is shifting, the long-term direction of change is far from obvious. Things feel shaky, but it is only in hindsight that the overall direction of movement becomes clear. That is why we can now suggest that it was during 1974 that the long-term trend of increasing equality was reversed (Dorling, 2010). It simply was not obvious except in hindsight and then only by viewing what occurred almost immediately after 1974.

Even though the excesses of the very wealthiest were still being curtailed in the mid- to late 1970s, their wealth did not cascade down very far. In 1976, just below the richest 1%, the next wealthiest 4% held in total 17% of all national wealth, which rose to 21% in 1988. Thus their increase in wealth perfectly absorbed the slight fall in the share of the very richest percentile. There was, in effect, redistribution among and within the very wealthiest twentieth of the population between 1976 and 1988, but Peter was most concerned with the very poorest.

Although there was clearly no conspiracy, the richest people of the 1970s in effect reallocated a little of their wealth to the not-quite-so-rich (some 4% of all national wealth changed between rich hands), and the remaining 45% of the best-off half of the population saw their share of wealth rise, to the detriment of the worst-off half of the population, who saw their share fall over the same period, 1976–88, from just 8% to 6% of all personal wealth in the UK (Townsend, 1991). That 6% was spread very thinly across half the population, a fall of a quarter in the relative value of their holdings. These figures are shown in Table 8.1. This was the 'new deal' of the late 1970s and early 1980s. It contrasts with Roosevelt's 'New Deal' of 1930s America, which saw redistribution from rich to poor, and Blair's 'New Deal' of the turn of millennium Britain, which was implied also to be redistributive (but on aggregate, wasn't). Peter presented

Table 8.1: Inequalities in wealth in the UK 1976–2008: shares of wealth

%	1976	1981	1986	1988	2006–08	
					(a)	(b)
Top 1% of the population	21	18	18	17	28	53
Next 4% (top 5% less top 1%)	17	18	18	21	13	10
Top half excluding top 5%	54	56	54	56	51	31
Bottom half of population by wealth	8	8	10	6	8	6
Total	100	100	100	100	100	100

Source: Townsend, 1991, p 33, marketable wealth at death from probate; and final columns calculated by author of this chapter, (a) excluding pension rights and (b) also excluding main residence housing equity from the wealth calculations.

the numbers but not the idea of a new right-wing shift or 'deal'. He didn't explain how growing inequality was being excused (and even condoned) politically and how those ideas that it was OK for a few to become extremely wealthy were again seeping into the fabric of our thinking.

So, how does the distribution of wealth in these figures for 1988 (revealed in 1991) compare to inequalities in wealth today? It turns out to be remarkably difficult to replicate Peter's early work because government statistics are very hard to unravel (Peter complained about this too), but the penultimate two columns of Table 8.1 show my attempt to replicate Peter's earlier work, given the most recently available data from the Office for National Statistics (ONS) surveys taken in 2006–08, and also incorporating data from *The Sunday Times* Rich List of 2010 (which reveals wealth inequalities of earlier years). The answer to the question 'By how much have the poor become poorer and the rich relatively richer?' is that it depends on what you now include as 'wealth'. The most comparable estimate to the marketable wealth at death estimate used in the first four columns of Table 8.1 is wealth excluding pensions, which is shown in the 2006–08(a) column.

Table 8.1 shows that by 2006–08, according to the estimate of wealth excluding pensions, the poorest half of all people living in Britain were a little richer than at their low point in 1988, by a tiny amount – some 2% of all national wealth had trickled down in the 20 years from 1988. Execution of the right-to-buy policy was a key part of the reason for this, but wealth trickled down very unevenly within this poor half. The poorest quarter were, by 2008, in much greater debt than before, but overall, 8% is an increase of one third on 6%. However, at the other end of the distribution, the gains have been far greater. The richest 1% have seen their share of national wealth grow from 1988 to 2008 to include an extra 11% of all wealth. Compared to the slight gains of the poor, this is five times more wealth for 50 times fewer people, or 250 times more riches each than the individualised gains of the poorest. By comparison with the deluge of wealth that rained on the very richest, the poor only received crumbs. However, for both a few of the poor to gain a little and most of the rich to gain a huge amount, others had to lose.

Those who were most squeezed from 1988 to 2008 were those in the middle and near to the top, but not in the very top 1%. The share of the best-off 5%, excluding the best-off 1%, almost halved.

Why are inequalities in wealth so much greater in the final column in Table 8.1, when both pensions and main residence housing equity are excluded? The very richest do not need pensions and usually do not have any. They are able to live off their wealth, so excluding pensions does not reduce their wealth much, if at all. Furthermore, the very richest do not need all of their homes to live in; they can easily sell off property without having to worry where they will sleep. They do not have large amounts of illiquid wealth held in the form of bricks and mortar that they cannot sell. The estimates of wealth that are quoted nowadays, by which the best-off tenth of Londoners are now 273 times better off than the poorest tenth, are made using all wealth estimates, including both main residence housing equity and pensions. This 'All' estimate is now misleading, however, and underestimates inequalities at the top end in that it makes the very wealthy look less wealthy because of the new reality that they do not need pensions, and are able to realise their assets in bricks and mortar.

How much richer are the rich?

Percentages of national wealth can be hard to interpret. It is easier just to look at how many times more wealth one person has compared to another. Across all of Britain in 1976 the richest single percentile had recourse to 131 times the wealth of the average person in the poorest half of the population. That ratio fell in 1986, to 90 : 1, as the result of previous decades of decreasing income inequalities. However, as income inequalities again began to rise, these wealth inequalities rapidly rose again, to stand at 142 : 1 by 1988.

Almost as shocking was the rise in the ratio between people in the top half, but not the top 5%, as compared to the bottom half, which rose to 10 : 1 by 1988, up from 8 : 1 in 1976 (see Table 8.2). But then, in contrast to the very rich, that share next fell in relative terms in the two decades to 2006–08 as, by then, the very rich were taking so much that the middle became squeezed when those in the top 1% each became 165 times richer than the poorest half of

Table 8.2: Wealth in the UK 1976–2008: comparison with the poorer half of the population

Ratio of wealth held	1976	1981	1986	1988	2006–08	
					(a)	(b)
Top 1% of the population	131	113	90	142	165	421
Next 4% (top 5% less top 1%)	27	28	23	44	19	20
Top half excluding top 5%	8	8	6	10	7	6
Bottom half of all people	1	1	1	1	1	1

Source: See Table 8.1 above. Wealth of each group is expressed in terms of multiples of the wealth of the average person in the poorer half of UK society. Final column (a) excludes pension rights and (b) also excludes main residence housing equity from the calculations.

the population, or 421 times richer when main residence housing equity was excluded.

The single richest percentile of people in Britain now have recourse to riches worth more than eight times the wealth of all of the poorer half of the population put together. If the richest percentile were to give up *half* their wealth, they could increase the wealth of the poorest half of the population *four times over*. Things have changed in a fundamental way when a single percentile of the population is (in terms of each average wealthy individual) worth 421 times more than average ordinary individual.

Within the wealthiest 1% of the population, to have recourse to only £2.6 million is to be the very poorest amongst this richest of groups. The average wealth of someone living amongst the richest 100,000 people in Britain (but not in the top 1,000) is £13.6 million. *The Sunday Times* Rich List of 2010 estimated that the richest 1,000 people in Britain hold average wealth of £335.5 million each. The wealthiest 10 have average wealth of £6.99 billion each, but 'only' £5.27 billion apiece if the single wealthiest individual is excluded. That difference is £1,718 million less each (apiece) for being in the top 10 but not being the top one. People with dozens or hundreds or thousands of millions of pounds are no overclass – they are a new class: a supernova class. Their wealth has been exploding in size over recent years but in a way which ensures the unstable rapid growth of enormous inequality even amongst themselves.

From ruling class to supernova class

What has happened since Peter Townsend wrote about underclass and overclass, since he exposed the wide and then growing gap between rich and poor in Britain and, later, worldwide?[2] Worldwide the position of most of the very poorest had appeared to be improving until very recently, when food prices spiked and inflation began to rise in the costs of basic everyday essentials following the 2008 economic crash. Locally many success stories began to emerge of people taking the initiative, introducing social security schemes, overthrowing right-wing governments through democratic means in Latin America, securing improving living standards through undemocratic means in China, and demonstrating to try to ensure some democracy in parts of the Middle East in 2011.

In recent years the World Health Organization's (WHO) estimates of the number of children aged under five in the world dying each year dipped under 10 million, but that was mainly the result of fewer children being born than of any fall in death rates. In April 2008 death rates rose around the world as speculators in New York and London hiked food prices in a desperate and, for them, successful attempt to keep up their profits during the financial crash (Mason, 2009, pp 108-9). So, just as in Britain, where the poor have been getting poorer since the late 1970s (using Peter Townsend's definition of poverty), now worldwide immiseration has begun to increase again. Price rises in the poorest areas of the planet represent absolute immiseration.

Why has this happened? The answers emerging suggest that suffering is rising worldwide because of the emergence of a new super-rich stratum. This is now an argument that is often presented in mainstream media and by television news economists such as Paul Mason (2009). It is because of the speculation of those managing the hedge funds of the super-rich that so many are being made poorer around the world. It is because of the speculation the super-rich have to engage in to continue to grow their wealth that global incomes fall. This is self-destructive behaviour; it is unlikely to be long lived. It cannot last.

The supernova class are the people who rely on hedge funds to keep their wealth growing at rates no one else is able to achieve. Their wealth has to grow rapidly because they have to spend so much of it so quickly in disparate ways if they are to maintain their rank order amongst the immensely affluent. They must invest in speculation over world food prices that results in the slow and painful starvation of millions because, when other routes to investment are exhausted, there is no other way to go, and because so many have come to believe that what is most profitable is what is best, regardless of the consequences. The supernova class have emerged above the ruling class because, in hindsight, they had to. If people as a whole do not curtail profiteering, then one small group or another will emerge (Booth, 2010), almost randomly, with enormous shares of wealth, and that group will become smaller as its wealth becomes larger. It is, however, too tiny a group of people to constitute a ruling class, and it is not an organised group. Billionaires do not meet on giant super-yachts and plan the future of the globe. Inequalities grow when entire ways of thinking become corrupted to excuse such growth.

The old ruling class may have preserved a system that allowed a supernova class to be born but they too did not plan for this, nor did they envisage it. The world as we see it today is not even the utopia imagined by far-right economic neoliberals. It is a disaster that could have been prevented, but was not devised by human mind. It was not planned. Again, knowing now a little about complex systems, about that 1968 computer program, the 'Game of Life', we can see this in ways which were, until recently, very hard to imagine.[3]

Complicity with the rich

Very rich individuals are often very concerned about status (Edwards, 2008). Often they had very troubled pasts (Peston, 2008). Quite often these have been almost as troubled as the pasts of despots. Continued and growing world inequality contributes to millions more premature deaths than even genocide has achieved, and so comparing those who advocate giving free rein to what they call market forces with those responsible for mass direct killing is neither trite nor unwarranted. It is easy to link the millions of annual deaths in China from lung cancer to the companies that continue to profit by selling tobacco. It becomes a little more controversial when we consider purveyors of baby milk powder as net contributors to mass infant mortality when they campaign to encourage mothers to use milk powder, which often means using unclean water.

Leaders of industry and commerce in general have come to argue that there is no alternative to what clearly amounts to mass exploitation and now the re-emergence of absolute immiseration. Listen carefully to the words of those who go so far as to claim that such exploitation is good and efficient and will eventually benefit all, cleansing society of inefficiency and the 'feckless' (those not included in 'alarm clock Britain', for instance – a phrase introduced by Nick Clegg, Deputy Prime Minister, in early 2011). Think what value they might put on different segments of their markets; think how so many have been led not to see people as people, but as market segments. Then you can begin to see how, in a time of mass killing, such killing can be made to be seen as an inevitable, unfortunate but necessary, part of what makes the human world work. This is an evil idea, but almost all who propagate it are not intent on evil, they just cannot see any alternative as possible; they are blinkered (Scott Cato, 2009).

Because greed is now seen as warranted, even Members of Parliament (MPs) try to excuse their greed when found out. For what service might a company offer to pay an MP £5,000 a day? Is it only in a few cases where the company is fictitious and has been established to reveal wrong-doing by journalists that we find out (Booth, 2010)? The company is buying complicity, to align the interests of a few people with a little money, MPs in this case, to more closely match the interests of an even smaller group with even more money: businessmen (and in a few cases businesswomen). People without money cannot buy this complicity unless they pool their meagre resources, which is why unions also sponsor MPs. The interests of those whose time is being bought have been changed. Money corrupts. If they had not, then there would not be any need to pay them a fee in the first place. Inequality cannot survive without continued complicity with those among the very affluent favouring its extension. Neither that complicity nor such favouring is carefully organised. It would be easier to prevent if it was, but it extends far beyond simply bribery and corruption.

Global and national income curves slope smoothly because of a structure of complicity and coercion. For every man at the top there are two a little way down earning much less than him but much more than almost everyone else. For both of them this pattern is reciprocated. Further down a few women are included in the ranks, growing in number as the branches spread. Most people in these positions look up to their boss and his income and feel inferior in some way (Wilkinson and Pickett, 2009). They are hardly being greedy when they compare themselves to him. They then look sideways at their rivals and strive to compete against them. They tell those below them to work harder and say that one day soon they too might be promoted upwards. But what they don't say is that for every two places below there is only one above. People are optimistic and think that odds of fifty–fifty are good. How many times do you think you might repeatedly toss a coin and see heads repeated? We have a tendency to be short-sighted, to be optimistic, to think we will get the job, the promotion, the pay rise, and often not to look too far ahead, or to look down, other than occasionally in fear.

Looking down in fear

It is hard to get to talk to someone who could tell you what it is like to be paid £5,000 or more for a single day's work – there are so few people in this position. When you earn that much money you don't have to think in the way most other people think. Your concern is not the taxi fare but getting a taxi quickly. Your decision over whether to fly is not the price, but the time it will take out of your 'schedule'. You do not clean, you do not cook your own food, you need not care for your children or your garden or your home. Your money pays others to drive you, to fly you, to clean for you, child-mind, garden, decorate, build, do all manner of tasks to satisfy your requirements and whims.

A tenth of a per cent of your £5,000 for a day's 'work' is used to demand an hour of a self-employed taxi driver's time: most of that hour the driver spends driving around waiting for someone like you to put their hand out: you only pay £5 for the short 10-minute trip. On a slow day the driver makes £60 working 12 hours a day (and has to pay tax, and for the car and petrol out of that sum before food and rent). "There's a recession on," the taxi driver tells you. "Fewer people want cabs so more of us drivers are out on the roads for longer each day to pay the bills." She reads the *Daily Mail*. She votes Conservative. She believes in free enterprise. She used to be a social worker but driving is less stressful. She is complicit with the rich. The rich quote taxi drivers often because they talk so little to so few other people on low wages. Taxi drivers vary greatly of course, but in more equal countries there are far fewer taxis.

Policy and belief

Divisions of labour can be very efficient. Markets can be very efficient. What is not efficient is allowing some people to profit and to grow richer not through any effort themselves, but simply because they already have riches. Most world religions became established in places where inequalities had newly grown wide, and many of the new religions were established to abate or reverse that growth in inequality. Religions were often created to curtail even getting into a situation where the super-rich could again exist (Ruddiman, 2005, pp 73, 134). Messiahs often railed against newly established hierarchies, often imposed after invasion and colonisation.

Most well known among religious laws against greed are those that explain why usury, gaining money by lending money, is a sin. It is fine to lend money, but not fine to profit by such lending – you should only profit by your own efforts. People establish and then recreate and reinforce the apparent naturalness of their laws and religions in attempts to curtail greed and to ensure continued caring as societies grow larger. We continue to do that. It is in our nature to try to survive and we have become quite good at spotting threats to our common survival. The supernova class is one such threat to survival. They are also a threat to themselves and they suffer fears most people do not: kidnap, for instance, or deteriorating relationships with their families (thus threatening their inheritance).

In building a reasoned case for reducing the wealth of the supernova class it is worth trying to help at least a small number of the rich to understand that redistribution is in their self-interest. Collectively, for survival, we need to ensure redistribution occurs even if most of the rich do not understand why it is in their best interest. Maintaining riches depends not on building up wealth but on denying it to others. The rich must therefore breed selectively to maintain their wealth (and so they place limits on their freedom to love); they must restrict entry into the professions (and so limit their freedom to do other work that may be less well paid); they must ensure 'severe restriction on the opportunity to acquire land and property' (Townsend, 1979, p 365), and so end up having to manage property and land themselves to remain rich.

The rich cannot become artists, although a tiny number of artists become rich, they usually cannot write novels that are any good or do much else other than try as hard as they can to remain rich. Theirs is not a good life, and we have known it is not a good life for some time (for at least as long as the major world religions have preached against greed, and they must have got the idea from sometime a little earlier). It requires the most conspicuous consumption, having to constantly buy the right things to appear rich, and not only that, you have to maintain what are called 'high-bred manners' (Veblen, 1925, p 75), to talk, act and behave 'posh' just to fit in. For the very rich what 'the right things' are in terms of behaviour may differ, but codes of behaviour still exist.

What can be done?

Raising minimum income standards, universal provision of benefits and limiting privilege were the three groups of policies Peter advocated when asked what should be done to redistribute wealth (Townsend, 1976, pp 286-90). Peter would not have known he was then writing about such things in the year in which people in Britain were most equal, when it became most easily possible to imagine a better world: 1976. Of these three courses of action Peter had most to say about limiting privilege: 'The relief of poverty is secured by lower managerial and professional incomes, relative to the average, as much as by higher minimum wages and benefits' (Townsend, 1976, p 288). Had his words been listened to more widely then, we would not find ourselves in the economic crisis we are in now, and now is a very good time to look again more carefully at Peter's words and those of like-minded individuals who have so painstakingly and carefully, decade by decade, century by century, tried to teach and explain why inequality is bad.

What are the key messages for future research, teaching, campaigning and policy making? As well as Peter Townsend's three policy areas to consider, there are three places to look for such messages. First, we can look at what we did when we were last faced with the emergence of a super-rich class in Britain, from 1876 to around 1926. It is not as if this is the first time people on these islands have confronted rapidly growing inequality and had to try to find ways to overcome it. In the end those who argued for greater equality were so successful that for 60 years from 1918, Britain became more equal: in fits and starts at first, but then much more solidly (Dorling, 2010).

In many ways we have been here before. Go to the grave of Sir Titus Salt (1803–76), or read the plaque by Miller's Dale in Derbyshire that describes how many orphans were brought up from London to die in its mills, or hear tales of how the Factory Acts were only brought in after children perished in large numbers sleeping where they worked when fire broke out. All this gives a sense of previous injustices overcome, but the scope is now global. However, the global is also very local – the world's super-rich are especially concentrated near London. We have more power to control their greed than almost any other people alive today. On 25 April 2010 it was announced that the richest 1,000 people in Britain had seen the largest ever recorded increase in their wealth, jumping by about 30% in that one financial year![4]

The second place to look is abroad. It is harder in countries like Japan, Norway, the Netherlands, Italy, Canada or Korea (or more than another dozen I could mention) to ask how inequality can be reduced because these countries are already so much more equal when compared to the UK. In contrast, all the British need do is look almost anywhere other than the US, and all the Americans need do is look at almost any other affluent country for a better way to live.

The British have tended to look to the US because public debate in Britain has been so harmed by growing inequality, but there are signs that ignorance is slowly reducing (Wilkinson and Pickett, 2009). The Americans, for similar reasons, often look nowhere else because their sense of geography and wider understanding is famously even more limited than that of the British. One joke often repeated during the early 21st century was that the only advantage the US gained by going to war was a slight improvement in its people's abysmal understanding of world geography.

The third place to look for policies to deal with inequality and to again disperse the super-rich is our own imaginations. *All the policies there have ever been were imagined by someone.* Most we could use have already been imagined, discussed and debated. Many policies that we currently think it would be impossible to introduce are currently in place somewhere in the world in a country not too different from ours, or else we once had such a policy but have forgotten it. It takes only a few minutes to work out that the introduction of a land value tax of 7p a square metre a year would wipe out UK national debt in 10 years (do the calculations yourself, and see Margo and Bradley, 2010, for why such a tax would work). The tax is so small for the vast majority of people that they would not notice they were paying it. Raise it to 10p a square metre a year and you could abolish Council Tax too, and then perhaps most would notice! Those who said they could not pay a tax based on the value of the land they own could sell a small portion of that land to pay it. The tax is based on the value of land so it would never be too high. It is also very hard to evade a land tax by hiding your land. This was first understood when the country was surveyed for tax purposes in 1086 (Wright, 2009). Why are we so slow to learn in Britain? Or did we recently know better and have forgotten?

Redistribution for the benefit of the rich

A land value tax is one way of dealing with the urgent need to redistribute wealth in Britain now rather than waiting until death duties might begin the process. Death duties are a very slow mechanism, even if they were made harder to avoid and more effective in the first place. Why wait until death? We now know that *for the good of the rich* it is not in their own interest to hold so much wealth. Instigating new public policies to redistribute wealth is morally akin to outlawing smoking in public places. It is in the interest of both the smoker and their neighbours to outlaw smoking in public buildings. Allowing the hoarding of a little wealth in private can be defended as a way of stopping a black market in wealth emerging (as occurs under communism). However, our current excesses of wealth inequalities and the flaunting of wealth are obscene, damaging and indefensible.

Before smoking in public buildings and bus shelters could be banned, it was necessary to establish that smoking really was harmful. Tobacco company bosses worked hard to try to prevent that understanding becoming widespread, but through a great deal of very good academic work, their objections were overcome (in Britain at any rate).

Before the flaunting of wealth in public can be banned, widespread redistribution reintroduced and policies become accepted to slowly make each year a little more equal than the last, it will be necessary to establish in the minds of many more people that wealth inequalities really are so harmful compared to most of the other threats we now face. Some of the wealthy are working hard to prevent that. Some directly fund right-wing parties, or what they insultingly call 'taxpayers' alliances'. Others control newspapers and television stations. They are most successful at this in countries which are already most unequal, where they try to stoke up fears around immigrants, Muslims and those they call 'scroungers' and 'delinquents'. They do this partly to avert attention from their own behaviour, their own scrounging off the poor and the delinquency of their philosophy of greed.

Addressing the advocates of inequality

Most advocates for inequality will continue to be advocates until the day that they die, but no human beings live for very long, even the richest. It is our ideas that can have much longer lives, both good and bad. The supernova class has been here before and they have burnt themselves out before: Pharaohs and emperors, cardinals who built churches larger than any palace, kings who squandered kingdoms. All their dynasties were either removed or imploded as they became unsustainable.

The existence of today's supernova class is again unsustainable. It is not in doubt that this class will end – there are not enough riches on the planet for its wealth to continue to increase indefinitely. The current 30% annual increases in the wealth of the most affluent require their assets to more than double in value every four years, to rise much more than one hundred fold in 28 years. We only have one planet. We cannot all become slaves. It is simply not politically possible for what we currently measure to continue.

What is at stake is whether the greater *equality* to come is achieved in ways that involve more or less immediate suffering. How many more children have to die of starvation worldwide and how many more of the rich will be kidnapped and blackmailed out of a small share of their wealth before the trend returns to a narrowing gap?

So what else could you do in policy terms were you so minded? Here is a short list. There are other wealth taxes that can be applied. Land tax is the hardest to evade but inheritance tax can be re-established at its previous higher levels and at a much lower kick-in rate. Capital gains taxation, including business taxes on profit, can be raised (from, in some cases, rates as low as 18%), back up to at least 50%.

It should be established as a principle that if people make money out of doing no work – from inheritance, shares, stocks and lending – then, *as a minimum,* half of the profit should go to government – to be spread out among everyone else. There is also the opposite to tax – hand-outs – but these are expensive rather than saving money, so unless they are funded by significant redistribution from the rich, they are likely to be paltry.

Reintroducing the Child Trust Funds (that the new Coalition government abolished in their first £6.24 billion of cuts in May 2010) would be one example of improving hand-outs. Such things may help but it may be more efficient simply to ensure that people do not need to think they must accumulate wealth to be cared for. Nor should they see it as likely that they will be allowed to accumulate great wealth by a society that tolerates selfishness less in future. This would reduce the desire of those working hours that are too long to begin with to work even longer.

In the medium term, reducing income inequalities would also help reduce wealth inequalities, but this route is no short-term solution. If income inequalities were reduced substantially, without other action it would still take millennia for the huge inequalities in wealth that have been amassed to be eroded back to the levels Peter Townsend first described. For Child Trust Funds (the last government's much vaunted solution) to result in a net fall in wealth inequalities, children would have to live for many hundreds of years and to spend none of their fund when they become adults to see the interest on it grow enough to result in inequalities falling.

Learning to value equality

In the long term, education is needed, a curtailment of the wider forms of racism that allow inequality to be seen as good. This is needed to try to prevent cycling round again to the same old problems, even after redistribution has been achieved. This current crisis will end, soon, hopefully without the widespread suffering that would occur if the concentration of the vast majority of wealth in the hands of so few was allowed to continue to grow. Even before it has ended, however, we should be thinking forward to how to prevent the super-rich emerging again, looking down on everyone else again, and others copying their behaviour up and down an elongated social scale. Education is often in the form of stories so I will end with one of Peter's.

In 1958 Peter Townsend watched a man working a fairground ride. He was making a roundabout turn using his own strength and doing so for hours. He watched as one young girl started to wail on the ride. The man retrieved her, and was hurt in the process: 'he took a terrible blow in the middle of his back' (Townsend, 1973, p 24). The child's mother and father did not thank him but instead talked about how their daughter was especially sensitive. They did not really see him as human. They were rich. Their attitudes to others were early signs of what was later to become much more common.

It is now over 50 years since Peter watched the indifference to others at that fairground ride, and the very richest are no longer just emotionally callous. As their wealth explodes they now often behave as if they were a different species. However, the very nature of a supernova is to be short-lived. The atoms that make up a supernova explosion do not have this collective intent; they simply act to maximise certain forces given the positions they find themselves to be in. Atoms do this just as the super-rich themselves simply act individually to protect and expand their wealth, wealth they have been allowed to amass in such huge quantities. As with exploding stars, for supernova social classes their destruction is implicit in their creation. Supernovae exist only at the end of a process: 'Supernovae are extremely luminous and cause a burst of radiation that often briefly outshines an entire galaxy, before fading from view'.[5]

Notes

[1] Supernovae are dying stars. They explode with a burst of radiation that often briefly outshines an entire galaxy. Then they fade from view. See note 5 below for the origin of the term.

[2] See www.wider.unu.edu/ — part of the United Nations University website which provides links to download the World Income Inequality database and also to the first estimates made of worldwide wealth inequalities.

[3] The 'Game of Life' was a computer simulation of a very simple life form, a cell, which dies if it has too few neighbours but which reproduces if it has just the right number. The creators of the game never realised that what they had created was a system which could replicate basic logic gates ('AND', 'OR', 'NOT' and so on) and hence could itself form a synthetic computer and recreate the game within the game.

[4] BBC News at 10pm, 25 April 2010, which reported the news at 10.28pm (the very final national story) as being a positive sign that economic recovery might be on the way, expressing not a fraction of doubt that such wealth was warranted. The BBC presents the super-rich as great business leaders, or worthy members of royalty. Apparently the Queen saw her

fortune rise by £20 million in the year to 2010, as her subjects became poorer and her country slipped into additional debt of hundreds of billions.

[5] The term 'supernova' is attributed to Swiss astrophysicist and astronomer Fritz Zwicky. First appearing in print in 1926 it coincided with the last time the richest people in the world became so very rich before losing most of their wealth. On the stars see: http://en.wikipedia.org/wiki/Supernova

Further resources
For a series of graphics on the super-rich and their relationship to others see:

Dorling, D. and Pritchard, J. (2010) 'The geography of poverty, inequality and wealth in the UK and abroad: because enough is never enough', *Applied Spatial Analysis and Policy*, vol 3, no 2-3, pp 81-106.

Gordon, D. (2009) 'Global inequality, death, and disease', *Environment and Planning A*, vol 41, no 6, pp 1271-2 (www.envplan.com/epa/editorials/a42118.pdf).

Sutcliffe, B. (2001) *100 ways of seeing an unequal world*, London: Zed Books.

Worldmapper: 'People earning over $200 a day' (www.worldmapper.org/display.php?selected=158).

References

Booth, J. (2010) 'Ministers insist "cab-for-hire" Byers had no influence', *The Times*, 22 March (www.timesonline.co.uk/tol/news/politics/article7071347.ece).

Dorling, D. (2010) *Injustice: Why social inequality persists*, Bristol: The Policy Press.

Edwards, M. (2008) *Just another emperor? The myths and realities of philanthrocapitalism*, London: Demos and The Young Foundation.

Hills, J., Brewer, M., Jenkins, S., Lister, R., Lupton, R., Machin, S., Mills, C., Modood, T., Rees, T. and Riddell, S. (2010) *An anatomy of economic inequality in the UK*, London: Government Equalities Office/Centre for Analysis of Social Exclusion.

Margo, J. and Bradley, W. (2010) *Wealth of opportunity*, London: Demos.

Mason, P. (2009) *Meltdown: The end of the age of greed*, London: Verso.

Peston, R. (2008) *Who runs Britain? How the super-rich are changing our lives*, London: Hodder & Stoughton.

Ruddiman, W.F. (2005) *Plows, plagues, and petroleum: How humans took control of climate*, Princeton, NJ: Princeton University Press.

Scott Cato, M. (2009) *Green economics: An introduction to theory, policy and practice*, London: Earthscan.

Sutcliffe, B. (2009) 'The world distribution of gross national income, 2007', *Environment and Planning A*, vol 41, no 4, p 764.

Townsend, P. (1973) *The social minority*, London: Allen Lane.

Townsend, P. (1976) *Sociology and social policy*, London: Penguin Education.

Townsend, P. (1979) *Poverty in the United Kingdom: A survey of household resources and standards of living*, London: Penguin.

Townsend, P. (1991) *The poor are poorer: A statistical report on changes in the living standards of rich and poor in the United Kingdom, 1979–1989*, A report from the Social Policy Monitoring Unit, Bristol: Department of Social Policy and Social Planning, University of Bristol.

Townsend, P. (1993) 'Underclass and overclass: the widening gulf between social classes in Britain in the 1980s', in G. Payne and M. Cross (eds) *Sociology in action: Applications and opportunities for the 1990s*, London: Macmillan.

Townsend, P. (1994) 'The rich man in his castle', *British Medical Journal*, no 309, 24 December, pp 1674-5.

Veblen, T. (1925) *The theory of the leisure class: An economic study of institutions*, London: Allen & Unwin [3rd edn published in 1957].

Wilkinson, R. and Pickett, K. (2009) *The spirit level: Why more equal societies almost always do better*, London: Penguin.

Wright, A. (2009) *Hoax! The Domesday hide*, Leicester: Matador.

NINE

Addressing health inequalities: building on Peter Townsend's legacy

Margaret Whitehead

Introduction

Peter Townsend has been an inspiration to me and to many others in using his science and his art to press for more effective action, no more so than on the issue of health inequalities. This has always been a highly charged field politically, and sometimes it has felt like playing a game of snakes and ladders – making some advances then slipping back down again – but Peter's example has helped us all persevere despite set-backs.

This chapter therefore starts by paying tribute to how much Peter has shaped the health inequalities policy debate in this field, before looking to the future and singling out key academic and political challenges. On the academic front, the chapter argues that there is an enormous research challenge in devising ways of evaluating the health and health inequalities impact of major social policies that have the potential to have the greatest impact on the wider social determinants of health. These include both universal welfare policies and the health effects of the 'poor social policies and programmes, unfair social arrangements and bad politics' identified as causes of health inequalities by the global Commission on Social Determinants of Health (CSDH). On the political front, the chapter focuses on an issue that unites Peter's concerns for global poverty with those of health: how poor health generates poverty and what can be done about it. One particularly disturbing development is singled out for closer scrutiny: that of the 'medical poverty trap', in which having to pay for essential health services out-of-pocket impoverishes households: that is, the health system itself is a poverty generator. This is a growing problem affecting an alarming number of people in many low- and middle-income countries, brought on, as the chapter argues, by aggressive policies of privatisation and the commercialisation of healthcare services pushed by international institutions. The final section of the chapter discusses what needs to be done to make a start on addressing this issue.

Campaigning in a cold climate

Today, we have a climate that has never been more sympathetic towards tackling inequalities in health. More and more countries are accepting that they have unacceptable and sometimes widening inequalities within their countries and they are concerned to take action. The UK has had national strategies, national targets and performance monitoring on the issue of health inequalities (Acheson et al, 1998; DH, 2003, 2005, 2008a, 2008b, 2009; Marmot, 2010). The World Health Organization (WHO) has passed resolutions calling for action, agreed by all the ministers of health of the constituent countries (WHO, 2002). At the end of 2009, the European Union (EU) announced a new policy of solidarity in health and reducing health inequalities, with a programme of work on that issue (European Commission, 2009), and the Spanish presidency of the EU in January 2010 took up the theme as a priority. So, on the one hand, we have 'never had it so good' but, on the other, how much of it is real substance and how much merely rhetoric?

The current favourable climate is a far cry from the time when many of us came into the health inequalities field. It is a tribute to Peter and his continuing work that he has kept that flame alive to influence the inequalities policy agenda over many years.

What has influenced that policy agenda to make it fashionable today to talk about tackling health inequalities? Thirty years ago, Peter was a key member of a Research Working Group, along with Jerry Morris, Douglas Black and Cyril Smith, commissioned in 1977 by the then Labour government to explain the worrying trends in inequalities in health and to relate these to the policies in the country intended to promote as well as restore health. The idea that a government would authorise such an exercise represented a world first at the time. The conclusions of the Working Group were submitted to the new Conservative government in 1980 (Black et al, 1980). The Black Report recommended a thorough information and research strategy, redressing the balance of the healthcare system towards prevention, primary care, community health, and giving children a better start in life. In addition, it recommended improving the material conditions of life of poorer groups, especially children and people with disabilities, through cash benefits, day care and improving housing and working conditions. In other words, it emphasised tackling the social determinants of health inequalities, although that term had not come into common use at that time.

Reading the original Black Report, Peter's influence can be discerned on nearly every page, both in its substance and in the eloquent style. The Report was published just as a new Conservative government came into power and there is a most telling one-page Foreword to the report by the then Secretary of State, Patrick Jenkin. He said:

> I must make it clear that additional expenditure on the scale which could result from the report's recommendations – the amount involved could be upwards of £2 billion a year – is quite unrealistic in present or any foreseeable economic circumstances, quite apart from any judgement that may be formed of the effectiveness of such expenditure in dealing with the problems identified. I cannot therefore endorse the Group's recommendations. (Black et al, 1980, Foreword)

In effect, not only was it too expensive but also the minister was casting doubt on the evidence on which it was based. Under normal circumstances, such a damning judgement would have killed off a lesser report in lesser hands, but Peter took up the challenge to keep its message alive. He created the ripples that spread out internationally. He called press conferences, he brought in the medical authorities, the unions, he inspired different activists to take this report seriously. The original report was issued as a flimsy typescript of 260 copies, yet it has entered the mythology of health inequalities. These 260 copies are now collectors' items – I am certainly hanging on to mine! Peter was astute enough to do a deal with Penguin to publish it and when my report *The health divide* came out, it was also published along with the Black Report within the same cover (Townsend et al, second edition, 1992). It became a Penguin non-fiction bestseller, bought by successive generations of students and others seeking to understand the issue. So, if Patrick Jenkin in his Foreword wanted to kill the report, he did the opposite and made it a bestseller. At the same time it spread right across Europe and North America. It created policy interest in many quarters, to such an extent that several countries announced the intention to do their own 'Black Report'. At the same time that the report was being given the cold shoulder in this country, it was being taken very seriously indeed. It has gone on to shape the global health inequalities agenda, with it being taken up most recently by the global CSDH (CSDH, 2008).

It is a wonder and an inspiration to me to see how Peter operates. I have my own experience of this when *The health divide* was published and I witnessed Peter's extraordinary kindness. I will never forget his words to the Advisory Group I had round me when he said "We can't let Margaret face the flak alone". That was 20 years ago and I was very naïve. I did not even know that there was going to be any flak. However, Peter was right and he organised a protective group to help me face the media onslaught and to carry out the numerous interviews.

Fast forward 30 years from the seminal Black Report to another landmark report, that of the global CSDH, which was published in 2008. This contains the strongest statement yet in any WHO document:

> Health inequalities are caused by the unequal distribution of power, income, goods and services, globally and nationally. The consequent unfairness in the immediate visible circumstances of people's lives ... their access to health care, schools and education, their conditions of work and leisure, their homes, communities, towns and cities and their chances of leading a flourishing life,

> poor and unequal living conditions are the consequence
> of poor social policies and programmes, unfair social
> arrangements and bad politics. (CSDH, 2008, p 1)

The global Commission recommended three main strands to the strategy to tackle inequalities in health: to measure and understand the problem of health inequalities and assess the impact of action; to improve the conditions of daily life; and to tackle the inequitable distribution of power, money and resources. This is in many respects a continuation of the themes in the Black Report and the sorts of remedies that were being advocated in 1980 are clearly reflected again 30 years later in this WHO report. It is unfortunate that 30 years later we still have so much to do, academically and politically, as the rest of this chapter discusses.

Rising to the research challenge

One of the burning issues in public health internationally is the recognition of the need to take action on the wider social determinants of health in efforts to reduce health inequalities (Townsend, 1990). As a consequence, the global Commission called for health equity assessments of all policy reforms across all government sectors (CSDH, 2008). This includes the 'poor social policies and programmes, unfair social arrangements and bad politics' that the Commission identified as fundamental causes of health inequalities.

At the same time, there is a common lament that we lack evidence of what works to reduce health inequalities – a conclusion based on reviews from controlled experiments of specific interventions (for example, Health Select Committee, 2009). That pessimistic conclusion can be challenged if broader types of evidence are employed. There is no doubt, however, that there is a mismatch between what *should be* evaluated and what *is* being evaluated, and also in the concepts and methods of evaluation employed. Micro-analysis using experimental designs predominates in the health literature, in which the effects of specific interventions on individuals are assessed and cost-effectiveness is evaluated from the perspective of the health sector. This may be appropriate when the effectiveness of a specific drug or medical procedure on a patient suffering a particular disease is evaluated, but it is entirely inadequate for the assessment of complex social interventions and policies that are needed to tackle social inequalities in health. In such cases, broader macro-analysis of the range and distributional effects of policies on society and systems is required. What we are beginning to get in this field, however, as Smith and Petticrew (2010) argue persuasively, is micro-analysis methods applied to the evaluation of macro-level interventions.

There is also a tendency, even in the social determinants of the health field, to evaluate small-scale behavioural interventions, which are easier to fit into traditional experimental study designs, while ignoring wider policies dealing with structural factors, which may be much more difficult to evaluate but are potentially of greater impact. When we interviewed policy advisers and senior researchers about the type of evidence that would help them in their efforts to tackle inequalities in health, this message about structural factors was reinforced (Petticrew et al, 2004; Whitehead et al, 2004). Participants expressed frustration with the existence of 'the inverse evidence law', that is to say 'the availability of evidence tends to be inversely related to the potential impact/importance of the intervention' (Nutbeam, 2003).

Figure 9.1 illustrates a social model of health, with the main determinants of population health depicted as layers of influence, one on top of another, and each one interacting with the others. In terms of the 'inverse evidence law', evaluations of interventions to tackle social inequalities in health tend to be concentrated on factors in the innermost layer – the lifestyle factors – with declining numbers of evaluations in the successive outer layers. More sophisticated ways need to be found to assess policies and interventions that may have a profound effect on these wider social determinants.

The evaluation challenge is even more pressing in relation to universal welfare policies, which, by definition, cover the whole of the population and therefore cannot be evaluated by the use of an unexposed control group within that population. Yet such policies are potentially of great importance for reducing health inequalities and promoting the well-being of citizens across the social gradient. Methods need to be developed and refined for assessing the impact of such universal policies on public health and health inequalities. In the absence of such evaluations, politicians in Europe are prone to look to the US, where small-scale social welfare interventions are applied in a specific sub-population and compared, using randomised controlled trials (RCTs), with people who have no provision at all. Even though such interventions may be meaningless in the context of European welfare systems, this does not stop politicians importing the ideas and imposing them on the existing universal systems in ways that can even be counter-productive or damaging.

Figure 9.1: The main determinants of health

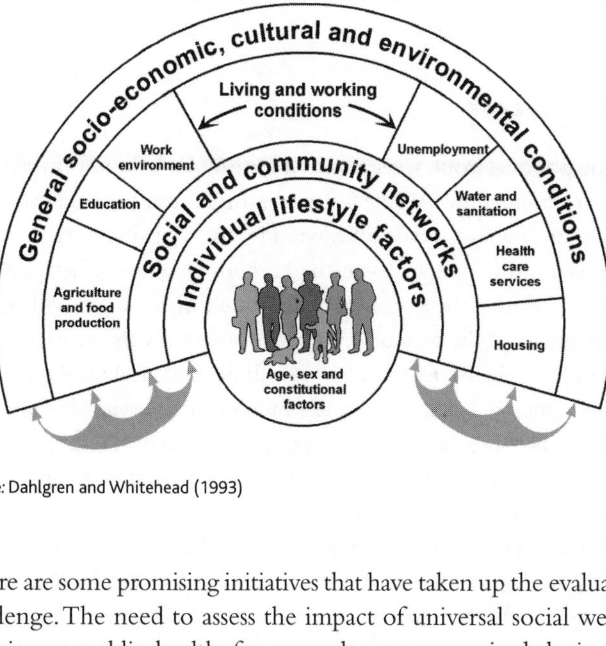

Source: Dahlgren and Whitehead (1993)

There are some promising initiatives that have taken up the evaluation challenge. The need to assess the impact of universal social welfare policies on public health, for example, was recognised during the early stages of the CSDH, and the NEWS project was set up to study the long-term impact of Swedish and Nordic welfare and egalitarian policies on health, funded by the Swedish Ministry of Health and Social Affairs (Lundberg et al, 2008). This provides a valuable example of an analytical approach that combines historical and comparative analysis and the study of qualitative differences between specific policy schemes, not only comparing clusters of countries. Other approaches use individual-level data to trace how specific sub-groups fare under the influence of different policy contexts (see, for example, Whitehead et al, 2000, 2009).

If the international experiences so far tell us one thing above all, it is that cross-county collaboration is more vital than ever to move forward on the vast agenda for tackling social inequalities in health. No one country has the opportunity or capacity to test and evaluate effective strategies to reduce health inequalities. We need collaborations to increase learning speed by: pooling research capacity, exploiting 'natural policy experiments' and continuing to exchange intelligence on questions of what works, for whom and within which context.

Political agenda

On the political front, we are entering treacherous waters in relation to health inequalities. While political momentum has been building globally in the last decade, illustrated by the worldwide response to the CSDH, the climate has changed considerably with the global economic crisis. Most pressing is the question of what will be the health impact of the economic crisis and especially the impact on the most vulnerable. We also have an assault on universal public services and benefits, and a drift towards individual lifestyle and targeted solutions and away from wider social determinants. Globally, there is a growing medical poverty trap, meaning that when people are ill and they need to access essential services, they have to pay so much for those services out of their own pocket that it is a major cause of poverty in a growing number of countries. All these problems are looming on the horizon. One challenge in particular unites Peter Townsend's concerns for global poverty issues with those of health: how poor health generates poverty and what can be done about it. The second half of this chapter explores this issue further.

Falling into the medical poverty trap

There is a two-way path between poverty and ill health: poverty causes ill health but equally ill health causes poverty. Peter Townsend's meticulous work has helped, on the one hand, to measure material deprivation and demonstrate its causal link to poor health (Townsend et al, 1988), and on the other hand, to champion income maintenance policies to prevent chronically ill and disabled people falling into poverty (for example, Walker and Townsend, 1981).

Globally, a problem of catastrophic proportions is developing: poor health is currently a major cause of poverty in many low- and middle-income countries where families have extremely limited public welfare support to help compensate income lost due to illness. At the same time, poorer groups have substantially increased expenditures, as they have to pay a high proportion of (or all) medical expenses out-of-pocket. This rise in out-of-pocket costs for health services that has driven many families into poverty and has deepened the poverty of those who were already poor can be conceptualised as a 'medical poverty trap' (Whitehead et al, 2001). WHO estimates that 100 million people per year are impoverished by having to pay out-of-pocket for their medical care (WHO, 2007). This estimate is the tip of the iceberg, as it only relates to catastrophic payments for acute hospital care, while many millions more are affected by having to pay for long-term conditions treated at primary care level and by self-care. In China, for example, medical expenditure since the mid-1990s has become an important cause of transient poverty, and one of the major poverty generators in rural areas (Liu et al, 2003; Hu et al, 2008; Tang et al, 2008). Between 1993 and 1998, the proportion of the population having to pay out-of-pocket for healthcare increased from 28% to 44%, and was estimated as being as high as 90% in poor rural areas (Tang et al, 2008). This has led to situations where payment for healthcare by tuberculosis patients for medical services in rural China in 2003 amounted to 45% of annual household income for the low-income group and 16% for the high-income group (Zhang et al, 2008). Other chronic diseases can eat up the equivalent of 100% or more of annual household income. How is that possible, one might ask. The answer is crippling debt.

The consequences of the medical poverty trap can be profound. In extreme cases, people are denied essential health services completely because they cannot afford the user fees demanded, and their illness goes untreated. This leads to a further deterioration in their health, and inability to work and earn a living leads to further poverty in a downward spiral. Then there are the cases where people delay care until a less serious condition that could have been treated in primary care becomes an emergency needing expensive hospital treatment. In many cases, the high fees lead to a cutting down on the amount of treatment, or dropping out before completion. This leads to inadequate control of the health condition, the use of cheaper, ineffective treatments, or even inappropriate or unsafe remedies, leading to problems such as the development of antibiotic resistance in the whole community. Long-term impoverishment may result from family members falling into debt by taking out crippling loans or selling off their assets that they need to make a living – such as cattle or land (McIntyre et al, 2006).

The roots of the problem

The medical poverty trap is not a chance occurrence. It is the result of aggressive policies pursued over more than 30 years, during which time broad-based economic growth has been promoted as a solution to poverty around the globe (Dollar and Kraay, 2002). Townsend and Gordon's book *World poverty* details the common prescription underlying these particular types of economic growth policy, pushed by international institutions such as The World Bank and International Monetary Fund (IMF): boosting exports and free trade by privatisation, by deregulation to open up local markets to competition, by capital market liberalisation and by market-based pricing, at the same time as cuts in public expenditure, including subsidies for basic foodstuffs and spending on health and education sectors. For countries in financial crisis, public spending has been further eroded by the necessity to keep up crippling debt repayments (Townsend and Gordon, 2002).

The adoption of such macro-economic policies has been reflected in the reforms of the health sector (Macintosh and Koivusalo,

2005). The provision of healthcare has increasingly been treated as a commodity that can be subjected to the same prescription as other goods: privatisation, competition, deregulation, decentralisation, accompanied by cuts in public expenditure. These have included direct cuts in health budgets, wages and employment, and indirect cuts by shifting costs onto patients. This includes the widespread introduction of user fees for health services (sometimes euphemistically called 'co-payments'), which has shifted the burden of payment more and more onto people who fall ill, rather than spreading it equitably across the population in proportion to ability to pay. The World Bank's 1987 'Agenda for Reform' in Africa, for example, was highly influential in promoting user fees for health services as a solution to the shortfall in public sector resources for healthcare (Akin et al, 1987), a shortfall in large part brought about by the wider macro-economic policies pursued at the time.

Even in some countries that have not been forced into these measures by a debt crisis, the introduction of neoliberal macro-economic reforms has led to similar problems within the health system. In China, for example, which has instigated wide-ranging reforms since the late 1970s, rapid economic growth coupled with unprecedented commercialisation of the health system led, among other effects, to the collapse of the previously well-functioning rural health insurance scheme. At its worst, health insurance coverage dropped to less than 10% in rural areas from the late 1980s to 2000, coupled with the fact that the proportion of costs reimbursed by insurers was very low for the minority who were insured. Over the same period, user fees and profiteering by providers (both public and private) led to dramatic increases in the proportion of medical costs that patients had to pay out-of-pocket (from 20% to 50%) (Tang et al, 2008). The profiteering, by prescribing drugs and procedures that make the most profit for the provider, caused knock-on effects including cost escalation, unnecessary or even dangerous treatments and poorer quality care. In recent years, the Chinese government itself has diagnosed that the market-oriented reforms of the healthcare system went too far and too deep and were based on 'a wrong concept' which did not meet the needs of the people (Tang et al, 2008). China now faces a mammoth task to turn the system around.

Breaking the poor health–poverty link

Escaping the medical poverty trap

The medical poverty trap is only one symptom of a broader problem of a dysfunctional healthcare system. Where there is a medical poverty trap, there are also grave problems with sections of the population not being able to get access to the healthcare that they need, exploitation of patients for profit, inefficiencies and ultimately the unsustainability of the system as a whole.

Merely getting rid of user fees to reduce the out-of-pocket expenses of sick people will therefore not solve the underlying problem. It may even make matters worse in the short term if services which relied on user fees to pay staff and maintain facilities are suddenly deprived of that income and no other source of financing is put in place to replace the fees (McIntyre et al, 2007). System failure requires a system-wide response. Unfortunately, as the Chinese government is discovering, a reasonably equitable healthcare system is not easily restored once dismantled. For those countries that had a relatively weak system to begin with, reversing the effects of years of marketisation, with the attendant corruption from under-the-table payments, is even more daunting. A start can and needs to be made, however, by the following:

- International institutions and advisers from high-income countries need to stop exporting the neoliberal model of health sector reform. Teams of consultants are still going into low- and middle-income countries to 'advise' on reforms and promoting the same, discredited prescription. Sometimes, this appears to be more to do with creating opportunities for profit rather than meeting the needs of the population.
- A firmer evidence base for health sector policies needs to be built by assessing the validity of the assumptions on which these market-oriented prescriptions for reform are based. For too long, the rhetoric about the merits of health sector policies advocated by The World Bank for countries with ailing economies has been accepted without question. Policy research is urgently needed to

distinguish the myths from reality, and to assess the alternative options for achieving efficient and equitable healthcare systems.

- The effects of reforms need to be assessed from a household perspective. We should be looking at what is really happening in individual countries to access and affordability of care for different groups in the population. Careful monitoring is needed of the experience of people trying to cope with illness and trying to access the health services they need, to form a proper evaluation of how the system is working and where it is failing the people it is meant to serve.

- Starting to (re-)build a more equitable system by:
  - devising more equitable mechanisms for financing services, including pooling of financial risk across the population, progressive financing in which contributions are in proportion to ability to pay, and pre-payment schemes replacing user fees so that use is free or low cost at the point of need for the service;
  - equitable distribution of resources for services, including the ability to cross-subsidise services from richer to poorer groups and areas of the country;
  - re-investment in good quality public health services (after decades of neglect and disinvestment in some countries), including improved planning and budgeting;
  - stronger government regulation of the system including essential drugs programmes and control of private sector activities.

- Fighting corruption. Informal (under-the-table) payments for public health services constitute a major burden of payment for many low-income patients. As well as adding to the medical poverty trap, such payments undermine the possibility of maintaining and developing public healthcare systems. One strategy that would help is an expansion of compulsory health insurance systems, linked to efforts to inform patients about their right to free or almost free health services at the point of delivery. Another is increased salaries for low-paid health professionals linked with strict rules and controls on informal payments.

Integrating health into poverty reduction strategies

On a wider front, poverty reduction strategies in low- and middle-income countries rarely consider the various links between poor health and increased poverty, not to mention the substantial contribution that improved health could make to financial and social well-being.

These poor health–poverty links need to be integrated into national strategies for reducing poverty, for example:

- Building into poverty reduction strategies regular assessments of the total burden of payment for healthcare as well as the social and health consequences of these payments for households.
- Reforming the financing system for health services, based on equity principles (as above), to prevent household impoverishment associated with healthcare costs.
- Developing social security systems to maintain income in the event of sickness.
- Promoting improved health as a route out of poverty. This is particularly pertinent for low-income countries, where the burden of disease is high from conditions potentially treatable or preventable by health service interventions. Disease prevention and health promotion strategies therefore need to take account of the heavier disease burden among poorer groups. This includes supplementing general health strategies with extra health promotion and prevention efforts to reach socioeconomic groups at greatest risk.
- Attention also needs to be paid to the way that available resources can be deployed more equitably. Even in situations where poverty is widespread, some countries have made impressive improvements in health by skilful action on the social determinants of health – such as living conditions, education and food security – across the whole population. The past success of countries such as Vietnam, Sri Lanka and Costa Rica in boosting their populations' health has been attributed to the priority they have given to ensuring that social services, particularly healthcare and basic education, reach everyone (Sen, 2001).

Protecting the equity gains already made

While the poor health–poverty link is strongest in low- and middle-income countries with market-oriented healthcare systems, the issue is still extremely pertinent to European welfare states. It is worth remembering that historically an important spur to the development of comprehensive social welfare systems was the need to break the links between poor health and poverty. Thus social security systems have been built to maintain income in the event of sickness, and universal health systems have been designed to pool financial risk and to provide services free or at a very low cost at the point of delivery. The positive effects of these reforms have been remarkable in many European countries, where poor health is no longer a cause of major financial problems and poverty.

This positive trend, however, is now slowly being eroded in some European countries, where financial support systems are weakening – for example, due to the requirement to pay an increasing share of medical expenses out-of-pocket. At the same time, market-oriented reforms to universal health services are chipping away at the underpinning equity principles on which the systems are built, and income maintenance schemes are under attack in the search for cuts in public expenditure. In such circumstances, we must be continually vigilant and fight to preserve the equitable universal systems we have. Now, more than ever, is the time to carry forward Peter Townsend's international work to tackle the ill health and poverty link globally and locally.

References

Acheson, D., Barker D., Chambers J., Graham H., Marmot M. and Whitehead M. (1998) *Report of the Independent Inquiry into Inequalities in Health (Acheson Report)*, London: The Stationery Office.

Akin, J., Birdsall, N. and Ferranti, D. (1987) *Financing health services in developing countries: An agenda for reform*, Washington, DC: The World Bank.

Black, D., Morris, J.N., Smith, C. and Townsend, P. (1980) *Inequalities in health: Report of a Research Working Group*, London: Department of Health and Social Security.

CSDH (Commission on Social Determinants of Health) (2008) *Closing the gap in a generation: Health equity through action on the social determinants of health*, Final report of CSDH, Geneva: World Health Organization.

Dahlgren, G. and Whitehead, M. (1993), accessible in G. Dahlgren and M. Whitehead (2007) *European strategies for tackling social inequities in health: Levelling up Part 2*, Studies on Social and Economic Determinants of Population Health, no 3, Copenhagen: World Health Organization Regional Office for Europe.

DH (Department of Health) (2003) *Tackling health inequalities: A programme for action*, London: DH.

DH (2005) *Tackling health inequalities: Status report on the programme for action*, London: DH.

DH (2008a) *Tackling health inequalities: 2007 status report on the programme for action*, London: DH.

DH (2008b) *Health inequalities: Progress and next steps*, Review for the Secretary of State for Health, London: DH.

DH (2009) *Tackling health inequalities: 10 years on*, London: DH.

Dollar, D. and Kraay, A. (2002) 'Growth is good for the poor', *Journal of Economic Growth,* vol 7, pp 195-225.

European Commission (2009) *Solidarity in health: Reducing health inequalities in the EU*, Communication from the Commission to the European Parliament, COM (2009) 567/4, Brussels: European Commission.

Health Select Committee (2009) *Third report – Health inequalities*, London: The Stationery Office (www.parliament.the-stationery-office.co.uk/pa/cm200809/cmselect/cmhealth/286/28602.htm).

Hu, S., Tang, S., Liu, Y., Zhao, Y., Escabar, M. and de Ferranti, D. (2008) 'Reform of how health care is provided, financed and organised in China: challenges and opportunities', *Lancet*, vol 372, pp 1846-53.

Liu, Y., Rao, K. and Hsiao, W.C. (2003) 'Medical expenditure and rural impoverishment in China', *Journal of Health, Population and Nutrition*, vol 21, pp 216-22.

Lundberg, O., Åberg Yngwe, M., Kölegård Stjärne, M., Björk, L. and Fritzell, J. (2008) *NEWS: The Nordic Experience Welfare States and public health*, Health Equity Studies no 12, Stockholm: Centre for Health Equity Studies (CHESS)/Karolinska Institutet.

Macintosh, M. and Koivusalo, M. (2005) *Commercialisation of health care: Global and local dynamics and policy responses*, Basingstoke: Palgrave Macmillan.

McIntyre, D., Thiede, M., Dahlgren, G. and Whitehead, M. (2006) 'What are the economic consequences for households of illness and paying for health care in low- and middle-income country contexts?', *Social Science and Medicine,* vol 62, pp 858-65.

McIntyre, D., Whitehead, M., Gilson, L., Dahlgren, G. and Tang, S. (2007) 'Equity impacts of neoliberal reforms: what should the policy be?', *International Journal of Health Services*, vol 37, no 4, pp 693-709.

Marmot, M. (2010) *Fair society, healthy lives. The Marmot review: Strategic review of health inequalities in England post-2010*, London: The Marmot Review (www.ucl.ac.uk/marmotreview).

Nutbeam, D. (2003) 'Evidence-based public policy for health: matching research to policy need', *IUHPE Promotion and Education*, vol 2 (suppl), pp 15-27.

Petticrew, M., Whitehead, M., Macintyre, S., Egan, M. and Bambra, C. (2004) 'Evidence for public health policy on inequalities: 1: the reality according to policymakers', *Journal of Epidemiology and Community Health*, vol 58, pp 811-16.

Sen, A. (2001) 'Economic progress and health', in D. Leon and G. Walt (eds) *Poverty, inequality and health: An international perspective*, Oxford: Oxford University Press., pp 333-45.

Smith, R. and Petticrew, M. (2010) 'Public health evaluation in the twenty-first century: time to see the wood as well as the trees', *Journal of Public Health*, vol 32, no 1, pp 2-7.

Tang, S., Meng, Q., Chen, L., Bekerman, H., Evans, T. and Whitehead, M. (2008) 'Tackling the challenges to health equity in China', *Lancet,* vol 372, pp 1493-501.

Townsend, P. (1990) 'Individual or social responsibility for premature death – current controversies in the British debate about health', *International Journal of Health Services*, vol 20, pp 373-92.

Townsend, P. and Gordon, D. (2002) *World poverty: New policies to defeat an old enemy*, Bristol: The Policy Press.

Townsend, P., Phillimore, P. and Beattie, A. (1988) *Health and deprivation: Inequality and the North*, London: Croom Helm.

Townsend, P., Whitehead, M. and Davidson, N. (eds) (1992) *Inequalities and health: The Black Report and the health divide* (2nd edn), Harmondsworth: Penguin Books.

Walker, A. and Townsend, P. (1981) *Disability in Britain: A manifesto of rights*, Oxford: Martin Robertson.

Whitehead, M., Burström, B. and Diderichsen, F. (2000) 'Social policies and the pathways to inequalities in health: a comparative analysis of lone mothers in Britain and Sweden', *Social Science & Medicine*, vol 50, pp 255-70.

Whitehead, M., Dahlgren, G. and Evans, T. (2001) 'Equity and health sector reforms: can low-income countries escape the medical poverty trap?', *Lancet*, vol 358, pp 833-6.

Whitehead, M., Burström, B., Diderichsen, F., Dahl, E., Ng, E., Clayton, S. et al (2009) *Helping chronically ill or disabled people into work: What can we learn from international comparative analyses?*, Final Report to the Policy Research Programme, London: Department of Health (www.york.ac.uk/phrc/papers).

Whitehead, M., Petticrew, M., Graham, H., Macintyre, S., Bambra, C. and Egan, M. (2004) 'Evidence for public health policy on inequalities: 2: Assembling the evidence jigsaw', *Journal of Epidemiology and Community Health*, vol 58, no 10, pp 817-21.

WHO (2007) *Everybody's business: Strengthening health systems to improve health outcomes*, Geneva: WHO.

Zhang, T., Tang, S., Jun, G. and Whitehead, M. (2007) 'Persistent problems of access to appropriate, affordable TB services in rural China: experiences of different socio-economic groups', *BMC Public Health*, vol 17, no e19.

TEN

Towards a new sociology of ageing: from structured dependency to critical gerontology

Chris Phillipson

Introduction

Peter Townsend can rightly be viewed as both the founder in the UK of the sociology of ageing and in his writing in this area a key figure in the development of what came to be known as 'critical perspectives' on ageing. The purpose of this chapter is to set out both a manifesto for developing new approaches to work in the field of ageing and in particular that relating to 'critical gerontology' (Estes et al, 2003; Baars et al, 2006a; Bernard and Scharf, 2007). The chapter is divided into five main sections:

- an examination of a central element of Townsend's contribution to work in the field of old age, namely, his development of 'structured dependency' theory;
- an exploration of the development of critical perspectives in gerontology, locating these in the context of sociological and related disciplines;
- the development of an analysis of key areas influencing the development of critical gerontology;
- the identification of new inequalities and divisions affecting the lives of older people;
- the presentation of a manifesto for change, focusing on three major areas for development.

From structured dependency to critical gerontology

In 1981, in the first issue of the journal *Ageing and Society*, Peter Townsend contributed what was to become a highly influential piece of writing dealing with the social and economic inequalities facing older people. This article – 'The structured dependency of the elderly: a creation of policy in the twentieth century' – represented a systematic attempt to provide a new theoretical framework for understanding policies affecting elderly people. Certainly, its publication in 1981 proved to be a watershed in sociological and critical thinking about ageing. Prior to this time, research had focused, as Townsend observed (1981, p 6), on 'individualistic instead of societal forms of explanation' or 'acquiescent functionalism', as it was described. Townsend, however, challenged this approach, arguing that it was social processes that created: '… the framework of institutions and rules within which the general problems of the elderly emerge and, indeed, are manufactured' (p 9). For Townsend, in common with a number of other writers developing work on ageing around this time (cf Estes, 1979; Walker, 1980), the marginalisation and dependency of older people could more properly be viewed as 'socially created', a product of forced exclusion from work, poverty, institutionalisation and passive forms of community care. Although not without its critics (see, for example, Johnson, 1989), the concept of structured dependency was to provide a foundation for the development of what subsequently came to be known as 'critical gerontology' (Minkler and Estes, 1999; see further below). The approach developed by structured dependency was important in highlighting ageing as a form of 'social construction', shaped by sociological, economic and political institutions. The underlying factors 'manufacturing old age' were subsequently examined in a variety of studies (see, for example, Phillipson, 1998; Estes and Associates, 2001; Walker, 2009) and will only be summarised for the purpose of this chapter. In essence, however, the argument ran as follows: for most Western societies, the period stretching from the early 1950s through to the mid-1970s created new institutions for supporting and managing the rising numbers of people entering their 60s, 70s and beyond. During this time, with variations across European countries, responses to ageing were formed around the institutions and relationships associated with mass retirement and the welfare state. This was a time when nations in the industrialised world identified older people as worthy beneficiaries of support, mindful of the sacrifices and deprivations associated with the economic depression of the 1930s and the world war that followed (Macnicol, 1998).

Despite the achievements associated with postwar reforms, Townsend (1981) highlighted major concerns about many of the policies linked with the development of retirement and the provision of state pensions. Retirement, he suggested, could be viewed as a form of 'mass redundancy', imposed on workers to solve the needs of employers keen to reduce wages and/or shift manufacturing to poorer countries overseas. The rise of retirement could also be related to new forms of technology that were leading to an 'over-valuation of the productive capacity of younger workers and under-valuation of the productive capacity of older workers' (p 11). Such arguments were prescient in many respects: the former anticipating debates about the impact of globalisation in the field of social policy (Yeates, 2008); the latter foreshadowing research in the 1990s and early 2000s examining discrimination against older workers (Platman and Taylor, 2006). The dependency created by retirement was, Townsend argued, further intensified by chronic poverty in old age, with at least 10% of older people living directly in poverty and a further 30% or 40% living on the margins. Pensions, he pointed out, were defined in relation to subsistence needs, and were invariably placed below net earnings during the period of paid employment. Private or occupational pensions also tended to be low relative to the earnings of younger and middle-aged people in employment (Townsend, 1979). Townsend concluded his article with a challenge for older people to 'continue in paid employment ... find substantial and productive occupations [and] to achieve rights to much larger incomes' (p 23).

Whatever the historical or sociological challenges that might be made to aspects of Townsend's case, the underlying argument came to be broadly accepted: namely, that through retirement and the welfare state a distinctive category of older people/pensioners had emerged, a group who could be seen to be in a 'dependent' status relative to other age groups. Such arguments chimed in with wider concerns that the post-Second World War institutions associated with the welfare state had failed to transform the lives of poorer groups in society. Older people had been integral to the development of ideas about a more 'inclusive society', one that would erase the link between old age and images of poverty and decrepitude. Yet concern about excess expenditure on older people had been ever-present in public policy from the 1950s onwards (Phillipson, 1982). Beveridge's strictures about avoiding the 'extravagance [of] giving a full subsistence income to every citizen, as a birthday present on his or her reaching the age of 60 or 65' (cited in Macnicol, 1998, p 381) was taken to heart by most governments (and reinforced in the Thatcher years). And older people were the largest single group of those 'rediscovered' as living in poverty in the early 1960s, although governments, along with senior civil servants, took some persuading that this could possibly be the case (Townsend and Wedderburn, 1965).

At the same time, the possibility of transforming old age, through guarantees to income and services, was a significant component of the postwar social contract. Care for older people was viewed, first, as a fair exchange for past work and services; second, as an essential element of reforms protecting people from hazards experienced over the life course; and third, as part of the intergenerational contract with support from the welfare state complementing that provided by the family (Townsend, 1957; Phillipson et al, 2000). Yet if the welfare state provided 'security' (albeit of a limited kind) in exchange for 'dependency', new challenges were to emerge in the period following the publication of Townsend's paper. We can now in fact see the late 1970s/early 1980s as a crucial period when many features of the postwar welfare state began to unravel, with numerous threats to the economic and social security of older people.

Old age and crisis construction

The crisis in ageing that took hold from the early 1980s onwards can be seen as an early indication of the loosening of institutional supports underpinning the life course. Population ageing was itself a creation of modernity, reflecting the achievements of industrialism, improved public health and the growth of social welfare (Thane, 2000). The steady expansion in the proportion of older people in the population was, up until the beginning of the 1980s, largely contained within the linked institutions of retirement and the welfare state. The unravelling of these arrangements can be traced to at least three types of crisis affecting the management of ageing populations in the last quarter of the 20th century: economic, social and cultural.

The economic dimension has been well rehearsed with successive crises from the mid-1970s onwards undermining: first, the goal of full employment and hence destabilising the institution of retirement, and, second, the fiscal crisis affecting the welfare state, accelerated with the onset of privatisation and deregulation from the 1980s onwards (Rogne et al, 2009). These aspects led to the development in the social sphere of what Estes and Associates (2001) defined as the 'crisis construction' and 'crisis management' of ageing, with old age presented as a burden and problem for society (Vincent, 2006). At its most extreme, demographic change came to be viewed as a factor behind the economic crisis of the 1970s and early 1980s (and continuing in different ways through into the early 1990s), notably in respect of the apparent imbalance between 'productive' and 'non-productive' sectors in the economy (The World Bank, 1994). Finally, at a cultural level, the modern life course itself came to be viewed as playing a contributory role in the alienation of older people in Western society. Thomas Cole (1992, p 241) set out the issues as follows:

> The idea of a society legitimately ordered by the divisions of a human lifetime is now under siege in large part because its view of old age is neither socially nor spiritually adequate and because the social meanings of life's stages are in great flux. Recent critiques of ageing in the modern life course have also reflected a dawning awareness that ageing is much more than a problem to be solved. In some quarters it is becoming clear that accumulating health and wealth through the rationalized control of the body is an impoverished vision of what it means to live a life.

Concern with all three aspects of the crisis affecting older people – economic, social and cultural – was to come together in the development of critical gerontology.[1] Faced with the variety of challenges affecting older people, given the depth of economic crisis in the 1980s and early 1990s, critical gerontology emerged as an attempt to extend arguments expressed in structured dependency theory and associated contributions. In making this attempt, critical perspectives drew on approaches that had been influential in other areas of sociology and political science – notably Marxism, feminism and critical theory (as represented in the Frankfurt School). These tools of analysis were picked up by those seeking to develop new approaches in the field of ageing and were applied to areas such as retirement, family life, pensions and community care (Estes and Associates, 2001; Baars et al, 2006b; Walker and Naegele, 2009).

The political economy perspective emerged as one of the most important strands within the critical tradition, drawing on many of the themes in structured dependency. Beginning in the late 1970s and early 1980s, with the work of Estes (1979), Guillemard (1983), Phillipson (1982) and Walker (1981), these theorists initiated the task of describing the respective roles of capitalism and the state in contributing to systems of domination and marginalisation affecting older people. This work extended the concept of structured dependency in two important ways: first, in relation to research on social inequality, and second, in developing ideas about the role of the state in the production of dependency. Social class became a major concern in respect of the former, this reflecting the influence of Marxism within the political economy model (Walker and Foster, 2006; Foster, 2010). Political economy theorists took the view that older people were as deeply divided along class (and other social fault lines) as younger and middle-aged adults. Walker (1996, p 33) contrasted this approach with functionalist theories that tended to view age as erasing class and status differentials. He argued that:

> There is no doubt that the process of retirement, not ageing, does superimpose reduced socio-economic status on a majority of older people ... but even so retirement has a differential impact on older people, depending on

their prior socio-economic status. For example, there is
unequal access to occupational pensions. Women and
other groups with incomplete employment records are
particularly disadvantaged.... There are also inequalities
between generations of older people, arising from their
unequal access to improved private and occupational
pension provision.

Political economy also emphasised the importance of other social
divisions affecting old age, notably those associated with gender (Estes,
2006) and ethnicity (Dressel, 1988). Minkler (1999, p 1) suggested
that these were best viewed as 'interlocking systems of inequality'
which determine the experience of growing old and which illustrate
the construction of ageing on multiple levels.

In relation to the role of the state in old age, research in this area
has been especially linked with that of Carroll Estes (1999; Estes and
Associates, 2001), who noted how the nature of state intervention
and the legitimacy of the state were issues that had hitherto been
kept apart from studies of older people. Estes (1999) took the view
that the study of the state was in fact central to the understanding of
ageing given its power to (a) allocate and distribute scarce resources;
(b) mediate between the different segments and classes of society;
and (c) ameliorate social conditions that could threaten the existing
order. Given these activities, Estes concluded that:

> The state and state policy on aging need to be examined
> more closely in terms of how each promotes and
> reproduces the dominant institution.... The political
> economy perspective renders the aged and state policy
> intrinsic parts of the phenomenon of crisis construction
> and management in advanced capitalism and considers
> how the aged and old age policy are used in these
> processes.... The task is to specify how the aged and state
> policy are implicated in crisis formation and trajectory
> and the role of ideology therein. (Estes, 1999, p 23)

Drawing on the perspectives developed by critical gerontology, and political economy in particular, the next section of this chapter considers challenges facing work in this area, especially in a context of economic and political crisis, one that is likely to intensify given substantial cuts in public expenditure.

Old age and economic crisis: new areas influencing critical gerontology

Older people have faced major changes to their lives over the past three decades, raising major issues for structured dependency theory and critical gerontology more generally. Three main areas for discussion can be identified:

* transformation of work and retirement;
* impact of privatisation and deregulation;
* influence of globalisation.

The above developments have created significant question marks for work in the field of ageing, and for the development of critical perspectives in particular. In respect of the first of these areas, Townsend described the postwar development of 'mass retirement' among men with dependency arising from the setting of chronological boundaries splitting work from non-work. In retrospect, however, the construction of old age through well-defined boundaries was confined to a relatively short period of time – roughly from the late 1940s through to the mid-1970s (Laczko and Phillipson, 1991). Following this, a number of changes can be identified arising from the development of flexible patterns of work running alongside rising levels of unemployment. The retirement transition itself became more complex with the emergence of different pathways (for example, unemployment, redundancy, disability, part-time employment, self-employment) that people followed before they describe themselves or are officially defined as 'wholly retired' (Chiva and Manthorpe, 2009).

Such changes raise complex issues about characterising the social and class status of people neither in work nor wholly retired in the conventional sense. By the mid-1990s, many European countries had labour participation rates among men aged 55-64 below or barely above 50% (for example, Finland 41.6%, France 41.5%, Netherlands 41.4% and Spain 54.9%). One response to this development has been to view this as representing a shift from the structured dependency associated with the period of industrial capitalism, to one of social and economic 'risk' characteristic of post-industrial capitalism (Phillipson, 2009). The distinction is important at a structural level but also in respect of the rewards and opportunities available to individuals. Modernity, from the late 1940s through to the early 1970s, reconstructed old age (at least in the case of men) around mass retirement (supported by the expansion of defined benefit pensions) underpinned by systems of public welfare. In the UK, employers used pensions (in the 1950s and 1960s) to cultivate a loyal workforce in a context of widespread shortages of skilled labour (Phillipson, 1982). Whiteside (2006) notes how some European countries, faced with the social and economic devastation arising from the Second World War, introduced citizenship pensions (illustrated by Sweden and the Netherlands) to prevent the spread of destitution. In the US, economic prosperity fostered the expansion of employer-based pensions, but with unions such as the United Mine Workers also influencing the adoption of pensions as a key item in collective bargaining (Sass, 1989).

How does this contrast with capitalism in its present post-industrial phase? A central feature here is the undertow of instability and crisis running through the system and the consequences for older workers and elderly people. Key features include accelerated job insecurity (Sennett, 2006; Hank and Erlinghagen, 2009); the large fluctuations in income experienced by workers from one year to the next (Hacker, 2008; Solow, 2008, p 79); the closure of pension plans to new employees (see further below); and governments pressing to 'extend working life' even while drastically reducing the employment options available to older workers (Blackburn, 2006; Phillipson, 2009).

The insecurities characteristic of capitalism in its present phase have been reinforced by the move towards privatisation/deregulation that gathered pace over the course of the 1990s and 2000s. There are a number of features here that require further analysis in respect of their impact on old age. In the first place, governments in post-industrial societies – under the influence of neoliberal ideology – grew steadily more conservative in respect of commitments to social reform. Tomasky (2010) makes this point in a US context, where he points out that it is necessary to go back to the 1960s and 1970s to identify the passing of major items of social legislation. The radical dismantling of the public sector was of course a characteristic of the Thatcher years in the UK but continued under New Labour, with noted failures to mount reforms in areas such as long-term care. Pension provision was subject to radical change but for present-day pensioners this was achieved through traditional means testing (although with a high proportion of benefits such as Pensioner Credits and Council Tax Benefit going unclaimed[2]) (see Chapter Seven, this volume), and for tomorrow's pensioners individualising risk through the shift from defined benefit to defined contribution pension schemes (Evandrou and Falkingham, 2009).[3]

Second, the unleashing of privatisation introduced a new language for the management of old age. Blackburn (2006, p 4) suggests that individuals and institutions were tasked with being 'weaned from the teat of public finance and [to] learn how to be "responsible risk takers"... rejecting the old forms of dependence of which the old age pension was a prime example'. Yet despite ambitious claims for the virtues of market as opposed to collective provision, the proportion of working-age people in the UK saving for their retirement actually *declined* over the period from 1999/2000 to 2005/06 (DWP, 2007). This reflects the long-term fall in occupational pension provision, yet to be offset by the growth of personal (defined contribution) pensions (DWP, 2008). There has been a substantial (and – in terms of rapidity – largely unforeseen) decline in the UK in membership of defined benefit schemes: in 2000, active members – that is, current employees accruing new benefits – in non-government (private sector) defined benefit schemes totalled *4.1 million*; this figure had dropped to *1.3 million* by 2007 (ONS, 2008). This figure was actually below the modelling assumptions used in the UK Pensions Commission (2004) first report, which suggested a long-term floor of around 1.6–1.8 million members. By 2009, 74% of final salary defined benefit schemes in the UK were closed to new employees, compared with just *17%* in 2001, with surveys suggesting that most of the remaining companies were likely to abandon their scheme in its current form (PricewaterhouseCoopers, 2010). Robert Peston's summary of the pensions crisis summarises the shift from collective to individual responsibility underpinning post-industrial capitalism:

> What has happened to corporate pensions funds reflects ... the abandonment of the notion that companies have a moral obligation to promote the welfare of their employees after a lifetime of service.... Company directors are no longer asking what it cost them to provide a comfortable retirement for staff. Instead, the majority of big companies are investigating the price of ridding themselves of any responsibility for their retired workforce. This is a less conspicuous but hugely important example of how the wealth of the many is being eroded, while that of the super-rich has soared. (Peston, 2008, p 255)

Third, all of this must be set within the context of globalisation, this producing new social forces and pressures transforming many of the relationships underpinning structured dependency. The impact of globalisation on ideologies and policies relating to ageing has been a highly significant development. A key aspect of this has been the move from debates that focused on ageing as a burden for national economies, to perspectives that view population ageing as a worldwide social problem. The report of The World Bank (1994) *Averting the old age crisis* was a crucial document in this regard, but more recent contributions have included those from the Central Intelligence Agency (2001) and documents such as *The global retirement crisis*, produced by the Washington-based Center for Strategic and International Studies (Jackson, 2002). There is insufficient space in this chapter to deal with the particular arguments raised by these papers (see, however, the discussion in Vincent, 2006), but the general point raised suggests what amounts to a *politicisation of ageing* generated by the intensification of global ties. This development has been driven by a number of factors: the growth of neoliberalism is one obvious dimension, this propagating hostility towards collective provision by the state or at the very least a view that private provision is inherently superior to that provided by the public sector (Walker and Deacon, 2003; Yeates, 2008). Politicisation has also arisen from the way in which globalisation fosters awareness about the relative economic position of one nation state compared with another. George and Wilding (2002, p 58) make the point here that: 'Globalization has created an economic and political climate in which national states become more conscious of the taxes they levy and their potential economic implications. Neoliberal ideology feeds and justifies these concerns'. Finally, the ideological debate has been promoted through key supranational bodies such as the Organisation for Economic Co-operation and Development (OECD) and the World Trade Organization (WTO), along with transnational corporations (notably pharmaceutical companies), all of which contributed to a distinctive worldview about the framing of policies for old age.

Critical gerontology: challenging new inequalities and social divisions

From collective to individual responsibility

Given the changes outlined above, what are the main areas that need to be developed in the spirit of the critical perspectives developed in structured dependency theory? Much has changed in the intervening decades: capitalist expansion and growth in the West has mutated into recession. In the UK, welfare services are facing 'the longest and deepest period of public spending cuts since the Second World War' (Crawford and Tetlow, 2010). From an intergenerational perspective, there is the prospect of long-term unemployment facing young people – with levels of 20%, 30% and 40% across many European countries – alongside increasing insecurity for those aged 50 and over. Tony Judt (2010, p 177) makes the point that:

> Mass unemployment – once regarded as a pathology of badly managed economies – is beginning to look like an endemic characteristic of advanced societies. At best, we can hope for 'underemployment' – where

men and women work part-time; accept jobs far below their skill level; or else undertake skilled work of the sort traditionally assigned to immigrants and the young.

All of this raises questions about how best to characterise the issues and challenges facing older people in the second decade of the 21st century. The institutional basis around which structured dependency theory was developed has now largely disappeared, with further major changes set to occur over the next five years. Arising from this will be the need for a radical re-assessment of sociological and policy aspects of growing old. Ageing is being reconstructed in a post-welfare state society, with the institutional pillars which once supported its development now largely removed. This process will transform the language and structures hitherto used to describe the lives of older people, with a particular challenge coming from new social divisions running through old age.

These developments can be best understood in terms of the shifting boundaries between collective support on the one side and individualism on the other. Provision for older people through the welfare state can be seen as part of the post-Second World War drive to institutionalise what Lowe (1993, p 21) described as 'a deeper sense of community and mutual care' or 'social citizenship' in the influential reading of T.H. Marshall (1950). Townsend (1981), however, highlighted the extent to which many of the outcomes associated with welfare provision had contributed to dependency and passivity in old age, with collective support undermining the status of older people, both in the workplace and in the wider community. Thirty years on we now seem to be examining these issues from the opposite end of the spectrum. The space previously occupied by welfare institutions has progressively shrunk, encouraging a new individualism to shape responses to what were previously seen as collective responsibilities. *Accompanying this development is the sense that we are entering a distinctive period in the history of ageing, one that looks set to deepen the experience of growing old as a time of personal risk and insecurity, reinforced by new structures of inequality.*

Poverty and inequality in old age

At first glance, it might be argued that a more positive picture can be inferred from recent trends in the financial circumstances of older people. For example, on the standard measure of relative poverty, defined as earnings below 60% of contemporary household income, the period from the late 1990s up to 2008/09 saw fairly consistent falls in pensioner poverty in the UK: from 24% of pensioners in 1996/97 to 20% before housing costs (BHC) or 29% to 16% after housing costs (AHC). Pensioner poverty would thus appear to have undergone a rapid decline over the past decade: a 13% drop since 1996/97 at 60% of median AHC, and a more modest 4.2% measuring incomes BHC. In their analysis of these trends, Joyce et al (2010, p 33) suggest that:

> In 2008–09, pensioner poverty fell by 200,000 (measuring incomes both before and after housing costs), about 30,000 to 40,000 of which can be attributed to the re-introduction of higher rates of the winter fuel payment in that year. Pensioner poverty is now at its lowest level since 1985 (BHC) or 1984 (AHC). Measuring incomes after housing costs, the rate of poverty amongst pensioners is now lower than the rate for any other population group.

The above picture does, however, need to be qualified in several respects: for example, we might still note the substantial population of elderly people living on incomes that fail to provide participation in society to any meaningful degree, a minimum of between 1.8 and 2.3 million elderly people but with many millions more living just above or around the poverty line. Research by Scharf et al (2002) highlighted the extent to which the risk of poverty was especially acute for those living in deprived urban areas. Using a broader definition of poverty based on access to activities and resources regarded as essential for daily living, the research found very high proportions of older people – up to three fifths of those aged 60 and over – experiencing moderate or multiple levels of deprivation. For this group, poverty in later life meant cutting back on the basics of life, including food, fuel and the telephone. For some it meant borrowing money from family and friends, and in isolated cases, looking for support from pawnbrokers or moneylenders (Scharf, 2009). For many older people, daily life was experienced as an intense struggle to achieve a decent quality of existence – something which may reflect the experience of poverty over the whole life course but which will almost certainly be intensified given the additional pressures accompanying old age.

But the 'decline' in poverty has itself been overshadowed by an even more significant trend – that which might be termed 'unequal ageing' – with the gap between those who are better off and those living in poverty moving ever further apart. In this context, social class is now playing a *more* influential role (as compared with previous decades) in differentiating groups of older people. *Old age is being reshaped through the influence of different types of inequality, those based around differences in wealth, pensions and access to care.*

Property ownership and different sources of income continue to serve as the basis for class divisions in old age in ways similar to earlier stages of the life course, reinforced, however, by the class-based nature of occupational and welfare benefits. This point was illustrated in findings on financial and health resources around retirement age from *An anatomy of economic inequality in the UK* (Hills et al, 2010). This demonstrated that by age 55–64, the top 10% of professionals owned on average £2.2 million in property and pensions, while the bottom 10% of manual workers owned less than £8,000 of resources of any kind (see also Banks et al, 2010). Drawing on data from the English Longitudinal Study of Ageing, and examining death rates over a six-year period, the same report found that more than twice as many men, and nearly four times as many women from lower income groups died within the six years as did those from the most wealthy groups.

Pension provision, with the move from defined benefit to defined contribution systems, will almost certainly produce greater income differentiation in old age, further compounded by the contrasting fortunes of public and private sector pensioners. Public sector workers (most of whom are already on low incomes) face reduced pensions through the move to uprating via the consumer price index (CPI) rather than the retail prices index (RPI) (the latter producing a higher inflation rate based on the inclusion of housing and related cost increases). In contrast, private sector schemes – especially those affecting higher salaried workers – may be bound into rules tying them to the RPI. Indeed, the inequalities between public and private schemes may be increased with the latter opting in some cases to increase pensions by CPI or RPI, whichever is higher at any one time.

But possibly the most important emerging inequality is that around access to social care, an area which is facing substantial cuts in public funding over the next five years. Reduced spending in this area has been a feature for a number of years, as reflected in a tightening in the eligibility rules and restrictions in the packages of support maintaining people at home. With substantial reductions in the Revenue Support Grant and Council Tax in England, as part of the planned cuts in public expenditure, the withdrawal of support from large groups of older people appears inevitable. Forder and Fernández (2010) modelled the impact of the first two years of likely spending cuts over the years 2011/12 and 2012/13. The impact of their 'reduced budget' scenario was measured against a comparator where eligibility thresholds and the financial means test in the current social care system remained unchanged. The results suggested that by 2012 councils would be able to support at home only half the number of people currently assisted. Crucially, the researchers note that this reduction will be offset to some degree by an increase in the number of private users of social care, with a projected increase in 2012/13 of around 300,000 of those paying for care, compared with the 490,000 fall in state-supported recipients. The conclusion from this is instructive:

> The modelling suggests that a reduction in public support would prompt more people to pay privately for care and/or seek informal care. However, the substitution from public to private expenditure is limited because of the limited financial resources available to individuals with needs, who cannot always afford the high costs of care. As a result, the overall (state and private) expenditure is lower when the level of public funding is reduced. There

> are also equity consequences – with more private funding
> required, the rich would do better and the poor would
> be the biggest losers. (Forder and Fernández, 2010, p 8)

A further major strand of inequality has come with changes affecting the institutions of work and retirement. In this area there are important contradictions within the research and policy debate. On the one side, the original formulation of structured dependency presented retirement as a 'euphemism for unemployment', highlighting the fact that 'many older workers deplore the termination of economic activity' (Townsend, 1981, p 10). This notion has subsequently been emphasised by governments wishing to extend working life in the context of concerns about shortages of skilled labour and/ or the financing of pensions. On the other side, the debate around the 'third age' presents retirement as a positive choice, with retirees presented as having the 'freedom to spend time and money in pursuit of individualized lifestyle goals' (Gilleard and Higgs, 2005, p 153; Jones et al, 2010).

From a critical perspective both the above approaches have major problems given the current crisis facing many older people. Structured dependency downplayed the extent to which retirement evolved as a 'hard-won' right for working people (Duncan, 2008), arguably producing a gain rather than a necessary loss in social status. 'Third age' perspectives have identified positive benefits from retirement, but at the expense of analysing class differentials in access to social, economic and cultural capital. Yet developments over the past decade have only served to reinforce a point made by Peter Stearns in his study of old age in working-class culture, namely that: 'in modern society one of the main functions of social class has been to prepare a differential response to aging, just as in earlier times social stratification served significantly to differentiate the trappings of death' (1977, p 42).

From a social class perspective, the increase in state pension age, increasing to 66 for men and women by 2020, highlights a number of concerns. The policy takes as self-evident the desirability of working additional years, this viewed as acceptable given increased life expectancy and necessary as a means of reducing the cost of pensions. But such a measure (increasingly adopted across many

European countries) is especially unfair on working-class groups whose lower life expectancy means that they will draw their pension for a significantly shorter period in comparison with those from professional and managerial groups. An additional concern is that increasing numbers of workers will be forced to remain in employment despite major health problems, with many experiencing downward mobility with an increase in low-paid, part-time working. In reality, many workers may find higher state pension ages an unfair exchange between guaranteed retirement benefits on the one side, and insecure employment on the other (see Ghilarducci, 2004, for evidence from the US on this point). Certainly, there is no evidence for an expansion in appropriate forms of paid work for most older employees, with very little 'flexible' employment available which properly takes account of the health and social changes affecting people in their 60s and 70s (Phillipson, 2009).

A manifesto for change

Given a context of radical change in the material and social circumstances affecting older people, what are the ideas and policies that need to be developed? First, and most important of all, greater recognition must be given to the realities and implications of unequal ageing (Cann and Dean, 2009). In this context, the idea of structured dependence contains a tension – reflected in work on ageing more generally – between institutional processes creating similarities among older people, and contrasting trends creating differences and divisions. The argument here is that the former have steadily weakened in influence, while the latter have expanded in scope and intensity. This development may be seen as a product of the interaction between increased within-cohort differentiation (with the ageing 'first wave' baby boom generation illustrative of this trend) and policy developments promoting stratification in old age (see further above). This has created a major challenge in sociological and policy terms: *How to define old age where the social, cultural and economic ties across different groups have been removed? How to identify common policy ground between those whose lives have been blighted by cumulative inequality as compared with those where 'successful ageing' builds on benefits enjoyed throughout the life course?*

The challenge posed by contemporary ageing is unique in both the above regards and raises serious doubts as to the value of shaping policy responses around conventional approaches to 'old age' and the 'older person'. In many ways this can be regarded as an inevitable consequence of the effect of the market in enhancing those vulnerabilities and risks associated with growing old. Scharf (2009) refers to the failure of the unregulated free market to deliver security in old age, a feature highlighted in the crisis affecting pensions and jobs arising from the global economic recession. But this raises questions such as: *How to insert security into lives undermined through lifelong poverty and marginalisation? How to strengthen resources depleted during major transitions through life?*

Various responses might be made in response to the above questions. Here, we will focus on just three.

The first is the need for continued emphasis on the maintenance of the basic state pension (BSP) as a fundamental building block to a secure old age. At the same time, it is essential that the BSP not only eliminates poverty, but also provides an adequate replacement in relation to wages and salaries. This raises a fundamental challenge given the direction of policy at the present time. In the UK, reforms to pensions introduced in 2007 will mean that an individual on median earnings retiring in 2055 can expect to achieve a replacement rate of just 32% from the BSP. Achieving a higher level of replacement (for example, to at least Guaranteed Credit level of the Pension Credit), in the context of the crisis affecting occupational and private pensions, should be a central goal for a social policy supporting older people through the economic recession. Such a policy would represent a major shift away from means testing and would ensure that many older people were automatically lifted out of financial hardship. Linked to this is the need for a new global discourse on pensions, one that challenges the view that government provision should be reduced, and reliance on the market increased. The experience to date indicates that market provision has led to a deepening of inequalities among different groups of workers and pensioners, that significant groups are likely to remain without the support of a viable additional pension, and that the volatility of the market is in direct contradiction to the need for security and certainty in old age. This discourse will need to challenge the neoliberal consensus around pensions, adopted in intergovernmental organisations such as The World Bank, the International Monetary Fund (IMF) and OECD. Such bodies have been able to exert a considerable influence on the pensions debate, but one that has marginalised views regarding the necessity of substantial public sector provision.

The second argument is the need for more radical policies directed at the poorest and most disadvantaged elderly – especially those living in inner cities and in areas experiencing major social and economic dislocation. Research by Scharf et al (2002) demonstrated the vulnerability of older people to physical and social changes within deprived neighbourhoods: higher proportions (compared with those living in other locations) experienced severe loneliness and intense social isolation; fear about and experience of crime was a significant feature of daily life; particular minority groups – Pakistanis and Somalis in this study – experienced very high levels of poverty and loneliness. All of these difficulties are likely to have been compounded by economic recession and its impact on urban areas already suffering from long-term industrial decline (Centre for Cities, 2009). Older people are experiencing the full force of these changes with the scaling back of regeneration programmes an additional threat to the quality of life in many urban areas. Elderly people are especially vulnerable to the withdrawal of services and amenities at a local level, spending a high proportion of their time at home or around their immediate neighbourhood. One response here would be to further develop discussions launched by the WHO (2007) on planning what have been called 'age-friendly cities'. This approach has developed a number of recommendations concerning the need to improve the physical environment of cities, and to promote improved transportation and housing. From a critical perspective, however, this discussion has been disconnected from influences on urban environments in the Global North, where private developers remain the dominant influence on urban planning. The result, according to Harvey (2008, p 31), is that the: 'Quality of urban life has become a commodity, as has the city itself, in a world where consumerism, tourism, cultural and knowledge-based industries have become major aspects of the urban political economy'. Blokland and Rae (2008, p 38) argue that such processes are leading to a different type of urbanism, one that is: 'confirming rather than challenging inequalities within cities and the various enclaves that can be found there – ranging from gated communities and gentrified neighbourhoods on the one hand to ghettos and poor enclaves on the other – and between central cities and their suburbs'.

One approach would be to link the discussion about 'age-friendly cities' to ideas about urban citizenship and rights to the benefits which living in a city brings. Painter, for example, cites the work of Henri Lefebvre, who explored issues relating to citizenship and rights in an urban context. Lefebvre:

> stressed the use-value of the city over its exchange value, emphasizing that citizens have a right to make use of the city, and that it is not just a collection of resources to enable economic activity. The uses of the city by citizens should be seen as valid ends in themselves, not merely as a means to produce economic growth.... The right to the city is the right to live a fully urban life, with all the liberating benefits it brings. [Lefbvre] believed the majority of city residents are denied this right because their lives are subordinated to economic pressures – despite being *in* the city, they are not fully *of* the city. (Painter, 2005, p 9)

This last point applies especially well to older people, who may find that despite having contributed to the urban environment in which they have spent most of their life, it offers few resources and many obstacles to achieving a fulfilling life in old age. Addressing how 'urban citizenship' can be extended into an explicit set of rights applicable to older people is an important agenda, the development of which might fulfil the potential of some of the discussion around 'age-friendly cities' and 'lifetime neighbourhoods'.

The third argument concerns the need to redefine the language and relationships that define ties between different generations. In the 1980s and 1990s, the balance of debate swung towards expressions of doubts about the benefits of population ageing (Vincent, 2003). Despite the radical critique offered by critical gerontology (Walker, 1981; Minkler and Estes, 1999), together with the activities of groups of older people themselves, the so-called 'burden' of population ageing became a dominant theme in much policy debate. For the 21st century, however, a process of renewal in generational politics is required. The basis for this will stem from recognition that presenting issues in terms of younger *versus* older generations will frustrate positive solutions to the needs of young *and* older people – in industrialised as well as industrialising countries. As Heclo (1989, p 387) observes:

> In an already fragmented society such a framework would be especially unconstructive. It would divert attention from disparities and unmet needs within age groups. It would help divide constituencies that often have a common stage. Above all, a politics of young versus old would reinforce an already strong tendency ... to define social welfare in terms of a competitive struggle for scarce resources and to ignore shared needs occurring in everyone's life-cycle.

Recognition that we are constructing a different type of life course may also help form the basis for a new generational politics. Here, the worker versus pensioner perspective is especially unhelpful in that it ignores fundamental changes to the distribution of labour through the life course. The labels 'worker' versus 'pensioner' are less easy to define when the stages that separate them are undergoing change. For many workers the predictability of continuous employment is being replaced by insecurity in middle and later life (Marshall et al, 2001). As already noted, these changes may be seen as part of the reconstruction of middle and old age, underpinned by the restructuring of work at different points of the life course (Phillipson, 2003). This development has underlined the need for a different type of language for describing relationships between generations in general, and workers and pensioners in particular. Emphasis should now be placed on the interdependency of generations, especially in the context of the radical changes accompanying global change. In essence, we should acknowledge ageing as a public concern shared equally across the life course. As Vincent argues (2003, p 108): 'A secure old age including income maintenance and health and social care can be achieved only within a framework of social solidarity'. The implication of this argument is that we cannot 'offload' responsibilities for an ageing population to particular generations or cohorts – whether old, young or middle aged. Ageing is an issue *for* particular generations, but it is also a question to be solved *across* generations. The role of nation states and global economic and social institutions will be central in the management of ageing populations (Estes and Phillipson, 2002). Social and political responsibility at all levels will be central to the task of developing appropriate policies for the 21st century.

Conclusion

The publication in 1981 of 'The structured dependency of the elderly' proved a vital stimulus for the development of critical perspectives on ageing. Hitherto, research and policy on older people had been sidelined in more radical thinking around social policy and hardly featured as a significant feature of wider debates within sociology and political science. But the 1980s and 1990s was a crucial period for attempting to apply approaches from Marxism, feminism and critical thought more generally, to the lives of older people. Given the context of economic recession, a likely backdrop to the decade from 2010, critical thinking about the place and futures of ageing is more than ever necessary. At present this re-assessment has only just began but the key issues will need to reflect the concerns and values that Peter Townsend addressed throughout his life. Among these we might include: the challenge of growing inequality among older people; the issues facing migrant groups managing ageing with minimal resources, often in the most deprived communities in the UK; the need to ensure that ageing leads to inclusion rather than exclusion from key areas of daily life; the continuing need to emphasise the importance of older people – and the contribution they make to families, neighbourhoods and society more generally; and the need to see ageing as a global issue with major policy tasks facing the Global South as much as the Global North. Ageing societies are now transforming the world but in circumstances of crisis and conflict: addressing the social and policy consequences is an urgent priority.

Notes

[1] For a review of the background to the development of critical gerontology see Baars et al (2006a).

[2] Around one third of pensioner households entitled to Pensioner Credit are not claiming it (1.3 million households); the figure for unclaimed Council Tax Benefits is two fifths (1.7 million households).

[3] Defined benefit scheme: a pension scheme in which the rules specify the rate of benefits to be paid. The most common defined benefit scheme is a salary-related scheme in which the benefits are based on the number of years of pensionable service. Defined contribution scheme: a pension scheme in which the benefits are determined by the contributions paid into the scheme, the investment returned on those contributions and the type of annuity purchased on retirement. Defined contribution pensions are sometimes referred to as 'money purchase schemes'.

References

Baars, J., Dannefer, D., Phillipson, C. and Walker, A. (2006a) 'Introduction: Critical perspectives in social gerontology', in J. Baars, D. Dannefer, C. Phillipson and A. Walker (eds) *Aging, globalization and inequality: The new critical gerontology*, Amityville, NY: Baywood, pp 1–16.

Baars, J., Dannefer, D., Phillipson, C. and Walker, A. (eds) (2006b) *Aging, globalization and inequality: The new critical gerontology*, Amityville, NY: Baywood.

Banks, J., Crawford, R. and Tetlow, G. (2010) *What does the distribution of wealth tell us about the future distribution of retirement resources?*, Research Report 665, London: Department for Work and Pensions.

Bernard, M. and Scharf, T. (eds) (2007) *Critical perspectives on ageing societies*, Bristol: The Policy Press.

Blackburn, R. (2006) *Age shock: How finance is failing us*, London: Verso.

Blokland, T and Rae, D. (2008) 'The end to urbanism: how the changing spatial structure of cities affected its social capital potentials' in T. Blokland and M. Savage (eds) *Networked urbanism*, Aldershot: Ashgate, pp 23-41.

Cann, P. and Dean, M. (2009) *Unequal ageing*, Bristol: The Policy Press.

Central Intelligence Agency (2001) *Long term global demographic trends: Reshaping the geo-political landscape* (www.cia.gov/library/reports/general-reports-1/Demo_Trends_For_Web.pdf).

Centre for Cities (2009) *Cities outlook 2009*, London: Centre for Cities.

Chiva, A. and Manthorpe, J. (2009) *Older workers in Europe*, Buckingham: Open University Press.

Cole, T. (1992) *The journey of life*, Cambridge: Cambridge University Press.

Crawford, R and Tetlow, G. (2010) 'The axeman cometh', *Public Finance*, 10 July (www.publicfinance.co.uk/features/2010/07/the-axeman-cometh/).

Dressel, P.L. (1988) 'Gender, race and class: beyond the feminization of poverty in later life', *Gerontologist*, vol 28, no 2, pp 177-80.

DWP (Department for Work and Pensions) (2007) *Family resources survey 2005-06*, London: DWP.

DWP (2008) *Pensions Bill: Impact assessment*, London: DWP.

Duncan, C. (2008) 'The dangers and limitations of equality agendas as a means of tackling old-age prejudice', *Ageing and Society*, vol 28, pp 1133-58.

Estes, C. (1979) *The aging enterprise*, San Francisco, CA: Jossey-Bass.

Estes, C. (1999) 'Critical gerontology and the new political economy of aging', in M. Minkler and C. Estes (eds) *Critical gerontology: Perspectives from political and moral economy*, Amityville, NY: Baywood, pp 17-36.

Estes, C. (2006) 'Critical feminist perspectives, aging and social policy', in J. Baars, D. Dannefer, C. Phillipson and A. Walker (eds) *Aging, globalization and inequality: The new critical gerontology*, Amityville, NY: Baywood, pp 81-102.

Estes, C.L. and Associates (2001) *Social policy and aging*, London: Sage Publications.

Estes, C.L. and Phillipson, C. (2002) 'The globalisation of capital, the welfare state and old age policy', *International Journal of Health Services*, vol 32, pp 279-97.

Estes, C.L., Biggs, S. and Phillipson, C. (2003) *Social theory, social policy and ageing: A critical introduction*, Buckingham: Open University Press.

Evandrou, M. and Falkingham, J. (2009) 'Pensions and income security in later life', in J. Hills, T. Sefton and K. Stewart (eds) *Towards a more equal society? Poverty, inequality and policy since 1997*, Bristol: The Policy Press, pp 157-78.

Forder, J. and Fernández, J.-L. (2010) *The impact of a tightening fiscal situation on social care for older people*, PSSRU Discussion Paper 2723 (www.pssru. ac.uk/pdf/dp2723.pdf).

Foster, L. (2010) 'Towards a new political economy of pensions: the implications for women', *Critical Social Policy*, vol 30, pp 27-47.

George, V. and Wilding, P. (2002) *Globalization and human welfare*, London: Palgrave.

Ghilarducci, T. (2004) *The political economy of 'pro-work' retirement policies and responsible accumulation*, Indiana, IN: University of Notre Dame (www. havenscenter.org/real_utopias/2004documents/Ghilarducci%paper.pdf).

Gilleard, C. and Higgs, P. (2005) *Contexts of ageing*, Cambridge: Polity Press.

Guillemard, A.-M. (ed) (1983) *Old age and the welfare state*, New York: Sage Publications.

Hacker, J. (2008) *The great risk shift*, New York: Oxford University Press.

Hank, K. and Erlinghagen, M. (2009) *Perceptions of job security in Europe's ageing workforce*, MEA Discussion Paper (176-09), Mannheim: University of Mannheim.

Harvey, D. (2008) 'The capitalist city', *New Left Review*, vol 53, pp 23-42.

Heclo, H. (1989) 'Generational politics', in T. Smeeding and B. Torrey (eds) *The vulnerable*, Washington, DC: Urban Institute Press, pp 381-441.

Hills, J., Brewer, M., Jenkins, S., Lister, R., Lupton, R., Machin, S., Mills, C., Modood, T. Rees, T. and Riddell, S. (2010) *An anatomy of economic inequality in the UK: Summary*, London: Government Equalities Office/ Centre for Analysis of Social Exclusion.

Jackson, R. (2002) *The global retirement crisis*, Washington, DC: Citigroup/ Center for Strategic and International Studies.

Johnson, P. (1989) 'The structured dependency of the elderly: a critical note', in M. Jeffreys (ed) *Growing old in the twentieth century*, London: Routledge, pp 62-71.

Jones, I.R., Leontowitsch, M. and Higgs, P. (2010) 'The experience of retirement in second modernity: generational habitus among retired senior managers', *Sociology*, vol 44, pp 103-20.

Joyce, R., Muriel, A., Phillips, D. and Sibieta, L. (2010) *Poverty and inequality in the UK 2010*, IFS Commentary C116, London: Institute for Fiscal Studies.

Judt, T. (2010) *Ill fares the land*, London: Allen Lane.

Laczko, F. and Phillipson, C. (1991) *Changing work and retirement*, Milton Keynes: Open University Press.

Lowe, R. (1993) *The welfare state in Britain since 1945*, London: Macmillan.

Macnicol, J. (1998) *The politics of retirement in Britain 1878–1948*, Cambridge: Cambridge University Press.

Marshall, T.H. (1950) *Citizenship and social class and other essays*, Cambridge: Cambridge University Press.

Marshall, V., Heinz, W.R., Kruger, H. and Anil, V. (eds) (2001) *Restructuring work and the life course*, Toronto: University of Toronto Press.

Minkler, M. (1999) 'Introduction', in M. Minkler and C.L. Estes (eds) (1999) *Critical gerontology: Perspectives from political and moral economy*, Amityville, NY: Baywood, pp 1-14.

Minkler, M. and Estes, C.L. (eds) (1999) *Critical gerontology: Perspectives from political and moral economy*, Amityville, NY: Baywood.

ONS (Office for National Statistics) (2008) *Occupational Pensions Scheme Survey 2007*, London: ONS.

Painter, J. (2005) *Urban citizenship and rights to the city*, Durham: International Centre for Regional Regeneration and Development Studies, Durham University.

Pensions Commission (2004) *Pensions: Challenges and choices. The first report of the Pensions Commission*, London: The Stationery Office.

Peston, R. (2008) *Who runs Britain? How the super-rich are changing our lives*, London: Hodder & Stoughton.

Phillipson, C. (1982) *Capitalism and the construction of old age*, London: Macmillan.

Phillipson, C. (1998) *Reconstructing old age*, London: Sage Publications.

Phillipson, C. (2003) *Transitions from work to retirement*, Bristol: The Policy Press.

Phillipson, C. (2009) 'Pensions in crisis: aging and inequality in a global age', in L. Rogne, C.L. Estes, B. Grossman, B. Hollister and E. Solway (eds) *Social insurance and social justice*, New York: Springer, pp 319-40.

Phillipson, C., Bernard, M., Phillips, J. and Ogg, J. (2000) *The family and community life of older people: Social networks and social support in three urban areas*, London: Routledge.

Platman, K. and Taylor, P. (2006) 'Training and learning in the workplace: can we legislate against age discriminatory practice?', *Social Policy Review 18*, Bristol: The Policy Press, for the Social Policy Association, pp 269-92.

PricewaterhouseCoopers (2010), www.ukmediacentre.pwc.com/News-Releases/Fresh-wave-of-pension-scheme-closures-expected-as-94-of-employers-intend-to-reduce-or-axe-current-defined-benefit-provision-eac.aspx

Rogne, L., Estes, C.L., Grossman, B., Hollister, B. and Solway, E. (2009) *Social insurance and social justice*, New York: Springer.

Sass, S. (1989) 'Pension bargaining: the heyday of US collectively bargained pension arrangements', in P. Johnson, C. Conrad and D. Thomson (eds) *Workers versus pensioners: Intergenerational justice in an ageing world*, Manchester: Manchester University Press, pp 92-112.

Scharf, T. (2009) 'Too tight to mention: unequal income in old age', in P. Cann and M. Dean, *Unequal ageing*, Bristol: The Policy Press, pp 25-52.

Scharf, T., Phillipson, C., Smith, A. and Kingston, P. (2002) *Growing older in socially deprived areas*, London: Help the Aged.

Sennett, R. (2006) *The culture of the new capitalism*, New Haven, CT: Yale University Press.

Solow, R. (2008) 'Trapped in the new "you're on your own" world', *New York Review of Books*, vol LV, no 18, pp 79-81.

Stearns, P. (1977) *Old age in European society*, London: Croom Helm.

Thane, P. (2000) *Old age in English history*, Oxford: Oxford University Press.

Tomasky, M. (2010) 'The money fighting health care', *New York Review of Books*, vol LXVII, no 6, pp 10-15.

Townsend, P. (1957) *The family life of older people*, London: Routledge and Kegan Paul.

Townsend, P. (1979) *Poverty in the United Kingdom: A survey of household resources and standards of living*, London: Penguin.

Townsend, P. (1981) 'The structured dependency of the elderly: a creation of policy in the twentieth century', *Ageing and Society*, vol 1, no 1, pp 5-28.

Townsend, P. and Wedderburn, D. (1965) *The aged in the welfare state*, London: Bell.

Vincent, J. (2003) *Old age*, London: Routledge.

Vincent, J. (2006) 'Globalization and critical theory: political economy of world population issues', in J. Baars, D. Dannefer, C. Phillipson and A. Walker (eds) *Aging, globalization and inequality: The new critical gerontology*, Amityville, NY: Baywood, pp 245-72.

Walker, A. (1980) 'The social creation of poverty and dependency in old age', *Journal of Social Policy*, vol 9, pp 49-75.

Walker, A. (1981) 'Towards a political economy of old age', *Ageing and Society*, vol 1, no 1, pp 73-94.

Walker, A. (1996) 'Intergenerational relations and the provision of welfare', in A. Walker (ed) *The new generational contract: Intergenerational relations, old age and welfare*, London: UCL Press, pp 10-37.

Walker, A. (2009) 'Aging and social policy: theorizing the social', in V. Bengston, D. Gans, N. Putney and M. Silverstein (eds) *Handbook of theories of aging*, New York: Springer, pp 595-614.

Walker, A and Deacon, A. (2003) 'Economic globalization and policies on ageing', *Journal of Societal and Social Policy*, vol 2, no 2, pp 1-18.

Walker, A. and Foster, L. (2006) 'Ageing and social class: an enduring relationship', in J. Vincent, C. Phillipson and M. Downs (eds) *The futures of old age*, London: Sage Publications, pp 44-53.

Walker, A. and Naegele, G. (2009) *Social policy in ageing societies: Britain and Germany compared*, Basingstoke: Palgrave Macmillan.

Whiteside, N. (2006) 'Occupational pensions and the search for security', in H. Pemberton, P. Thane and N. Whiteside (eds) *Britain's pensions crisis*, Oxford: Oxford University Press, pp 125-40.

World Bank, The (1994) *Averting the old age crisis*, Oxford: Oxford University Press.

WHO (World Health Organization) (2007) *Global age-friendly cities: A guide*, Geneva: WHO.

Yeates, N. (2008) *Understanding global social policy*, Bristol: The Policy Press.

ELEVEN

Disability: prospects for social inclusion

Carol Thomas

Introduction

Disability was a topic of interest to Peter Townsend from the earliest days in his academic and policy-oriented career. From the 1960s onwards he recognised that disability was always present somewhere in the mix that sculpted poverty and socioeconomic disadvantage in communities – especially among old people and in families with disabled children. His long-standing interest in social conditions, social relationships and the unequal distribution of resources meant that social groups who faced particular disadvantages in achieving decent standards of living won his lasting attention and unwavering political commitment (Walker et al, 2010). Thus, in Townsend's conceptual and methodological approach to studying the social world, disability was always part of what he called the 'big picture': 'the specialised cannot be disentangled from the generalised; the general and the special go together whether you approach it from one end or the other' (extract from transcribed interview between Peter Townsend and John Welshman, London, 3 July 2006, p 5).

In the broad sweep of his analysis of poverty in British society in the 1970s, Townsend carefully and meticulously drilled down into information on those structural and distributional features of state practices and economic arrangements that created the conditions for relative poverty among disabled people:

> In general, the greater poverty of disabled people is explained by their uneven or limited access to the

principal resource systems of society – the labour market and wage system, national insurance and its associated schemes, and the wealth-accumulating systems, particularly home ownership, life insurance and occupational pension schemes; by the indirect limitation which disability imposes upon the capacities of relatives, pooling resources in full or part in the household or family, to earn incomes and accumulate wealth themselves; and by the failure of society to recognize, or recognize only unevenly or fitfully, the additional resources that are required in disablement to obtain standards of living equivalent to those of the non-disabled. (Townsend, 1979, pp 734-5)

Townsend's commitment to relieving poverty among '*the disabled*' was most clearly expressed in his work for a campaigning organisation that he co-founded in 1974: the Disability Alliance. By this time in his academic career he was involved in building a new Department of Sociology at the University of Essex, on one of the new 1960s campuses (Busfield, 2010, p 28; see also Welshman, 2007). Indeed, Townsend chaired the Disability Alliance for more than 20 years and was the organisation's President when he died in 2009. Today's Disability Alliance website illustrates this legacy with characteristic clarity and directness:

Disability Alliance is a campaigning organisation. We are particularly concerned with disability, social care and tackling poverty....

We provide information on social security benefits, tax credits and social care to disabled people, their families, carers and professional advisers....

We are a membership organisation with around 300 members ranging from small, self-help groups to major national charities. We are controlled by disabled people who form a majority of our Board of Trustees....

We are best known as the authors of the *Disability Rights Handbook*, an annual publication with a print-run of 26,000....

We also play an important role in advising and lobbying the Government on matters concerning disability benefits, tax credits, social care and tackling poverty. Where necessary we also undertake research into the needs of disabled people and use findings to influence central and local Governments. (www.disabilityalliance. org/about.htm)

Given this personal history, readers may find it surprising that the Disabled People's Movement in the UK has never seen eye-to-eye, as it were, with Peter Townsend, and his work is not celebrated in the academic discipline known as Disability Studies. Is this fair?

Understanding disability

The UPIAS meets the Disability Alliance story

Let us try to uncover the reasons for this apparent paradox. To do so we must go back, once again, to the 1970s, because these were the years in which disabled people began to create *their own* organisations to embark on the struggle for disability rights and equality of opportunity. It is necessary to consider developments in some detail because the positions taken in subsequent decades were forged here (Thomas, 2007).

In the British context, the key organisation concerned was the Union of the Physically Impaired Against Segregation (UPIAS), founded in 1972 by Paul Hunt, Vic Finkelstein, Ken Davies and other disabled activists. This was the forerunner of the British Disabled People's Movement. It must be noted that most of the activists involved developed their ideas about disability, and how to fight for self-determination, through *secret correspondence* because their lives were socially restricted in residential establishments; that is, their lives were marshalled and controlled by medical and professional officers and 'carers' (for details, see Campbell and Oliver, 1996). Paul Hunt and Vic Finkelstein, in particular, turned to Marxism for inspiration – leading UPIAS to eventually formulate and publically articulate a radically new *social relational* understanding of disability:

> In our view, it is society which disables physically impaired people. Disability is something imposed on top of our impairments, by the way we are unnecessarily isolated and excluded from full participation in society. Disabled people are therefore an oppressed group in society. It follows from this analysis that having low incomes, for example, is only one aspect of our oppression. It is a consequence of our isolation and segregation, in every area of life, such as education, work, mobility housing etc. Poverty is only one symptom of our oppression, but it is not the cause. For us as disabled people it is absolutely vital that we get this question of the cause of disability quite straight, because on the answer depends the crucial matter of where we direct our main energies in the struggle for change. We shall clearly get nowhere if our efforts are chiefly directed not at the cause of our oppression but instead at one of the symptoms. (UPIAS and Disability Alliance, 1976, pp 3-4)

It is important to cite this passage at length here because it is actually a record of words spoken by members of UPIAS *directly* to Peter Townsend and selected members of the Disability Alliance. The context and occasion for this personal address was an organised meeting and debate between members from UPIAS and the Disability Alliance in November 1975 – recorded and documented in *Fundamental principles of disability* (UPIAS and Disability Alliance, 1976). From Townsend's perspective, the meeting offered a valuable opportunity to unite with an organised group of disabled people so that forces could be combined in favour of the Disability Alliance's *common platform* campaign for raised incomes for disabled people. Indeed, we know that Townsend already knew and respected Paul Hunt because some 10 years earlier he had written the following in the Foreword to Hunt's collection of essays written by disabled people and published as Stigma: *The experience of disability* (Hunt, 1966). There Townsend had said:

> [The *Stigma* essays] reflect a much deeper problem of a distortion of the structure and value-system of society itself. Achievement, productivity, vigour, health and youth are admired to an extreme. Incapacity, unproductiveness, slowness and old age are implicitly if not explicitly deplored. Such a system of values moulds and reinforces an elaborate social hierarchy. The disabled are as much the inevitable victims of this system as the young professional and managerial groups are its inevitable beneficiaries. The question that is therefore raised is not a straightforward one. It is complicated and immense. Is it possible to secure real gains for those who are disabled without calling for a reconstruction of society and schooling new attitudes in the entire population?...
>
> ... [The authors of these essays] disentangle themselves from conventional expressions of gratitude for services rendered and propose introducing new patterns of rights into a situation which has traditionally been dominated by condescension and patronage on the one hand and inferiority or deference on the other. By insisting on these rights they are saving many from a benevolent but indifferent superiority and laying the basis for a general pattern of more equal and less discriminatory social relationships. Some new and important steps have been taken to establish a common humanity. (Townsend, 1966, pp vii-viii)

To return to the UPIAS/Disability Alliance meeting in November 1975, we find that, despite the common ground on the *social* character of disability, agreement could not be reached on joining forces on the income question. In short, Townsend would not sign up to UPIAS's Policy Statement on the *causes* of disability as outlined above, and UPIAS would not sign up to joining the Disability Alliance *incomes legislative change* campaign. As documented in *Fundamental principles*

(1976) – in quasi-verbatim form – disagreements could not be overcome on the purpose and scope of the meeting:

> FINKELSTEIN: Forming an umbrella organisation [the Disability Alliance] has not touched the fundamental issues, and unless you raise and investigate these questions – 'what is disability, and how come we are impoverished in the first place' – you are not going to deal with the causes of disability, and it may well be that your approach will help to perpetuate them.
>
> PETER TOWNSEND said that statements of policy, etc, were 'open to different and acceptable meanings'. But PAUL HUNT reminded him that they were talking about absolutely fundamental principles, and PETER TOWNSEND then replied, 'You must understand, a social scientist who is asked to make a declaration about cause and effect takes up a very complicated position about factors which are associated as to make it difficult, in lay terms, to distinguish cause from effect – I have to make that point'...
>
> VIC FINKELSTEIN interrupted to say, 'That's just not acceptable, because it's implying that disabled people can put their necks out by making a declaration of what we feel is cause and effect, but you as a social scientist can't'. (UPIAS and Disability Alliance, 1976, pp 7-8)

In his subsequent commentary on the face-to-face meeting (also printed in *Fundamental principles*), Townsend explains that he had not anticipated a requirement to formally agree to UPIAS's analysis of the causes of disability, and he restated his conviction that the incomes question was the fulcrum of leverage for social change:

> [the Disability Alliance has] drawn attention to the disproportionate effect that the continual denial of a reasonable income has upon the lives of disabled people, whilst at the same time illustrating how this and other attitudes as expressed through current legislation and

administration result in their segregation, and their condemnation to the status of a second class citizen....

... the absence of an income as of right for disabled people is – in our view – more than just one more symptom of their oppression and segregation.... (UPIAS and Disability Alliance, 1976, p 22)

Showing sensitivity to the accusation that the Disability Alliance was in danger of replicating oppressive practices by allowing non-disabled *experts* to lead the way, Townsend also noted in his commentary that plans were in place to ensure that disabled people and their organisations became not just members of the Disability Alliance, and that half the places on the Disability Alliance Steering Committee were taken by disabled representatives (UPIAS and Disability Alliance, 1976, p 23). Indeed, as noted above, the Disability Alliance today states forcibly that it is controlled by disabled people.

Nevertheless, from this time onward,s the advocacy, campaigning and research undertaken by Peter Townsend on the one hand, and the activities of the Disabled People's Movement on the other, went their separate but parallel ways. Townsend's sociological and social policy research continued to systematically document disabled people's limited and constrained access to income and related recourses (Walker and Townsend, 1980). The nature and effects of disablement, especially in childhood or old age, continued to occupy Townsend as he carefully documented social deprivation in all its forms over the decades; and his membership of the team that produced the seminal Black Report on health inequalities in 1980 (see Chapter Nine, this volume) resulted in the creation of an important raft of evidence that highlighted the association between socioeconomic disadvantage and poor health – an approach that led to successive government-sponsored research programmes on the *health gap* under Labour administrations (Townsend, 1979; Townsend and Davidson, 1982; Graham, 2007).

In contrast, the academic discipline that emerged from the Disabled People's Movement – Disability Studies – set itself the task of researching and theorising disability in *all* of its social manifestations, under the *social model of disability* banner headline (see, for example,

Swain et al, 2004; Barnes and Mercer, 2006; Thomas, 2007). The struggle for independent living, and thus freeing lives from traditional professional and service control, remained a constant campaigning theme and analytical priority. For those in the Disability Studies camp, Peter Townsend was never one of their own, and was sometimes referred to, perhaps unjustly, as a representative of the *not to be trusted* non-disabled academic elite. Thus, in essence, key differences between the perspectives of Peter Townsend and activists/writers in Disability Studies persisted for decades.

New times

It is somewhat ironic, therefore, that in recent years Townsend and those in the materialist wing of the Disabled People's Movement and Disability Studies came to share a *sceptical* assessment of the apparently enormous gains made by disabled people in their campaigns for disability rights in the 1990s and 2000s – especially under successive Labour governments. For example, the passage of the Disability Discrimination Acts (1995, 2005), the setting up of the Disability Rights Commission – with its disabled leaders and champions (Disability Rights Commission Act 1999) – and the introduction of legislative support for direct payments (1996) and individual budgets (Welfare Reform Bill 2009) all seemed to be ushering in disability equality, inclusion and independent living in the new century. Moreover, in 2001 the Labour government published *Valuing People: A strategy for learning disability in the 21st century* (DH, 2001), which was based on the key principles of independence, inclusion and greater self-determination, and then in 2004 the (Labour) Prime Minister's Strategy Unit published a report entitled *Improving the life chances of disabled people*, proposing that disabled people in Britain should have full opportunities and choices to improve their quality of life and to be treated as respected and equal members of society (Cabinet Office, 2004, p 7). The creation of the Office for Disability Issues (ODI) – a unit accountable to several key government departments – in 2005 reflected this commitment.

Our vision – By 2025, disabled people in Britain should
have the same opportunities and choices as non-disabled
people to improve their quality of life and be respected
and included as equal members of society. (www.
officefordisability.gov.uk/index.php)

Nevertheless, it was the degree of *real change* that had occurred in the
lives of disabled people that both Townsend and powerful voices in
Disability Studies questioned. For example, Disability Studies writers
Mike Oliver and Colin Barnes wrote the following particularly
pessimistic assessment in 2006:

> ... the drift towards a rights based approach that now
> dominates disability politics [has meant that] we have
> witnessed the growing professionalisation of disability
> rights and the wilful decimation of organisations
> controlled and run by disabled people at the local and
> national level by successive government policies despite
> rhetoric to the contrary. As a result we no longer have
> a strong and powerful disabled people's movement and
> the struggle to improve disabled people's life chances has
> taken a step backwards. (cited in Oliver, 2009, p 135)

Thus, rather than being transformed by the legislative developments
and policy initiatives noted above, Oliver and Barnes argued that the
lives of the great majority of disabled people remained essentially the
same: located on the social margins, tied down by the consequences
of socioeconomic disadvantage and hemmed in by a myriad of
social exclusionary processes and practices. Moreover, they noted
that the Disabled People's Movement was fragmenting; the hard-
won independent living initiatives were often unsuccessful because
they were starved of resources by local authorities, and some leading
campaigning figures in the Disabled People's Movement had been
incorporated into the bureaucratic work of official agencies. In
short, the disability rights agenda – and the social model of disability
– had been hi-jacked, incorporated and rendered ineffective by

non-disabled representatives of the capitalist state (Finkelstein, 2007; Oliver, 2009).

Townsend similarly exposed the fictitiousness of governmental claims about the reach and extent of social change that had occurred under New Labour. Official rhetoric about social inclusion and human rights did not deflect Townsend's measured assessments of contemporary social conditions (Walker et al, 2010), which he illustrated in a lengthy interview with the historian John Welshman in 2006. Reflecting on the huge tasks, past *and present*, involved in achieving decent standards of living for all, Townsend noted the following about the ongoing scourge of child poverty in British society and beyond – just before the global financial crash occurred in 2008:

> [New Labour] haven't delivered on child poverty – because the truth is that compared with the rest of Europe we have covered less than a quarter of the ground that we lost in the Thatcher years. If that is Gordon Brown's claim to fame, I don't think too much of it. The claim is bolstered by the luck with full employment, and, frankly, if we didn't have the continuing stream of ill-paid immigrants, we would be in a very poor way indeed. (extract from transcribed interview between Peter Townsend and John Welshman, London, 3 July 2006, p 8)

So, for both Townsend and influential figures in Disability Studies and the Disabled People's Movement, the prospects for full social inclusion did not look encouraging at the close of the new century's first decade. There was agreement that New Labour's neoliberalism was genuine in its support of *user control* because transferring responsibilities to service users fitted into pluralistic models of service provision. The (1997–May 2010) Labour governments' ideological promotion of mixed economies of welfare could accommodate groups of disabled people commissioning and/or managing their own support services in their quest to live independently. However, as Barnes and Mercer (2006) reported in their detailed study of *outcomes* in situations where disabled people employed models of user control – particularly Centres for Independent/Integrated/ Inclusive Living (CILs) – the initiatives were routinely undermined by the provision of woefully inadequate resources (direct payments, individual/personalised budgets, CIL grants, staff resources, CIL facilities, etc). Barnes and Mercer concluded as follows:

> Given the limited ambition of recent government initiatives in this regard, little significant progress will be made without further changes. It must be recognised that these will have significant resource implications, as effective barrier removal cannot be achieved 'on the cheap'. These short-term costs must be offset against the long-term gains of a barrier-free environment in which socially created dependence is considerably reduced if not eliminated altogether. (Barnes and Mercer, 2006, p 191)

The record of the Labour administrations is one of good intentions in the promotion of equal rights and opportunities for disabled people, restricted by a lack of resources. This occurred at a time when there was unprecedented investment in social welfare. The climate has now changed fundamentally. The Conservative–Liberal Democrat Coalition government that assumed power in May 2010 immediately announced changes to the benefits system that would affect the access to benefits of disabled people. It seems inevitable that disabled people will be particularly vulnerable to fall-out from the programme of spending cuts, which will have been announced while this book is in print. These concerns have been expressed by the Disability Alliance:

> [T]he new coalition Government's plans have sparked widespread fear amongst many disabled people and their representative organisations. The proposals announced to date could amount to a triple-jeopardy for disabled people of:
>
> • Forced ineffective tests to prove the impact of health conditions/impairments.

- A lack of support under a one-size-fits-all 'Work Programme' that may abolish some help for disabled people to find suitable work.
- Reduced in-work support through cuts to tax credits and potential watering down of obligations on employers to support disabled employees through a proposed employment law review. (www.disabilityalliance.org/welreform2.htm)

Thus, it seems that full social inclusion is but a distant prospect. I shall return to this theme at the close of this chapter.

Disability, health inequality and the prospects for disabled children

In this section, I would like to honour Peter Townsend's memory and contribution to the struggle for the abolition of disabled people's relative poverty by linking together a number of key themes in his writings on social inequality: disability, childhood, families and health inequality. The recently acquired insights reported here are based on quantitative data compilation and analysis by colleagues with whom I work in the Centre for Disability Research (CeDR) at Lancaster University: Eric Emerson, Chris Hatton and Janet Robertson (sometimes with others in international teams). The amassing of an evidence base to demonstrate that disabled children and adults continue to be at excess risk of poor health – because they are at excess risk of living in poor socioeconomic circumstances is an important development in the study of disabled people's relative deprivation. The findings of an extensive literature review that was submitted to the *Strategic review of health inequalities in England post 2010* (Marmot Review) would not have surprised him, although they would have disappointed him, coming as they did nearly 40 years after the founding of the Disability Alliance, 30 years after the Black Report and 13 years of Labour government:

Findings: *disability and health inequality*

- Disabled people experience significantly poorer health outcomes than their non-disabled peers, including in all aspects of health that are unrelated to the *specific* health conditions associated with their disability. Poorer health outcomes are also experienced by the carers of disabled children and adults.
- There are strong social gradients, across the life course, in the prevalence of disability.
- These gradients are likely to result from a combination of factors including:
  - the impact of adversity and disadvantage on the onset of health conditions associated with disability;
  - intergenerational transmission of socially patterned health conditions associated with disability;
  - the impact of disability on social mobility.
- As a result, disabled children and adults are more likely than their peers to be exposed to general socioeconomic conditions that are detrimental to health. A significant proportion of the risk of poor health of the disabled person themselves and carers appears to be attributable to their increased risk of exposure to socio-economic disadvantage.
- Some health conditions associated with disability or impairments may specifically impede the attainment of positive health.
- In addition, disabled children and adults are at risk of experiencing social exclusion and discrimination associated with their disability (disablism). The direct effects of such discrimination on health include reduced access to appropriate healthcare. Indirect effects of such discrimination on health operate through increased social exclusion, restricted social mobility and the psychological impact of direct personal experience of disablist actions.

Source: Emerson et al (2009)

A related illustration concerns children with intellectual disabilities. Emerson and Hatton undertook secondary statistical analyses of cross-sectional data extracted from Wave 4 (2002) of the Department for Work and Pensions' Families and Children Study. This involved working with a nationally representative sample of 12,916 British children in 7,070 families. Of these children, 593 (4.7%) were identified as having an intellectual disability (see Emerson and Hatton, 2007, for a detailed account of methods and measures). The Wave 4 study also contained a great deal of data on socioeconomic status. In summary, Emerson and Hatton found that children with intellectual disabilities were significantly more likely to live in disadvantaged households than their non-disabled counterparts. It was also evident that such children had poorer health (as reported by patents) than non-disabled children, and it was estimated that 31% of this increased risk of poor health could be attributed to (a) the household's socioeconomic position, and (b) the household's level of social capital (also measured). After carefully qualifying their findings, Emerson and Hatton's conclusion about the policy and practice implications of their findings in the 21st century echoed the social determinants of health arguments underpinning the Black Report:

> social policies aimed at reducing the inequity in health outcomes between people with IDs [intellectual disabilities] and their nondisabled peers will need to address the social inequalities that contribute to health status. This would require improving the socio-economic position of more disadvantaged children and young people with IDs by, for example, targeted tax transfers and removing barriers to maternal employment (Graham, 2005). Second ... approaches to health promotion and ensuring appropriate access to acceptable standards of health among young people with IDs will need to be targeted at more deprived families and communities. Otherwise, there is a risk that, through selective uptake, such interventions will serve to increase social inequalities within the population of people with IDs. (Emerson and Hatton, 2007, p 872)

Given all that is known about the link between disability and poverty, the same conclusion would have been drawn when comparing the circumstances of disabled children *with any impairment type* with their non-disabled counterparts. Once again, the evidence base is strengthened for the contention – held by both Townsend and the Disability Studies' community – that disabled people continue to face particular social disadvantages which have pernicious consequences for their ability to live as equal citizens in today's society.

Prospects?

This chapter has offered some observations on Peter Townsend's contribution to research and campaigning on disability, with his focus on income and living standards, and has considered some recent data on the relationship between disability and health inequality, which illustrate the truth in his arguments about disability and social disadvantage first raised several decades ago. We have seen that Townsend and the leaders of the Disabled People's Movement in Britain followed parallel but closely interrelated paths on the disability question from the 1970s. The potential for the full social inclusion of disabled adults and children has certainly been strengthened by continued pressure both from the Disabled People's Movement and Disability Studies and from the Disability Alliance and scholarly advocacy. Nevertheless contradictory signs and pressures are evident today.

On the one hand, in 2007 the UK government signed up to *The United Nations Convention on the Rights of People with Disabilities* (2006) – a very important international agreement about protecting and promoting the rights of disabled people throughout the world. It is also of note that the World Health Organization (WHO) is soon to release a landmark World Report on disability and rehabilitation across the globe (due summer 2011). In the words of Mike Smith, Commissioner and Chair of the Disability Committee at the Equality and Human Rights Commission:

> The Convention is not just a paper 'declaration' without
> any teeth. It requires government to take action to

remove barriers and give disabled people real freedom, dignity and equality. We can use it in lots of different ways to make sure our rights are respected and to get a better deal. (EHRC, 2010, p 2)

Moreover, the UK's Equality Act 2010 is now in force, bringing disability anti-discrimination law into alignment with equality legislation covering other groups in need of protection – on the grounds of 'race', gender, age, sexual orientation or religious belief.

On the other hand, disability activists in Britain are currently struggling to make sense of, and to resist, the impact of governmental 'austerity measures' designed to reduce the British financial deficit. If Peter Townsend was with us today, there is no doubt that he would have drawn detailed attention to the detrimental impact of legislative measures on the incomes and living standards of disabled people, young and old – forces propelling many individuals and families into deeper relative poverty. He would have deplored the undermining of the life chances of disabled children and young adults in the 21st century, and called for the careful tracking of this unfolding process through academic research and campaigning. Similarly, the Disabled People's Movement in the UK anticipates a barrage of actual and probable attacks on disabled people's life circumstances and human rights – especially with regard to independent living, income levels, resource distributional arrangements, employment opportunities and the configuration of health and social care services. If Oliver (2009) is correct about the fragmentation of the Disabled People's Movement, then the prospects for disabled people appear particularly grim. However, some user-led organisations point to enhanced opportunities for *user control* embedded in the government's agenda for the deregulation or jettisoning of state services: much debate is under way (*NCIL Newsletter*, 2010).

Thus, in the present climate of contradictory *fine words but hard truths*, it is difficult to assess what the next decade has in store for disabled people. However, it is certain that Townsend would have agreed with Disability Studies academics and user-led organisations that pressure must be maximised to protect and advance disabled people's social interests and status, and that this pressure must be exerted in a variety of forms, especially: political campaigning, research, teaching, advocacy and community action. The advances hard fought and hard won by and on behalf of disabled people over the last 40 years should not so easily be lost.

References

Barnes, C. and Mercer, G. (2006) *Independent futures: Creating user-led disability servicers in a disabling society*, Bristol: The Policy Press.

Busfield, J. (2010) 'Obituary: Peter Townsend 1928–2009', *Network – British Sociological Association*, no 104, Spring, pp 28-9.

Cabinet Office (2004) *Improving the life chances of disabled people*, London: Prime Minister's Strategy Unit.

Campbell, J. and Oliver, M. (1996) *Disability politics: Understanding our past, changing our future*, London: Routledge.

DH (Department of Health) (2001) *Valuing people: A strategy for learning disability in the 21st century*, Cm 5086, London: The Stationery Office.

Emerson, E. and Hatton, C. (2007) 'Poverty, socio-economic position, social capital and the health of children and adolescents with intellectual disabilities in Britain: a replication', *Journal of Intellectual Disability Research*, vol 51, pp 866-74.

Emerson, E., Madden, R., Robertson, J., Graham, H., Hatton, C. and Llewellyn, G. (2009) *Intellectual and physical disability, social mobility, social exclusion and health*, Submission to *Strategic review of health inequalities in England post 2010 (Marmot Review)*, CeDR Report 2, Lancaster: Lancaster University.

EHRC (Equality and Human Rights Commission) (2010) *The United Nations Convention on the Rights of People with Disabilities: A guide for disabled people and disabled people's organisations*, London: EHRC.

Finkelstein, V. (2009) 'The "social model of disability" and the disability movement', in M. Oliver (ed) *Understanding disability: From theory to practice* (2nd edn), Basingstoke: Palgrave Macmillan, pp 57-64.

Graham, H. (2005) 'Intellectual disabilities and socioeconomic inequalities in health: an overview of research', *Journal of Applied Research in Intellectual Disabilities*, vol 18, pp 101-11.

Graham, H. (2007) *Unequal lives: Health and socioeconomic inequalities*, Maidenhead: Open University Press.

Hunt, P. (ed) (1966) *Stigma: The experience of disability*, London: Chapman.

NCIL (National Council for Independent Living) (2010) 'Independently', *Newsletter*, August/September, London: NCIL.

Oliver, M. (2009) *Understanding disability: From theory to practice* (2nd edn), Basingstoke: Palgrave Macmillan.

Swain, J., Barnes, C., French, S. and Thomas, C. (eds) (2004) *Disabling barriers, enabling environments* (2nd edn), London: Sage Publications.

Thomas, C. (2007) *Sociologies of disability and illness: Contested ideas in disability studies and medical sociology*, Basingstoke: Palgrave Macmillan.

Townsend, P. (1966) 'Foreword', in P. Hunt (ed) *Stigma: The experience of disability*, London: Chapman, pp vi–viii.

Townsend, P. (1979) *Poverty in the United Kingdom: A survey of household resources and standards of living*, London: Penguin.

Townsend, P. and Davidson, N. (1982) *Inequalities in health: The Black Report*, Harmondsworth: Penguin.

UPIAS (Union of the Physically Impaired Against Segregation) and Disability Alliance (1976) *Fundamental principles of disability*, London: UPIAS.

Walker, A. and Townsend, P. (eds) (1980) *Disability in Britain: A manifesto of rights*, Oxford: Martin Robertson.

Walker, A., Gordon, D., Levitas, R., Phillimore, P., Phillipson, C., Salomon, M.E. and Yeates, N. (eds) (2010) *The Peter Townsend reader*, Bristol: The Policy Press.

Welshman, J. (2007) *From transmitted deprivation to social exclusion: Policy, poverty and parenting*, Bristol: The Policy Press.

TWELVE

Putting the lawyers in their place: the role of human rights in the struggle against poverty

Conor Gearty

Introduction

Peter Townsend came to 'human rights' as a term late in his career, but its spirit had been with him from the start. As early as 1958, in his contribution to the well-known *Conviction* volume, Peter was writing like a human rights activist:

> If that overdone phrase 'a classless society' means anything it is a society where differences in reward are much narrower than in Britain today and where people of different backgrounds and accomplishment can mix easily and without guilt; but also a society where a respect for people is valued most of all, for that brings a real equality. (Townsend, 1958, pp 93, 120)

With his wife Jean Corston as Chair of the newly established Joint Committee on Human Rights, there was no shortage of energetic human rights support in the Townsend household in the first decade of the 21st century. Here was an ideal way for Peter to carry on his battles against poverty at a time when the traditional socialist ethic seemed so much in eclipse and when (as a result of such decline) progressive language of any sort was very hard to find. His support for me as the incoming Director of the London School of Economics and Political Sciences' (LSE) Centre for the Study of Human Rights was immense: helping me navigate the perils of a new university environment on my arrival in 2002; securing Mary Robinson to give the lecture to launch my directorship (and packing out the Peacock Theatre as a result); chairing the Centre's advisory board for the first five years of my tenure as director; throwing himself into all our activities (I particularly remember him holding forth as Mahatma Gandhi in front of 450 enthralled students to win a Centre debate over who was the greatest human rights person of the 20th century – beating Eleanor Roosevelt, Nelson Mandela and many other distinguished activist icons in the process); and teaching a hugely popular course on children's rights which drew admiring attendees from across LSE's entire spectrum of postgraduate students. One meeting among many stands out: early in my tenure and at the height of New Labour's popularity, I brought a colleague from my barristers' chambers (and LSE governor) Cherie Booth together with Peter to talk about poverty and how to reduce it: for two engrossing hours in my office Peter sought to persuade her that government could do more, and Cherie tried as best she could to explain why what her husband Tony Blair had already done – slight though it seemed to Peter – was revolutionary by the standards of the international political culture in which, as Britain's Prime Minister, he was then moving.

In this chapter I want to explore a position that Peter unequivocally adopted, but I acknowledge immediately both that it is a hard one to maintain and also that few non-lawyers (much less lawyers) have argued for it: can we be strongly *in favour* of human rights but at the same time be firmly *against* the lawyers' exclusive appropriation of the term? It is a difficult stance because the idea of human rights has been so indelibly associated with the legal profession from the moment of its re-emergence in 1948 (with the Universal Declaration of Human Rights) and particularly since 1989, when the collapse of the Berlin Wall brought down not just Soviet communism for ever but (let's face it) old-style democratic socialism as well, for a generation (or two) at least. The core of human rights was for Peter to be found not in the courtroom but on the streets, in the souls of the activists and campaigners who were seeking by their human rights-inspired actions to change society for the better. But how can we resist the lawyers' plundering of human rights, their transformation of it from a source of emancipatory power into an arid mechanism for the resolution of disputes? Not only are they powerful but they are also well resourced, have a straightforward story to tell (forget the tedium of politics and persuasion – we can deliver individual rights by court order!) and are usually (this type of lawyer anyway) well meaning. The law is now so deeply entrenched in the field of civil and political rights that the once eccentric US system of judicial oversight of legislation is these days regarded as practically the democratic norm rather than the tool of reaction it so obviously was to people of Peter's generation (Griffith, 1997). With their control of political rights secure, the lawyers are now moving onwards and upwards towards their next goal, the legalisation of social rights. The momentum towards transforming social rights from a political idea into a series of individual rights that fall to be enforced by the courts is very strong. A feature of the collapse in radical political confidence in recent times has been this dash to the law as a panacea for ills thought to be both deep and (nowadays) unreachable by political action. This counsel of despair must be resisted: lawyers are never the answer to any serious question about social policy that any progressively minded person might ever care to ask.

In the spirit of Peter Townsend, and following in his footsteps, I will argue three propositions in this chapter. The first assertion is that the idea of human rights in general (and social rights in particular) is valuable, that such entitlements deserve not just our protection but also to be respected and promoted. Peter was right that the left needs to embrace human rights even if (as I argue below) it involves taking a cleaver to some sacred Marxist preconceptions. My second point is that the value of this notion of social rights lies principally in the political arena, this being the world in which the good that these words do can be best concretised or (to use a more bucolic image) most fruitfully deployed. Nowhere is this more true than in relation to poverty reduction, the focus of Peter's work over so many generations. Third, and following directly from this second assertion, and occupying most of what follows, I argue that the least effective way of securing social rights is via an over-concentration on the

---

243

legal process, with the constitutionalisation of such rights being an especial disaster wherever it occurs.

Why care?

Social rights are primarily about everyone having the right to a chance to thrive in life, to have sufficient resources, education and leisure time to live a fulfilled life. A prior question presents itself, frequently skirted around, skated over or ignored altogether: why does it matter that so many are currently lost to the world on account of their impoverishment, either because they die unnaturally young or lead lives of unyielding grimness? Why should we not think of this as simply the (bad) luck of the species birth lottery? In times past it was easy to grasp why we both cared for others and ought to care for them: it was God's direction. This was whether or not we rooted our faith in Christianity, in Islam or in one or other of the great religions of the world. At least since Marx, however, secular society has had the greatest of difficulty with absolutes of any sort, a scepticism that has extended to a reluctance to explore any of the supposed ethical foundations that might lie at its core. The inclination to feel for others, to care about their situation and to act to improve their lot has somehow survived the decline of religion in such cultures, but is this just the death rattle of organised religion, likely to wither away completely as the memory of what faith-based moral duties necessitated is gradually forgotten? If it is, human rights will die with it.

It is important to the future health of rights-based activism that something deeper than this is going on, reflecting at a fundamental level a part of what is entailed in our being human, of which religion is not the source but merely just a possible (albeit for a time hegemonic) reflection. Human rights need foundations deeper than the latest social practice. After decades in the doldrums, when all was thought to be constructed and the human mind a mere creature of the social forces into which the body containing it was born, the power of this kind of intuitive thinking has been making something of a comeback (Ridley, 1996). Its attraction lies in its link to human nature, that we think certain things because of what we are, not how we have been composed. Foreign though it is to so much social sciences teaching over so many years, this can be made into an attractive ally of the caring characteristic which, when it is then linked to entitlement, produces the underlying explanation of human rights: that many of us want to care for others, feel compelled to do so in a way that seems to flow not from any conscious decision but simply from how we are, and (taking this insight further) that we claim on behalf of those who are the subjects of our sympathy (including the billions whom we do not know) a right to its receipt, together with the actions that flow from recognition of it.

If we think of ourselves not as members of a special species but as each of us composed of a bundle of genes on the look-out for survival, then it by no means follows that in this field we have to commit ourselves to the rather loaded idea of the 'selfish gene' – there are many routes to survival and not all of them are marked 'me alone'. The way we are is not all self-oriented: as Adam Smith put it, 'How selfish soever man may be supposed, there are evidently some principles in his nature, which interest him in the fortune of others, and render their happiness necessary to him, though he derives nothing from it, except the pleasure of seeing it' (Smith, 1761). What Darwin allows us to do is locate an insight of this sort within science and then to see it as part of an animal (rather than uniquely human) approach to living. Far from being something spilt into us at birth from which we then learn how to behave, 'the building blocks of morality' are, as the great primatologist Frans de Waal put it in his Tanner lectures, 'evolutionarily ancient' (de Waal, 2006, p 7). The intuition to help others that is the product of this evolutionary dynamic, and its offshoot into a more general empathy and outreach to the other that de Waal describes in his lectures, is clearly close to the desire to achieve the kind of flourishing towards the other at which contemporary human rights practice is aimed. Of course not all of us care all the time or even (some of us) at all: there are very nasty competing instincts out there as well (tribal solidarity; hostility to the stranger; fear of the different), and these always threaten and often manage to swamp the better side of our nature, both individually and collectively.

An achievement of culture has been to erect obstacles to the success of these contrarian impulses. Since we first began to think about more than merely the next meal, our species has been good at erecting barriers to what it has been quick to see as 'bad' behaviour. Law, custom and religion have all played a part in this. In our contemporary culture, human rights is one of the best of these, an effective 'commitment gadget' (Boyer, 2001, p 211) available to those whose life project or immediate ethical task is the generalisation of the propensity to help the other into something beyond kin, beyond immediate community, beyond nation even, into the world at large. It is the habit of mind that flows from the far-seeing activist's capacity to grasp that in our shrunken world we are all affected by actions in a way that requires us all to be seen: the island people whose homes are destroyed by an inundation precipitated by the industrial world's greed and recklessness are the contemporary equivalent of the newly arrived neighbour whom some grunting but imaginatively wired pre-linguistic human types thought it better to befriend and help rather than to kill. The term 'human rights' works so well to capture this feeling because it is multi-purpose: seeming to make sense at the level of philosophy ('here is why you ought to help the stranger'), in the realm of politics ('they have a human right to this or a human right to that – therefore arrangements must be made for them to get it'), and in the sphere of law ('the right is set out in the charter or in the covenant or in the constitution that our forefathers created to keep us in check').

How should we care?

The primary way of embedding human rights properly (and social rights particularly) in any given culture, of making this commitment check work, should be via the political process. The tension between acceptance of the necessity of political work and a hankering after the quick-fix of a judicial *Deus ex machina* is a feature of human rights generally but has become especially evident in the field of social rights, where outcomes have proved stubbornly difficult to achieve in the political domain. The preoccupation with judicial solutions is not just a matter of the activists' impatience with politics;

it is a consequence as well of the culture in which human rights work is immersed. As I earlier briefly noted, immediately from its re-emergence at the end of the Second World War, the field of human rights has been one which has been very much the preserve of lawyers. This has been entirely understandable, given that the main way in which the subject has expressed itself has been via international, regional and domestic documents which have, of necessity, required the sort of expert textual elucidation (frequently in the context of litigation) at which lawyers naturally excel. The United Nations (UN) human rights industry (using that term in a consciously non-disparaging sense) has been peopled by lawyers: they have been prominent in the oversight committees, served as special rapporteurs and been natural choices as independent experts. Of course this has been a great credit to the legal profession, proudly sending its secular missionaries into the world to do important ethical work. But these excellent people have taken with them into the field a partiality for the judicial process which is so deeply embedded within them that they think it to be a reflection of the natural order of things and not a (mere) consequence of how they themselves have been educated, and their subsequent lived experience. And for most lawyers, standards are not truly real unless their existence can be confirmed in legal proceedings before an independent and impartial tribunal. So the momentum in our subject has been away from the kind of political engagement that might deliver on the promise of the Universal Declaration and the subsequent covenants (on civil and political and economic, social and cultural rights respectively) and towards the idea that basic human rights are best protected by allowing individuals to hold their governments to account in judicial and/or quasi-judicial fora.

Peter knew very well the value of giving human rights a wider remit than this, as his framing of the issue of poverty in rights terms demonstrated so clearly (Townsend and Gordon, 2002; Gordon et al, 2003). The way the term has been used to underpin action against poverty is a very good example of the energy outside the law that is to be found in this very contemporary way of doing human rights. The UK's Joint Committee on Human Rights remarked that '[p]overty and inequality are the central concerns of economic, social and cultural rights' (Joint Committee on Human Rights, 2004, para 102), observing that 'a rights-based approach' is clearly of assistance to 'government in addressing poverty, and Parliament and civil society in scrutinising its success in doing so' (Joint Committee on Human Rights, 2004, para 106). To the leading charity Oxfam, another advantage is that a 'rights-based approach requires' not only 'a system of policy-making that is accountable in law and open to scrutiny' but a way of securing this that involves 'the active participation of those living within the jurisdiction, especially those living on the margins, whether citizens or otherwise' (Joint Committee on Human Rights, 2004, para 119ev para 3). The experience of Oxfam is 'that the realisation of economic, social and cultural rights can most effectively be achieved with the active participation of those affected' (Joint Committee on Human Rights, 2004, para 122ev para 18). The range of civil society groups and local communities that reach for the language of human rights to articulate this need for action and to express the solidarity that flows from collective engagement in tackling poverty is impressive and (although obviously each individually is very local) truly international in its reach. Good examples can be pointed to in Wales (the Gellideg Foundation Project) (Joint Committee on Human Rights, 2004, para 125ev paras 42-5), in Brazil (the shadow reporting on international social rights obligations in place since the early part of the last decade) (Donald and Mottershaw, 2009, p 25) and the Poor People's Economic Human Rights Campaign in the US (Donald and Mottershaw, 2009, pp 15-16).

There are many others (Donald and Mottershaw, 2009) – what unites them is not the language of international human rights *law* (sometimes they do not even locate their work in this terminology at all) but rather their use of human rights as an *idea*, a way of asserting dignity, respect for themselves and an insistence that they too (despite their disadvantage and often their misfortune) deserve to be treated properly.

This is exactly how Peter used the term, and how best it can be deployed to achieve socially valuable outcomes. A common commitment to human rights can enable the building of alliances that would be impossible without the sharing of a common vision that this term makes possible. What other language could, in the name of the moral imperative of poverty reduction, bring together figures from within civil society, government, trade unions, the poor themselves and even the Pope (whose position on social rights is entirely progressive, even mainstream) (Benedict XVI, 2009, para 27)? Human rights are authentic when they reflect the values and principles that are rooted in the instinct to help, the perceived obligation to care for the stranger that has been part of our species behaviour since the dawn of human time. The term is an open-textured one, its content changes over time as new ways of expressing basic values come to the fore, assuming a human rights shape in order both to capture the essence of what the right is about and at the same time to push for its further realisation in the culture in which the argument for it is being made. All of this is particularly true of social rights because it is the social that is now at the frontier of rights talk. In contrast to the now well-established and strongly embedded frameworks of civil and political rights, it is the porousness of the boundaries of social rights that are their main strength. The basic rights in the International Covenant on Economic, Social and Cultural Rights are there for all to see, but both what they entail in concrete terms and also the extent to which they are supported, complemented and supplemented remain open to discussion, debate and further action, at whatever level it might happen to be: the international, the regional, the state or even the purely local. The rights can also be added to as new challenges get successfully framed in the language of rights, on disability for example, or the rights of indigenous peoples. Viewed in this way, the framing, detailing and embedding of social rights are quintessential political activities.

Of course politics cannot be guaranteed to deliver the outcomes one desires. There are many examples of how imperfect is the political support afforded social rights: oversight bodies are overworked; vital resources are not forthcoming; new rights take an unconscionably long time to assert themselves, both as facts on paper and then (even more difficult) as realities on the ground. The tension in the mind of human rights protagonists between the certainty of the goal and the radical uncertainty of the political process designed to bring it about has produced a failure of nerve so far as the development of a mature politics of human rights has been concerned. It has been difficult for those who truly care about social rights to avoid being tempted into the belief that rendering their field subject to judicial enforcement will be the ideal way of avoiding the pitfalls of the political while securing all the benefits that ordinarily flow from success in such a process. This explains the momentum towards the judicial enforcement of social rights which has been such a feature of the post-1989 climate, at all levels of governance and to which we have earlier referred. But what is so wrong with that, it might be reasonably asked. Why not have *both* the politics *and* the law, operating in tandem?

How can we tame the lawyers?

The word is tame, not destroy. Clearly there is a role for the law in delivering social rights, just as there is in every field in all democratic polities. But it should never go so far as embedding in the constitution legally enforceable social rights of a general nature with the capacity to override statute law. The Joint Committee on Human Rights has elaborated on what it has called the three 'most common objections' to such an approach. First, it observed that the rights themselves would be 'too vaguely expressed', and would 'only raise expectations and encourage time-consuming and expensive litigation against public bodies' (Joint Committee on Human Rights, 2008, paras 183-4). Second, the move to law 'hands too much power to the courts and so is undemocratic' (Joint Committee on Human Rights, 2008, paras 185-7). Third, such an adjudicative power would involve 'the courts in making decisions about resources and priority setting that they are ill-equipped to take' (Joint Committee on Human Rights, 2008, paras 188-91). Several additional points of objection can be added to these. There is, fourth, the strong emphasis on the individual that is inherent in the whole idea of justiciability, with its inevitable focus on particular claimants at the expense of the wider public interest. This might be laudable in the arena of traditional litigation where two parties jostle to secure a reading of a specific law (or prior agreement) in their favour, but it fits less well when such proceedings are being regarded by one of the parties as a device through which to smuggle into court the interests of thousands of invisible claimants, however meritorious the moral arguments being made via their representative litigant might be. Judges are suspicious of 'test cases', not necessarily because they are opposed to the outcome that the litigant before them is pursuing on behalf of others so much as on account of the self-evident lack of fit between the narrow realm of such litigation and the broader issues that they are being asked covertly to deal with in such proceedings.

This mismatch is compounded, fifth, by the inappropriateness of the adversarial model to the resolution of broadly framed issues of social rights going beyond the litigant before the court. Courts are not suitable places to receive, much less assess, the kind of empirical data and guesses about future trends that should underpin all social policy (including on the provision of social rights). This is more than a reservation based on lack of equipment for the job (the Joint Committee's third objection, above) so much as it is an observation on the incompetence of the judicial forum, however seemingly well-provided for the decision it might appear to be: the point is that it is not the right site to decide these things and the more you fiddle with its procedures to make it the right place (special briefs on socioeconomic data and the like; advice from non-governmental organisations [NGOs]; expert evidence on the wider social impact of a proposed ruling; and so on), the more any such tribunal looks increasingly like an executive officer, but without the usual democratic necessities of electoral legitimacy and public accountability.

Without a proper enforcement arm as well, a sixth objection to assigning the development of social rights to the judicial branch emerges. Who is to follow up the court's decision to see that it has been effectively implemented? What happens when unexpected glitches in effecting a court's orders are encountered? Supposing the court's guesses about the cost of its intervention prove to be wrong, how are the new financial implications to be properly taken into account? As with the fourth and fifth objections detailed above, the answer to this has often been thought to be to switch the emphasis to ways in which the court process can be made better, more accommodating to the tasks it is now being asked to do, but once again this is to distort the court's mission and to drive it away from its core function.

A seventh objection is broader in nature. Even if the court process was sympathetic and able effectively to deliver social rights from time to time, it is still an avenue down which activists for social rights should not willingly go, however tempting it might seem when contrasted with the long and slow political slog that often seems the only democratic alternative. We are back with the seductive appeal of law as a speedy deliverer of solutions to problems that appear otherwise to be intractable. But changing the focus to law in this way does not come without cost. Even the most enthusiastically backed of human rights campaigns has only a finite amount of energy, and switching emphasis to the courts uses up organisational time, money and campaigner zeal, strengths that might have been better servants to the shared ideal if they had remained where they were, fighting the good fight in the legislature, in civil society, and if necessary, on the streets. Of course the two are not binary opposites in the way that it might be thought is being suggested here – but what is undeniable is that a twin-track approach (law and political activism) is one that is very difficult even for well-resourced groups to keep evenly balanced on the campaigning road. With its courtroom drama, its arguments and its inevitable individualisation of the issues to hand, above all with its prospect of a clean victory in a campaign that seems otherwise so bogged down in *realpolitik*, the lawyers have a tendency to shove all other travellers off to the side of the road.

And eighth, there is a possibility which is very familiar to old socialists but which has faded out of the limelight somewhat since the collapse of Marxist confidence in the aftermath of the Cold War: beware of empowering judges lest you give them an aggressive tool with which to hinder (rather than to facilitate) progress. Here social rights come up full square against the uncomfortable fact that to be fully realised, their proponents may well have to take on established interests whose power and determination to hold on to privilege is certain to make them dangerous enemies. The achievement of the kind of equal society in which social rights do truly allow all to flourish will not be cost-free, in financial or in political terms. The changes that most societies in the world would need to effect the radical transformation required to move to a situation in which all those within their borders truly enjoyed their social rights would be great indeed. Taxes would need to be raised, restrictions on individual freedom introduced, bureaucracies empowered. The legal obstacle that would be likely to arise would have two aspects. First, there would be the way in which civil and political rights holders would be able to deploy these rights in order to hinder progress and thereby to preserve their privilege. Under the cover of political speech, expensive campaigns against the 'erosion of individual freedom' would be mounted and these would be certain to enjoy some traction with a general public which would be at this point by definition schooled in the importance of human rights. Similarly popular would be invocations of the right to property and of the urgent need for 'fair procedures' in the face of executive action that would be vulnerable to being credibly attacked as too speedy and disrespectful of existing interests. Advocates of legalised social rights could hardly disparage the use in the courts of civil and political rights, even if the main intention was to block progress. The results would be quickly plain for all to see: slums would be cleared more slowly; unnecessarily large compensation would be paid to property owners, thereby reducing the pot available to the poor; and taxes would produce less revenue than if the right to property (for example, extending to inheritance) did not exist.

The second way in which entrenching social rights within the legal system supports this eighth objection to justiciable rights lies in the nature of social rights themselves, and in particular in the effects that flow from the focus on the individual that is (as I have argued here) inevitably entailed in such a move. We are not concerned now with the abstract effects of this individualisation, something that has already been covered above (the fourth in this litany of anxieties). Rather it is with what the powerful can do by way of assertion of their own social rights as an indirect means of resisting the social rights of others. Two well-known examples of this come to mind. Many states wrestle with the problem of privately funded education as a barrier to the achievement of a truly equal society, one in which social rights are available to all. This is because of the disproportionate hold the 'alumni' of such elite environments have on the society in which they are to be found. The UK is an outstanding example of this (Milburn, 2009), and yet because of the existence of the (social) right to education that happens to appear in a protocol to the otherwise civil and political European Convention on Human Rights, anyone seeking genuine reform finds an unnecessary roadblock strewn in their way in the form of a parental entitlement to an education of their choice. Of course a reformer could and indeed should make strong arguments the other way, but the point is that in doing so he or she is having to pit a known individual's freedom against the merely hypothetical social rights that unknown numbers of currently deprived children would (it has to be argued) enjoy in the future if the freedom of an actual, knowable set of children is limited now. The masses of pupils who are potential beneficiaries of the change are, despite their likely numbers, less visible as individuals than the named boys and girls who are being made to suffer now.

As was the case with the civil and political rights obstacles just discussed, reformers coming from outside the rights tradition would have no difficulty with this – of course the known few must suffer for the future unknown many, and the fact that there is a withdrawal of the privileges of the minority now so as to assist in their future flourishing is of the essence of policy making; this is exactly what planners ought to be doing. Even the most far-sighted and broadminded of those who embrace the language of human rights have difficulty with this; they are uneasy at such utilitarian calculations. And human rights proponents of a more traditional, individualist bent are all the more concerned. Where they happen to be judges, schooled in the application of justice not by reference to broad societal goals but in accord with what precisely configured individual cases before them appear to require by reference to legally enforceable human rights law, then the objections become all the greater. This is why the courts (to mention, albeit more briefly, our second example) have historically had such difficulty in so many jurisdictions with the concept of affirmative action, not so much with the partisanship shown to those in *groups* whom the state desires to support as with the consequent disfavouring of certain *individuals*, not for any reason related to themselves but solely on account of their membership of an abstract category of person who is being ruled out a priori: he is a man when a woman is required, a white applicant where some other ethnic identity is being insisted on, a person without disabilities when the job is required to go to one with such disadvantages, and so on. On whose side in such difficult matters of judgement lies the language of human rights? In the political environment it is possible to look to the future and defend the imposition of short-term injustice. But if the judges are given a front row seat in the management of these difficult issues, the outcome is likely to be very different.

Conclusion

What progress there has been in Britain in the alleviation of poverty and the delivery of social rights generally has been achieved by political action, by legislation forced on our rulers by determined and brilliantly dogged egalitarians like Peter Townsend. This includes the successful establishment of the National Health Service, the delivery of free education for all, and the guarantor of legal aid for those too poor to pay for such support themselves. But just to identify the gains is to remind oneself of the losses, of how each of these successes has been undermined by the recent antagonism of successive governments. Politics is inevitably a slow business, often poisoned by the influence of money and with seemingly endless setbacks along the way, various pitfalls that seem always to need to be negotiated and concessions made – all of this tries the patience of rights activists and drives many of them into the courtroom in search of a speedy dash to absolute victory. But the central argument of this chapter has been that such tempting short-cuts are in truth cul-de-sacs, and that there is no alternative to careful navigation of the traditional route, one that when it is successfully negotiated and the finish line reached has carried all its passengers with it to a destination that is both new and real, and where everybody now agrees it is right to be. Peter Townsend understood this very well: freed from the constraints of law, human rights work has the potential to be the single most important contributor to social justice and to equality in the decades to come. But first it must consolidate its intellectual foundations, celebrate the potential of politics and be perpetually wary of its noisy friends in their gowns and wigs.

References

Benedict XVI (2009) *Caritas in Veritate*, London: Catholic Truth Society.

Boyer, P. (2001) *Religion explained: The human instinct that fashions gods, spirits and ancestors*, London: Vintage.

de Waal, F. (2006) *Primates and philosophers: How morality evolved*, Princeton, NJ: Princeton University Press.

Donald, A. and Mottershaw, E. (2009) *Poverty, inequality and human rights: Do human rights make a difference?*, York: Joseph Rowntree Foundation.

Gordon, D., Nandy, S., Pantazis, C., Pemberton, S. and Townsend, P. (2003) *Child poverty in the developing world*, Bristol: The Policy Press.

Griffith, J.A.G. (1997) *The politics of the judiciary* (5th edn), London: Fontana Press.

Joint Committee on Human Rights (2004) *The International Covenant on Economic, Social and Cultural Rights*, Twenty-first report of Session 2003-04, HL 183, HC 1188, London: The Stationery Office, November.

Joint Committee on Human Rights (2008) *A Bill of Rights for the UK?*, Twenty-ninth report of Session 2007-08, HL 165, HC 150, London: The Stationery Office, August.

Milburn, A. (chair) (2009) *Unleashing aspiration: The final report of the Panel on Fair Access to the Professions*, London: Cabinet Office.

Ridley, M. (1996) *The origins of virtue*, London: Penguin Books.

Smith, A. (1761) *The theory of moral sentiments* (2nd edn), London: Millar.

Townsend, P. (1958) 'A society for people', in N. Mackenzie (ed) *Conviction*, London: MacGibbon & Kee, pp 93-120.

Townsend, P. and Gordon, D. (eds) (2002) *World poverty: New policies to defeat an old enemy*, Bristol: The Policy Press.

THIRTEEN

Radicalising social policy in the 21st century: a global approach[1]

Nicola Yeates and Bob Deacon

Introduction

We undertake four tasks in this chapter. First, we offer a brief review of Peter Townsend's work on global social policy and the stature of its contribution to its field. We highlight the innovativeness and breadth of coverage of Peter's work which was firmly grounded in a materialist, globalist and sociological analysis of social policy. Second, we reflect on the impact of this work, where we make reference to his academic and policy impacts. Third, we assess the implications of the key messages of Peter's work for current and future research, teaching and campaigning. We focus on the value and importance of a global approach to social policy research, teaching and campaigning, and make especial reference to the implications of his work both on child poverty and social security in the context of the current United Nations (UN) Global Social Floor strategy. Finally, we add some comments on what still needs to be done if Peter's vision of a meaningful global social policy grounded in democratic socialism is to be realised.

Scene setting: a review of the global dimensions of Peter's work

Peter was a pioneer of global social policy. Although global social policy is commonly attributed to a field of study and research that developed in the mid-1990s (see Yeates, 2008b), as early as the 1950s Peter was developing a *global* analysis of world poverty, combining the insights of global sociology with those of development studies and social policy. Peter's personal diary from January 1953 evidences that he reflected on the relationship between Britain and its colonies in the development of social policy:

> True social security and welfare can be brought about in Britain – at a cost. In a sense the level of welfare at present is subsidised by people in our Colonies. Should not their claims have greater consideration than our own? The right to freedom from want has no geographical boundaries. Moreover, a moral and social principle regarded as obligatory for the British is all the more obligatory for colonial peoples for whom we are responsible. We have shunned the rights of East Africans, for example, while pontificating about our own. I fear that in arguing for better and greater use of resources for the social services in Britain, as anyone who studies these services is bound to do, I will lack conviction, merely because I will feel the resources ought to be used for East Africans and others. (Walker and Walker, 2009, pp 5-6)

Peter developed his analysis of this relationship throughout the ensuing years and published it in *The concept of poverty*, where he set out an 'approach to development and stratification [to explain] how poverty arises, and is perpetuated, in low income and high income countries' (Townsend, 1970, p 30). It was this work that formed the basis of his influential theory of poverty, including *Poverty in the UK* (1979). Peter's analysis of poverty and social policy at this time laid the foundations for his later work that took centre stage in his work from the 1990s and was formative in the development of contemporary global social policy studies. This work was particularly influenced by Peter's involvement in the 1995 Copenhagen United Nations (UN) Summit. At this time Peter's work centred squarely on the 'new' global development context of world poverty and the articulation of comprehensive strategies to eliminate it. Peter rejected an academic career trajectory that insulated him from wider public engagement and policy activism, and the breadth and nature of his work evidenced *par excellence* the integration of research, scholarship, teaching and campaigning in the UK and internationally.

The globalist framework within which Peter worked meant he eschewed the conventional division between 'domestic' and 'overseas' social policy. He regarded these less as opposites than as inseparable realms of analysis and action. When it comes to explaining the production – and reproduction – of poverty, a globalist analysis, he maintained, was an indispensable part of any coherent programme of social research, policy formation and campaigning. Well known is his argument that poverty and wealth are directly related to one another (Townsend, 1979). But less recognised is that this relationship was articulated by him from the outset in global terms. The riches of (those living in) high-income countries are, he argued, inextricably linked to poverty (of those living) in low-income countries. This idea that poverty at home and abroad are directly connected is well articulated in the following quote taken from *The concept of poverty*:

> A wealthy society which deprives a poor country of resources may simultaneously deprive its own poor classes through maldistribution of those additional resources. (Townsend, 1970, p 42)

The core of Peter's work at this time and subsequently was directed towards demonstrating the connections and interdependencies between systems of social stratification around the world. This, he argued, necessitated looking 'outwards' beyond the UK or national context of social policy, and in two key ways.

First, it meant attending to the *extra*-national dimensions and effects of government policy. Peter was clear about the role of the advanced economies/rich countries in perpetuating world poverty and their responsibility to eradicate it. In the 1960s and 1970s he was especially concerned with the adverse effects of their trade, aid and development policies on poorer countries, and with how former British colonies had been urged to reproduce subsistence social security and poverty relief policies (see, for example, Townsend, 1970). In the 1980s and 1990s he was scathing of the shameful participation of the British government in helping forge a version of European integration that both propelled social polarisation within the European Union (EU) and worsened the terms of production, trade and labour in poorer and developing countries (see, for example, Townsend, 1992, 1993; Townsend and Donkor, 1996).

Second, Peter was clear that social policy analysis also had to focus more extensively on policy formation in cross-border spheres of governance. He recognised that a progressive national – UK – politics of poverty necessarily had to engage with the poverty and wider social policies of international organisations and transnational corporations (TNCs), and argued that not enough attention in UK academic and policy campaigning was being directed towards critical engagement with these organisations:

> The influence of international organisations and transnational corporations upon national economies and upon the distribution of national resources also requires a larger share in any theory of poverty than it has attracted hitherto. (Townsend, 1993, p 105)

The social and economic policies of multilateral bodies, whether the EU, The World Bank, International Monetary Fund (IMF) or the UN, became prominent in Peter's work in latter decades, when his deep-rooted internationalism focused squarely on the 'new' global context of social policy and development. The consequences of the rise of global markets, together with the role of policies and practices of international organisations and TNCs acting in tandem with national governmental and non-governmental organisations (NGOs) in perpetuating world poverty, all came within his analysis. Transnational institutions actively shape the distribution of resources between and within countries, but, he argued, they were not being given enough attention in explanations of polarisation, exclusion and poverty given that the policies of international organisations such as The World Bank, IMF and the UN agencies as well as the EU were intrinsic to the problem of poverty whether in rich or poor countries (Townsend, 1993; Townsend and Donkor, 1996).

He was particularly scathing of The World Bank (Townsend, 1992, 1993, 2008b), whose poverty policies, he felt, amounted to nothing less than a global poor law and which epitomised the 'self-importance and self-deception of current global institutions' (Townsend and Donkor, 1996, p 6). He particularly railed against prevailing discourses of 'social safety nets' that he regarded as a 'miserable diversion' (Townsend, 1992) from the need to develop comprehensive social protection systems. In the debate between those who wished to abolish global institutions such as The World Bank and those who wished to reform them, Peter was on the side of the latter – but he was no co-optee. What was needed, he argued, was a radical overhaul and thorough democratisation of The World Bank and other global institutions dominated by the Global North. These institutions must embrace the values of collectivism and public service, and establish comprehensive systems of social protection worldwide. Above all, what was needed was development-oriented *global social planning* as a prerequisite to the establishment of an international welfare state.

Peter took heart in some developments within the UN, notably the 1995 Copenhagen Declaration and the Millennium Development Goals that he regarded as landmarks in the formulation of a more coherent global social policy based on scientific measures of poverty.[2] He was also greatly heartened and energised by the growing interest of two particular UN agencies – UNICEF and the International Labour Organization (ILO) – in a human rights approach to child poverty (Townsend, 2006). But while Peter worked with these agencies in advancing the cause of evidence-based policy making, he was never complacent, and continually pressed the UN agencies to do more and to do it better. The failure of these organisations – and the rich countries that control them – to adopt a progressive social policy, to establish what Peter called an 'international welfare state' (Townsend and Donkor, 1996; Townsend, 2002) that institutionalised fairer systems of both distribution and redistribution, would inevitably mean adding hundreds of millions more people to the billions already impoverished. Later in this chapter we turn to the UN's Global Social Floor strategy to consider in detail what the implications of Peter's work were for this crucially important field.

The implications of Peter's work for social policy research and teaching

Major advances in globalising academic social policy in the ways that Peter advocated have occurred. Although he never used the term, the 'methodological nationalism' that compartmentalises social structures and processes – and accordingly knowledge about them – into discrete socio-political (nation state) units and fails to connect them to wider global social edifices has been somewhat loosened, and the methodological transnationalism that he implicitly advocated has gained much ground in teaching, research and scholarship. Global social policy is now established as a dynamic field of academic study and research in the UK and internationally with strong advocacy, campaigning and teaching traditions and leanings (Yeates, 2008a). The example of world poverty, an area on which Peter worked throughout his life, is an excellent example of the development of globalist political campaigns around policy reform. Here, Peter was a major contributor to scholarly campaigns for scientific analysis to focus much more on the role of Bretton Woods institutions, such as The World Bank, and UN agencies in addressing poverty and he made key interventions in debates about policy reforms needed to eradicate world poverty. Later in the chapter we return to consider these interventions and their implications for policy in more detail. Here we reflect a little further on the implications of Peter's work for academic social policy research and teaching.

Perhaps the most important point to make here is the imperative of a globalist analysis of social policy being concretised in research and teaching programmes. Although academic programmes that focus on the global dimensions of social policy have emerged, it is still the case that social scientists and funding bodies all too often fail to look outwards beyond the country in which they are located, to relate national systems of social stratification to global ones or to focus on transnational social policy. The vast body of academic work revolving around the conceptualisation, theorisation and empirical manifestations of welfare regimes is one example of this. Remarkably little of the vast literature to have emerged over the last two decades that points to the embeddedness of border-spanning social, economic and political formations in the formation of 'national' welfare settlements has been taken up in the welfare regimes literature. The welfare regimes literature unfortunately remains firmly tied to a conception of society (and social policy) that stops at political (state) borders. The welfare regimes literature initiated by Esping-Andersen (1990) has undergone numerous critiques and modifications over the last two decades to take better account of diverse systems around the world and of complex social divisions such as gender, 'race', ethnicity and class, but it remains centrally preoccupied with the business of typologising and categorising *national* welfare systems. As such, to the extent that this literature addresses poverty, exclusion and polarisation, it pinpoints national and local causes and fails to relate them to global structures. Nor does it in any way engage with relations of connectedness, cooperation, coordination and conflict in the wider world that have been so instrumental in the formation of ostensibly 'national' welfare states, or with social policy formation in spheres of cross-border governance that transcend individual countries.

If we take Peter's analysis seriously, more extensive and thorough engagement with a globalist analysis of social policy is needed. In his words, 'global policy analysis must now attract the predominant part of academic analysis of economic and social structural change' (Townsend, 2008a, p xxi). This includes challenging conventional distinctions between what is 'national' and what is 'international', and between what is 'domestic' and what is 'foreign'. By way of illustration, it is plainly evident that so-called domestic policy and decisions about 'domestic' matters have potentially major ramifications beyond the territory concerned. Take staffing policies, for example. The failure to institute adequate workforce planning and investment by wealthy countries has generated labour crises in their health systems that are filled by recruiting from poorer countries. The resources these countries invested in producing skilled qualified staff are lost through emigration and, depleted of labour, health services' needs remain unmet, resulting in adverse health outcomes and unnecessary deaths (Yeates, 2009). The importance of examining the role of international organisations in these extra-territorial impacts of domestic policy remains: 'fiscal policies imposed by international financial institutions (IMF, World Bank) restrict provisions for health and education in poor countries and often encourage brain drain. Despite a shortage of nurses in public facilities, many nurses are either unemployed or working outside the health sector – because of a freeze on recruitment' (Adepoju, 2007). Here also the most recent global financial crisis – which many foretold and the repercussions of which are now falling on rich Western economies and adversely impacting on standards of living of the non-rich – serves as a salutary reminder of the need to devote far more attention to matters of global social policy and governance than has hitherto been the case.

Meaningfully scrutinising global structures, processes, policies and actions of governmental and non-governmental actors shaping the (mal)distribution of resources within and between countries necessitates engaging with issues of international trade, finance, aid and investment policy as well as 'traditional' issues of health, education, employment and social protection policy. The former realm has important social policy outcomes in their own right – shaping the distribution as well as redistribution of resources within and between countries – as well as conditioning the latter. Thus, the conventional lines that demarcate social policy become blurred and the distinctions on which it is founded look increasingly untenable if the field is concerned with discerning the structural causes and effective remedies to social polarisation, exclusion and poverty. We need to be asking difficult and challenging questions about how international organisations' and TNCs' policies and practices affect who in the world gets what resources, by what means and with what effects. It is the potential harms and not only the benefits of global restructuring that need to be brought more regularly and more forcefully into the frame of attention (Townsend, 1993). This must become a central focus of academic social policy.

Assessing the implications of Peter's work in the context of the UN Global Social Floor

Peter was always clear that scientific analysis and policy action was but a means to an end, namely the eradication of world poverty. A sense of the task ahead and how to achieve it was clearly articulated in the 'Manifesto: international action to defeat poverty' (Townsend and Gordon, 2002). Among the various steps set out in this manifesto are the implementation of existing international human rights conventions and the introduction of new – and enforceable – rights where necessary. The manifesto also identifies the need to curtail TNCs' powers as part of any strategy of global redistribution. Here, the preoccupation with corporate self-regulation and the Global Compact must be replaced by the introduction of mandatory legal powers to regulate TNCs. Effective distribution requires funds, and two sources of international finance were advocated: an increase in development assistance from the 0.7% target to 1% of gross national product (GNP), and the introduction of new cross-border taxes to fund cross-national subsidies for social services and social security for children in all low-income countries and regions.

From the early 2000s Peter, with his colleagues at the University of Bristol, came to focus on the issue of child poverty (Gordon et al, 2003; Townsend, 2008c, 2009a). Peter's last collected work (Townsend, 2009a), published in the year of his death, follows up on many elements of the 2002 manifesto. This last book was uncompromisingly titled *Building decent societies: Rethinking the role of social security in development*. It was a collaborative project produced while working for the Social Security Department of the ILO, with contributions by leading ILO figures, by global social security experts, by scholars from the Global South, by international NGO spokespeople and by those working in Departments of International Development in the Global North. The very breadth of contributions is testimony to Peter's powerful standing in the field. But it is the 'Introduction' by Peter and his chapters on 'Social security and human rights', 'Investment in social security: a possible UN model for Child Benefit?' and 'Social security in developing countries: a brief overview' in that collection that we are most interested in here.

This assessment needs to be placed in the context of the emergence in 2009 of a new UN campaign for a Global Social Protection Floor that built on previous global campaigns to extend social security. We briefly review this development here before assessing Peter's work in the light of it. A recent public presentation of the campaign for a Global Social Floor brought together individuals from the UN Department of Economic and Social Affairs (UNDESA), the ILO,

HelpAge International and UNICEF on a public side event at the Doha Financing for Development Conference in December 2008. At this event it was argued that:

> The current global financial crisis is an opportunity to create a Global New Deal to deliver social protection in all countries through basic old age and disability pensions, child benefits, employment programs, and provision of social services.... Social security is a human right (Articles 22 and 25 of the Universal Declaration of Human Rights) and it is affordable, a basic package is estimated to cost from 2 to 5 percent of GDP as an average. It is feasible if the international system commits to providing financial support for a Global New Deal to jump start an emergency response to the urgent social needs of our times. (www.choike.org/2009/eng/informes/7194.html)

Several strands of activity fed into this 'campaign' for a 'global social floor' or 'minimum social protection package'. First was the work of the ILO in its Global Campaign on Social Security and Coverage for All (2003). The Socioeconomic Security work programme of the ILO, which culminated in the report entitled *Economic security for a better world* (ILO, 2004) that argued for a range of policies including a citizenship income, and categorical cash transfers, also advanced the case. Subsequently Michel Cichon, Director of the ILO Social Security Department, argued to combine the idea of universal cash transfers with the Campaign to Extend Social Security for All (the precursor to the UN Global Social Protection Floor campaign). Thus the call for a new Minimum Social Protection Package and a new ILO Social Protection Standard (ILO, 2008). The informal networking including public campaigning at the level of senior players in UNDESA, ILO, UNICEF and HelpAge International continued to take place and led to the adoption of this Global Social Floor policy by the Chief Executives Board (CEB) of the UN System in April 2009 at a meeting in Paris. This UN CEB meeting generated the CEB Issue Paper *The global financial crisis and its impact on the work of the UN system*. Initiative six in this paper was to work towards a global 'Social Protection Floor which ensures access to basic social services, shelter, and empowerment and protection of the poor and vulnerable'. This has subsequently been elaborated in the June 2009 UN CEB document (UN CEB, 2009) as a 'floor (that) could consist of two main elements: (a) public services: geographical and financial access to essential public services (water, sanitation, health, education); and (b) transfers: a basic set of essential social transfers ... to provide a minimum income security'. The ILO and WHO would lead on this policy supported by a host of other agencies such as UNICEF and UNDESA.

Peter's work, and especially the last book we are referring to here (Townsend, 2009a), was a key element of the intellectual inputs into the political process that enabled this movement to thrive. Peter, together with his colleagues in the Peter Townsend Centre for International Poverty Research, produced excellent campaigning papers on related topics but these did not always engage directly with the policy ideas emerging at the time from others. This meant that he did not feel constrained by the political compromises felt to be needed by those working in the UN system. An example is his work on a universal child benefit. The chapter in the 2009 book argues for 'a currency transfer tax for a universal child benefit ... [which would] ... pave the way for the emergence of social security systems in low-income countries on a scale that will eventually compare with that of the OECD [Organisation for Economic Co-operation and Development] countries' (Townsend, 2009c, p 164). Although desirable, this goes ahead of what many in UNICEF and other agencies would currently regard as realisable.

In his 'Introduction' and 'Overview' chapters addressing social security we find his view that:

> ... national and international bodies may be obliged in the next few years to choose between two alternative grand strategies in the developing countries: (1) staged progress towards a major public system of social security costing more than 10% of GDP; and (2) conditional public cash transfer schemes targeting the extreme poor

> and costing less than 3 % of GDP. (Townsend, 2009b, p 19)

Peter's sympathies lie with the former but there is unfortunately no detailed engagement with how the Global Social Floor campaign could move from the second to the first. The need, for example, for the ILO to shift focus from social security benefits based on work to social protection benefits based on citizenship or residence is needed to facilitate this and is something Peter would have been sympathetic to.

There are criticisms of the Global Social Floor campaign that would have resonated with Peter's vision for a comprehensive social policy and his cautiousness about seemingly progressive developments in the UN. For example, one of us has argued that 'The global social floor or minimum social protection packages being argued for by … the ILO and … UNDESA are still essentially packages for the poor' (Deacon, 2009). The issue to be addressed is the solidarity needed between the poor, the working class and the middle class, and especially the role of the middle class in building decent societies for all. Effectively functioning states that meet the welfare needs of their citizens and residents do so because they meet the welfare needs of all social groups. This idea was central to Peter's 2009 book, *Building decent societies*.

What remains to be done

Peter campaigned for all countries to establish comprehensive social security systems based on the most progressive examples in Europe. He foresaw a world that paid for child benefits for all children out of revenues raised from TNCs and the rich via an international currency transactions tax. He wanted the UN to be strengthened and The World Bank to be marginalised. He wanted TNCs to be held accountable for the damage they caused and for their policies to be socially responsible. He argued that new legal frameworks were needed to hold TNCs democratically accountable and to compel them to fund social insurance or tax-funded benefits in low-income countries (Yeates, 2010a).

What is needed is political action focused on the establishment of what Peter called an 'international welfare state' which would take the form of universal right of access to social security, basic healthcare, education, housing – the need to introduce schemes where they do not exist and develop them where they do but are not universal. To pay for these rights, countries should allocate 1% of their GNP for overseas development assistance. There should be new operational specification of fair trade; the removal of protective agricultural and other subsidies (tariff and non-tariff barriers) in rich countries; and the introduction of domestic food production and fair price standard for food commodities. In terms of UN reform, the representation of populous countries and the poorest 100 countries needs to be increased especially on economic and social committees: there should be progress in stages to equal representation of regions by population size. He wanted strong world–regional policy alliances – collaborative working relationships between regional/global policy actors – led by the UN. He emphasised the need for the UN to lead this, working in conjunction with governments, but also with inputs from scientific advisers and NGOs.

In this context, it is worth returning to the significance of the four-page manifesto that forms the Appendix to *World poverty* (Townsend and Gordon, 2002). This document remains one of the most progressive and far-sighted global social policy and governance manifestos available. A checklist of current global campaigns would include many if not all of these demands. Progress is now being made on an international financial activities tax that even the IMF report to the G20 in April 2010 considers could form a source of government revenues (http://blog-imfdirect.imf.org/2010/04/25/fair-and-substantial%e2%80%94taxing-the-financial-sector), on a global social protection floor, on strengthened regions and UN reform. But much more remains to be done if Peter's progressive globalist vision is to be realised. These steps include the delivery of promised increased overseas international development assistance; the earmarking of the funds generated by a new global tax for social protection and child benefit purposes to match the existing global health and education funds; the further democratisation of the UN and its strengthening with independent funds; and the replacement of the Global Compact with a global legal set of regulations and obligations placed on TNCs.

Peter's concerns were not only with global campaigning but also about the subject area of social policy, poverty and health and housing studies. Advancing Peter's vision of global social policy would require a shift in the focus of social policy. Most social policy remains parochial and British, at best comparative, with a focus on Europe. The global analysis of poverty in the UK and elsewhere that he pressed for has been ignored by many or only partially responded to. It was this issue rather than issues of domestic social policy that he emphasised as being of particular significance and concern at his 80th birthday celebrations at the London School of Economics and Political Science (LSE) and at the acceptance of his Social Policy Association Lifetime Achievement Award in 2009. If only a fraction of the intellectual effort devoted by academic scholars were refocused on social policy in other parts of the world, on the transnational processes that impact on social policy and social development, and the social and economic policies of international organisations, then Peter's long-standing vision of a globalist discipline would be realised. This would require too that such internationalised scholars followed in his footsteps and not only engaged with UK ministries and social movements and the EU Commission, but also talked to and worked with the ILO, WHO, UN Development Programme (UNDP), UNICEF, The World Bank and global social movements. It would require too an active dialogue with scholars of development studies, international relations and international organisations. Steps in this direction have been taken but much more work of this kind is needed. Funding authorities need to refocus too on the transnational and global aspects of social policy much more centrally. Too often what passes for 'global' programmes of social policy research by national and global institutions are no more than 'extended internationalism' (Yeates, 2008b, p 10) that simply seek to examine ever more varieties of national social policy around the world. Although the scope of analysis may have extended beyond the rich (OECD) countries, neither adherence to methodological nationalism nor ignorance of transnational processes of social policy formation have diminished.

Conclusion

We conclude by reiterating that Peter was a pioneer of global social policy analysis before the term was even invented. Since the 1960s his work evidenced a passionate commitment to a global analysis of poverty and to the eradication of poverty wherever it was manifested. Freedom from want, he argued, has no geographical limit. This analysis was undoubtedly made possible by his engagement with radical sociology and development studies as the field of social policy was beginning to emerge from its social administration origins. Part of his legacy to us is to have us understand better how the logics that inform the treatment of poverty in one place also realise themselves in other places. He made no distinctions between the worth of human lives based on social origin, national background or country of residence.

An articulate and passionate supporter of scholarly and political campaigns for a coherent global social policy based on democratic socialism, his agenda was far more radical than the pastiche of global social democracy that passes for contemporary global social policy. His commitment to a materialist analysis of world poverty and insistence on the need for comprehensive global social planning and investment alongside radical democratisation of global and national institutions, although often unpopular among elements of both the political left and the political right, found him many more friends and allies worldwide. Peter's policy contributions to the field remain desirable and far more radical than what is actually developing in practice and will stand the test of time. His legacy remains for the current and future generations of the international community of social policy scholars, students, activists and reformers to catch up on and – crucially – to act on.

A tall order, it may seem. But, perhaps, on closer inspection it is not so unrealistic. Politicians have injected unprecedented amounts of public money into supporting the banking industry, and are prepared to contemplate taxing financial transactions and massive cross-national subsidies to support the greening and cleaning of industry in the Global South. In this respect, Peter's policy manifesto for eradicating world poverty looks a reasonable and realisable programme for a global democratic socialist order that makes meaningful global social redistribution, regulation and rights a matter of the first priority.

Notes

[1] This chapter incorporates revised and extended versions of Nicola Yeates' plenary address to the Peter Townsend Memorial Conference at Conway Hall, London, 20 November 2009, parts of which were published in *Global Social Policy Forum*, vol 10, no 2, dedicated to the memory of Peter (Yeates, 2010b).

[2] Peter was a consultant to the UN (1993-95) during the preparations for, and at, the World Summit for Social Development at Copenhagen in March 1995. He felt that this influenced his later work on world poverty and policies to combat it. Thus, many of the activities in the last decade of his life revolved around the Copenhagen initiative, attempting to establish scientific measures of 'absolute' and 'overall' poverty.

References

Adepoju, A. (2007) *Migration in sub-Saharan Africa. A background paper commissioned by the Nordic Africa Institute for the Swedish Government White Paper on Africa* (www.sweden.gov.se/content/1/c6/08/88/66/730473a9.pdf).

Deacon, B. (2009) 'From the global politics of poverty alleviation to the global politics of welfare state (re)building', Presented at a Panel on the Role of Social Research and Social Policy (CROP-CLASCO-CODESERIA), World Social Science Forum (WSSF), Bergen, 10–12 May.

Esping-Andersen, G. (1990) *The three worlds of welfare capitalism*, Cambridge: Polity Press.

Gordon, D., Nandy, S., Pantazis, C., Pemberton, S. and Townsend, P. (2003) *Child poverty in the developing world*, Bristol: The Policy Press.

ILO (International Labour Organization) (2004) *Economic security for a better world*, Geneva: ILO.

ILO (2008) *Can low-income countries afford basic social security? Social security policy briefings*, Social Security Department, Paper 3, Geneva: ILO.

Townsend, P. (ed) (1970) *The concept of poverty*, London: Heinemann.

Townsend, P. (1979) *Poverty in the UK: A survey of household resources and standards of living*, London: Penguin.

Townsend, P. (1992) 'The international welfare state', *Fabian Review*, vol 105, no 2, pp 3-6.

Townsend, P. (1993) *The international analysis of poverty*, Hemel Hempstead: Harvester Wheatsheaf.

Townsend, P. (2002) 'Poverty, social exclusion and social polarisation: the need to construct an international welfare state', in P. Townsend and D. Gordon (eds) *World poverty: New policies to defeat an old enemy*, Bristol: The Policy Press, pp 3-24.

Townsend, P. (2006) '"Absolute" and "overall" poverty: the 1995 Copenhagen approach to the fulfilment of human rights', *Global Social Policy*, vol 6, issue 3, pp 284-7.

Townsend, P. (2008a) 'Foreword', in N. Yeates (ed) *Understanding global social policy*, Bristol: The Policy Press, pp xx-xxiii.

Townsend, P. (2008b) *The 2009 Minority Report on The World Bank*, London: Fabian Society.

Townsend, P. (2008c) *The abolition of child poverty and the right to social security: A possible UN model for child benefit?*, A report to the ILO, GTZ and DfiD, London: Lulu Press.

Townsend, P. (ed) (2009a) *Building decent societies: Rethinking the role of social security in development*, Basingstoke: Palgrave.

Townsend, P. (2009b) 'Introduction', in P. Townsend (ed) *Building decent societies: Rethinking the role of social security in development*, Basingstoke: Palgrave, ch 1.

Townsend, P. (2009c) 'Investment in social security: a possible UN model for Child Benefit?', in P. Townsend (ed) *Building decent societies: Rethinking the role of social security in development*, Basingstoke: Palgrave, ch 7.

Townsend, P. and Donkor, K. (1996) *Global restructuring and social policy: The need to establish an international welfare state*, Bristol: The Policy Press.

Townsend, P. and Gordon, D. (2002) 'Manifesto: international action to defeat poverty', in P. Townsend and D. Gordon (eds) in *World poverty: New policies to defeat an old enemy*, Bristol: The Policy Press, Appendix A.

UN (United Nations) CEB (Chief Executives Board) (2009) *The global financial crisis and its impact on the work of the UN system*, UN CEB Issue Paper.

Walker, A. and Walker, C. (eds) (2009) *Peter Townsend 1928–2009 (Memorial Booklet)*, Bristol: The Policy Press.

Yeates, N. (ed) (2008a) *Understanding global social policy*, Bristol: The Policy Press.

Yeates, N. (2008b) 'The idea of global social policy', in N. Yeates (ed) *Understanding global social policy*, Bristol: The Policy Press, pp 1-24.

Yeates, N. (2009) *Globalising care economies and migrant workers: Explorations in global care chains*, Basingstoke: Palgrave.

Yeates, N. (2010a) 'From welfare state to international welfare', Section II in A. Walker et al (eds) *The Peter Townsend reader*, Bristol: The Policy Press.

Yeates, N. (ed) (2010b) 'Human rights and global social policy: in memory of Professor Peter Townsend (1928–2009)', *Global Social Policy*, vol 10, no 2, pp 1-21.

FOURTEEN

Conclusion: building on the legacy of Peter Townsend

Alan Walker and Carol Walker

The main objectives of this book, set out in Chapter One, were, first, to encourage and support a concerted campaign against poverty, inequality and social injustice and, second, to provide a reasoned case for a new approach to social policy aimed at achieving the goal of social justice. The inspiration behind the book and its objectives is Peter Townsend and, specifically, his consistent, dogged pursuit of social justice in every aspect of his public life: education, research, writing and campaigning. The book's subtitle, referring to a 'manifesto', is intended to capture the idea of a public statement of policy on behalf of those who are, at the very least, offended by the present scale of inequality and social injustice in the UK and globally, and who want to do something about it. The form that such action might take should not be prescribed to allow for a multitude of different contributions aimed at changing society rather than expecting that there could be a single movement. Here we have followed Peter's lead and emphasised teaching, research/ scholarship and campaigning. It is also essential to recognise the very special nature of Peter Townsend. There are very few who can aspire to emulate his almost all-consuming passion, commitment and sustained campaigning zeal and, for health reasons, we would not recommend that anyone tries to do so!

The preceding chapters have provided the major contributions to the book's objectives. In this final chapter we summarise the key elements of the manifesto for social justice that the contributors have proposed. We then consider the challenges that this presents to the major constituency that Peter addressed throughout his life, policy makers. Finally, we turn inwards, to our own colleagues and students of social policy, to encourage them to be inspired by Peter's legacy, to take up the torch of social justice and, in doing so, to become more public in their campaign. As we approached this final chapter we were very conscious of what Peter might have said in particular about the Coalition government's programme of public expenditure cuts. We hope that we have represented him fairly.

The prize of social justice

The shared understanding of social justice among the book's contributors has remained implicit to this point, as it is in much of Peter's work. There is no doubt where he stood, however, and we are with him four-square: social justice should be understood and applied in terms of the equalisation of life chances (Townsend, 1958, 1979, 2009). This does not imply perfect equality, although it will be caricatured as such, but a clear distinction between individual or personal differences between people in terms, for example, of intelligence and identity, and social differences derived from the structure and organisation of society (and the wider global society). No one has captured this distinction more eloquently than R.H. Tawney, which is why this passage is so often quoted:

> So to criticise and to desire equality is not, as is sometimes suggested, to cherish the romantic illusion that men are equal in character and intelligence. It is to hold that, while their natural endowment differ profoundly, it is the work of a civilised society to aim at eliminating such inequalities as have their source, not in individual differences but in its own organisation, and that individual differences, which are a source of social energy, are more likely to ripen and find expression if social inequalities are, as far as practicable, diminished. (Tawney, 1964, p 57)

The evidence was scant on the last point when Tawney wrote it, but is now extensive (see, for example, Wilkinson and Pickett, 2009; Dorling, 2010; Hutton, 2010). The term 'fairness' has been so severely abused by politicians, not least Coalition ministers, that there is a danger that it will have to be forfeited. But its abuse and misuse must be challenged to avoid losing the rich Rawlsian interpretation of justice as fairness, in which inequality may be tolerated providing it is to the benefit of the least well-off, and 'injustice' is 'inequalities that are not to the benefit of all' (Rawls, 1973, p 62).

If it is to be achieved, this idea of social justice as equality must be embedded in institutions, as Rawls argued. But just institutions are not sufficient; there must be open opportunities for individuals and groups to take action to promote social justice, and there must be some social assessment and guarantee of realisation (Sen, 2010). Because of the vast number of interdependent interests that are globalised, it is essential too that the concept of social justice that is applied in practice is a global one. Arguably too, social participation should be at the heart of social justice (see below).

When Peter started out on his campaign for social justice he emphasised the moral case for equality – the fact that it is not acceptable, in a civilised society, for people to live in poverty or with reduced life chances. In the midst of postwar optimism this idealistic appeal was a natural starting point (Townsend, 1958). Throughout the main part of his career he built the empirical case for equality, alongside the moral one, demonstrating, for example, the social and economic costs of unemployment and health inequalities. In his late career he turned to a human rights orientation – it is a matter of human rights to abolish poverty and to reduce inequality.

A manifesto for social justice

In this chapter we can do no more than summarise the key components of this manifesto, as they are drawn down from the previous chapters. We must also acknowledge that, because our starting point is the work of one person, there are bound to be omissions from the following list. For example, Peter did not research, teach or campaign in the field of environmental justice and, therefore, it does not figure in this manifesto. It is to be hoped that others, from different fields, with a similar commitment to social justice, will add to this first manifesto draft to extend and refine it.

Developing the research agenda

In Chapters Two and Three Peter's special contribution as a pioneering social researcher was demonstrated. Paramount was his concern to ensure that the reality of the lives of normally powerless and excluded people were able to surface above broad generalisations and the quantitative data that increasingly was required to give research findings legitimacy in political debate. Despite, or because of, the political rhetoric and 'tick box' approach to user engagement and participation, the powerless and excluded still struggle to have their voices heard, other than through (predominantly middle-class) intermediaries. The need to continue to improve techniques to engage 'the researched' in the research process has been a recurring theme, most notably in respect to children (Chapter Six), older people (Chapter Ten) and disabled people (Chapter Eleven). Ruth Lister asks researchers to redress the marginalisation within poverty research of minority groups, for example Gypsies and Travellers, and refugees or asylum seekers and their children.

On poverty and inequality

- There must be a renewed campaign to provide an adequate income sufficient to enable people to live decently and with dignity, in work, out of work and in older age.
- A structural analysis of poverty must be reasserted to counter the resurgence of more individual and cultural explanations (Chapter Six), which not only dominate the debates around 'welfare' (Chapter Seven) but also on inequalities in health (Chapter Nine) and provision for older people and disabled people (Chapters Ten and Eleven).
- There is a need to influence public attitudes towards poverty. This requires, as Peter argued (1958, p 530), for the case to be made to restore 'a faith in people ... to give them the benefit of the doubt; to assume that they have good rather than bad motives when we know little or nothing about them, and to concern ourselves with their needs rather than their failings'. This necessitates constant rebuttal of the negative stereotypes of 'scroungers' and benefits as a 'lifestyle choice' that politicians and the media so like to promote.

- It is necessary to combat social divisions of class, age, gender, ethnicity and disability and also divisions between the 'deserving' and the 'undeserving', between workers and the workless, and between generations.
- Peter was committed to arguing that poverty could not be abolished without also addressing the problem of the rich. The excesses of income and wealth (Chapter Eight) must be redressed through an effective and progressive tax system. The incorrect perception of the UK as a high tax nation must be countered (see below). Tax avoidance and evasion exceeds the losses through benefit fraud many times over, and deserves to be treated with at least as much rigour and opprobrium. Further analysis is needed of how the rich and powerful exercise their agency to preserve their privileges and to pass them down to their children (Chapters Six and Eight).
- There should be greater integration of human rights and anti-poverty work, both nationally and internationally (Chapters Six and Twelve), which can reframe the poverty debate and influence the way public services treat people. Human rights should be taken out of the hands of the lawyers and put into the hands of civil society and social rights in particular, embedded in any given culture via the political (not the judicial) process.

A defence of universalism

- There should be a universal child benefit and a universal basic pension paid at a level that enables full participation in society.
- The widespread acceptance, nationally and internationally, that means-tested benefits are the more efficient and effective way of helping the poor must be countered (Chapters Four, Five, Six, Seven, Eight and Thirteen). Only universal benefits and services can reach all of the poor and have the potential, if paid at a sufficient level, to *prevent* poverty and to avoid the social divisions inevitable in any means-tested system or where the individual has to pay, for example, for healthcare (Chapter Seven).

The case for the welfare state

- The case for the welfare state as part of the solution must be pressed, countering its presentation as part of the problem – illustrated in the actions of the Coalition government in its first six months in office (see below).
- A scientific analysis is needed of the impact of the changing balance between private and public sectors in relation to the welfare state (Chapter Ten), and the impact that the neoliberal approach has had on many aspects of welfare provision and social inequality. There is a need for more policy research to distinguish the myths from the reality of market-oriented welfare reforms including, for example, the impact of 'the medical poverty trap' (Chapter Nine).
- The welfare state needs to be an instrument for the prevention of poverty and inequality rather than a reactive agency responding to the innumerable inadequacies of other social and economic policies.

International social policy

- The discipline of social policy should be less parochial (Chapter Thirteen), looking beyond Europe (Chapter Thirteen) and especially the US (Chapters Eight and Nine), and should follow Peter's example of working with international organisations such as the International Labour Organization (ILO) and the United Nations (UN). Social policy should engage more with development studies and international relations.
- Support should be given to the introduction of a financial transactions tax such as the Tobin tax, known popularly as the 'Robin Hood tax'.
- At least one per cent of gross domestic product (GDP) should be allocated to overseas development aid.

Realising social justice

To those familiar with Peter's work or seasoned in the campaign for social justice there will not be much that is novel in this manifesto.

Both the evidence concerning the damage that poverty and inequality do to individuals and society as a whole and the measures that should be taken to eliminate them are already well known, not least as a result of Peter's lifelong contributions (see also Wilkinson and Pickett, 2009; Dorling 2010; Marmot, 2010). The key question is, why has a progressive programme to promote social justice not been introduced long before now? This is essentially a political question which, posed in sharper terms, means: why has the political will to realise social justice been largely absent from Britain? The 1945–50 Labour government must be exempt from this question because it built the foundations of the welfare state in an unparalleled burst of social reforming zeal, despite a massive budget deficit and the mammoth task of postwar reconstruction (Timmins, 1995). Although minimalist with respect to social security (as intended by its main architect), the original British welfare state model contained clear universal principles with regard to health, education, child benefits (family allowances), National Insurance and employment.

The problem is that, first, as Peter pointed out originally (Chapter One), the policy makers, press and public were lulled into a false sense of security by the great social reforms of the immediate postwar period. As a consequence poverty had to be 'rediscovered'. Second, in comparison with most other forms of welfare state in Western Europe, the British one has always been a basic minimal Anglo-Saxon special case, usually grouped with Ireland (and non-European countries such as Australia and the US) in welfare regime typologies (Esping-Andersen, 1990). Subsequent governments set about welfare state reform by, at best, adding to the original structure in a piecemeal way, superannuation here, disability benefits there, until 1979 when the full force of neoliberal opposition to the very idea of a welfare state was given rein. From this point the vision of a society characterised by social justice withered as a part, that is, of a government programme, although not as an aspiration among many campaigning groups and, briefly, the Labour Party. The Thatcher governments pursued a strategy of inequality (Walker, 1990; Walker and Walker, 1981, 1997). The New Labour governments of Blair and Brown might have set about turning the tide of inequality, and there were important steps taken in this direction, notably the target to end child poverty by

2020, and some heart-warming rhetoric. Unfortunately, however, the scale of socioeconomic inequality climbed remorselessly during the first decade of the present century (Chapter Eight).

Those who shy away from the promotion of social justice, including apparently many at the heart of the New Labour project, opine that Britain is a conservative country ill suited for or unwilling to accept Scandinavian-style social institutions. The evidence points in another direction. Although public opinion is notoriously difficult to interpret (and after all, politicians are mainly interested in electoral salience), the British Social Attitudes survey data show a consistent majority in favour of the universal welfare state heartland, such as the NHS and National Insurance pensions, saying that they are willing to pay higher taxes and contributions to fund them (Park et al, 2008; Taylor-Gooby, 1998). While we may not expect Conservatives to pursue social justice when in office, the same cannot be said for Labour (or Liberal Democrat) administrations.

The failings of Labour governments on this front have been catalogued extensively, led by Peter himself in, for example, *Labour and inequality* (1972), and *Labour and equality* (1980), both with Nick Bosanquet. Like Peter we would not want to imply that the story is one of complete failure because, as noted above, there have been important progressive measures. But the failings are massive and take two forms. On the one hand, the response to vested interests, for example in private education, the media and the City of London, has been slavish. The growth of monstrous wealth holdings became an infamous cause for celebration. On the other hand, rather than seeking to encourage, develop and nurture the very decent strand of belief among British people favouring fairness and the public good, New Labour politicians joined their Conservative counterparts in following the path of least resistance. Rhetoric concerning public sector 'profligacy' and welfare 'scroungers' not only makes existing claimants feel bad, deters other potential ones and undermines staff morale, but it also performs an anti-social function to distance the claimant or service user from the rest of society, or to 'other' them (Lister, 2007).

It is too soon, as we write, to pass any considered judgement on the Coalition government elected in May 2010, but the early signs are not promising. Thatcher-style anti-welfare state rhetoric was in full flow following the general election (although not during it), and substantial cuts in social security benefits and a major transgression of the universalism of Child Benefit were early government announcements. The case advanced against universalism is a mixture of opportunism and more deep-running ideology. Thus, it is argued, for example, by Chancellor George Osborne in his Conservative Party Conference speech on 4 October 2010, that the removal of Child Benefit from those paying the higher rate of Income Tax has to be done in order to reduce the budget deficit. It is also argued that it is wrong and even 'morally unjust' for high earners to receive state support (or, in the word of the Secretary of State for Work and Pensions, 'bonkers'). The long-standing Conservative ideological opposition to universalism has been given an unexpected but clearly welcome opportunity by the deficit. In addition, the Liberal Democrats appear to be legitimating the government's essentially Conservative anti-welfare intentions. Add to this the absence of critical commentary by the mainstream press and broadcast media, and the prospects for a more enlightened approach look decidedly bleak.

The need for universalism

What, then, can be done to promote social justice, for example, the priority list of actions such as the one outlined above, in the midst of such political hostility to the idea? It is clear that a new approach is required to policy and politics, including the immediate politics of the budget deficit. First of all it is essential to restate unequivocally the case for universalism because that is the bedrock of a strategy to realise social justice. It was a huge failing of the 1997–2010 New Labour governments that this case was never made forcefully and in the persistent way necessary to embed it in the public consciousness. As Peter demonstrated countless times (restated in Chapters Four, Five and Seven), universal entitlement to social security is essential for two main reasons: to ensure, first, that all of those eligible actually receive it and, second, that the whole nation is involved together in the process of solidarity which supports those ends identified collectively as social priorities. This act of solidarity, which is also the most efficient method of social security benefit allocation, should be proclaimed as the cornerstone of a decent society. This does not mean that there should be no targeting of benefits but, unfortunately, this term has been hijacked in political usage as a euphemism for means testing. In fact child benefits are targeted at families with children and pensions at older people. It would be possible to make a big inroad into pensioner poverty by targeting a universal benefit on all those aged 80 and over where poverty is concentrated. Nor does the principle of solidarity mean that all existing universal entitlements are sacrosanct. It is debatable, for example, whether everyone should receive a Winter Fuel Payment when they reach the age of 60: these are poorly targeted universal benefits that were introduced to disguise the inadequacy of the basic pension. It would be much better to raise the basic pension to an adequate level and provide help to those in late old age, as already indicated.

A new approach to policy and politics would valorise universalism as an expression of solidarity, in recognition of common humanity and the shared national interest in minimising inequality and maximising the well-being of the worse off. A large body of evidence, which Peter pioneered, now demonstrates that the most unequal societies have the highest levels of social problems (Wilkinson and Pickett, 2009). Universalism acknowledges that there *is* such a thing as society, in direct contradiction of Margaret Thatcher's infamous contrary assertion. In practical terms this includes supporting the task of childrearing, ensuring that disabled people receive an appropriate income to meet their needs, as a right, and that people in retirement have adequate incomes. It also means providing income maintenance at times of unemployment. As argued above, in line with Peter's legacy, these social benefits must be sufficient to enable participation in society. There are individual responsibilities that match these social rights of citizenship, as argued by Beveridge (1942), and in a capitalist society, the chief responsibility is always paid work. But universalism entails responsibilities for governments too, extending beyond the organisation of social security or social services and the means to pay for them. This includes continuing education and training to ensure that workers are well equipped to compete in the labour market, with opportunities to update their skills, and regulation to promote not only safety but also the absence of discrimination and the payment of at least a living wage.

In these various ways universalism creates and reinforces social bonds and a common national interest in the promotion of well-being for all. In contrast, selectivity breaks down and prevents social bonds, and sets certain groups apart from the rest of society by labelling and stigmatising them. It reinforces inequality by providing a legitimation for differences in outcomes that may be the result of class-based privilege, such as inheritance, or good or bad luck, but which are boiled down to some variant of the deserving/undeserving dichotomy.

Fair taxation

Alongside universalism in social security and social services the realisation of social justice depends on a fair and progressive tax system. The myth that has survived for too long is that Britain's tax system is progressive. It is not, as government statistics have been showing for years. Public debate focuses on progressive Income Tax, but it is the total impact of all taxes that matters. Overall this is broadly proportional, but regressive for the poorest households. In 2008–09 36.2% of the income of the poorest fifth went in taxes, 33.5% of the average and only 33.9% of the richest fifth, and that is even after Council Tax relief and tax credits (Barnard, 2010, Table 3).

The myth is reinforced because the very system of progressive Income Tax that is widely assumed to reduce inequality also serves to maintain it by redistributing upward as well as downward. Tax reliefs are regressive, 'upside-down' benefits of much greater value to those paying higher rates of tax. So not surprisingly Income Tax receipts are reduced by at least 10% as the top 10% of taxpayers exploit the tax reliefs over and above the personal allowance with the help of an industry of tax advisers. In 2004–05 the top one tenth of the top 1% – some 47,000 people – were estimated to benefit by nearly £50,000 each. With a pre-tax income 31 times the average, they benefited from tax reliefs 86 times the average, considerably enhancing their already unequal position at enormous cost to the common wealth (Brewer et al, 2008, Table 1). A universal maximum of £5,000 or

£10,000 limit to benefits from tax reliefs over and above the personal allowance would be simple and fair.

In considering how the state redistributes life chances, let alone in tackling current budget problems, there has been a failure to recognise that who contributes and how is just as important as who benefits and how. The credit crunch crisis has revealed anew how in a market-dominated society some are better insulated both from sharing common risks and from contributing to the public resources needed to protect the quality of life for all, while others are deprived and many more made insecure. Tactics designed to reduce solidaristic contributions to public resources have been regarded as both smart and desirable – and not only by those using them – with little regard for the losses to the whole society.

The limits of redistribution

Universalism and a progressive tax system are two policy essentials for social justice but there is a further one that must be added if this goal is to be achieved. The Butskellite consensus of the immediate postwar years saw the welfare state as a form of redistribution within or across generations (mostly the former). In this consensus, which still holds today, it is believed that income is 'earned'. In other words, it is due to the efforts of the individual wage or salary earner and, therefore, it is their right to hold on to it. Their income is believed to reflect their innate and individually developed abilities and talents rather than being an accident of birth, say, or the bargaining power of their occupational group or sheer good or bad fortune. This individualistic notion of just deserts is a fundamental assumption of capitalism: individual effort results in an appropriate income level that is then, by right, converted into consumption. It implies a judgement concerning contribution. Those who contribute most (who work hardest) get the most back, and vice versa. The flaws in this simplistic model are obvious and well documented, not least by feminists who have pointed to the often hidden but essential contribution of unpaid labour. Also it is applied with widely different levels of intensity in different variants of capitalism that sanction different levels of de-commodification (Esping-Andersen, 1990). The Anglo-Saxon model tends to be the most individualistic in this respect, at least among Western European welfare states.

An alternative perspective is that income and wealth are generated collectively, the combined product of myriad social and economic relationships rather than individual 'wealth generators'. Therefore a collective judgement about distribution, not only redistribution, and just deserts is called for. We are following Peter in posing this alternative (see, for example, Cripps et al, 1981). Politicians, especially Labour ones, have tended to assume that redistribution alone can produce a more socially just society. (Under the New Labour governments even this modest concept of redistribution had to be disguised as 'redistribution by stealth' to avoid appearing too left wing.) There also has to be more social influence exerted over the original distribution of income and wealth. Again, the mechanisms to do this are available – a participation standard for earnings, going beyond a minimum wage; a maximum wage; abolition of regressive tax reliefs; social ownership of pension funds; taxes on land ownership; and a highly progressive wealth tax. The big question, however, concerns their translation into a formal policy programme and then legislation. This takes us back to the key question of political will and the equally important one of the scope for manoeuvre in a class-bound society that is dominated by vested interests wielding huge political power. It has been argued throughout this book that there must be a new approach to policy that builds on Peter's legacy. In reviewing the evidence presented earlier, we are forced to the conclusion that there has to be a new approach to politics as well if social justice is to be a realistic prospect. This would necessarily include more direct forms of democratic participation, such as citizens' juries (Coote and Lenaghan, 1997), or even more radical forms of empowered democratic governance (Wright, 2010).

Campaigning for social justice

It hardly needs restating that Peter was a Fabian socialist par excellence. He was part, therefore, of a train of thinking stretching back to the 18th-century European Enlightenment 'which saw clear-headed reasoning as a major ally in the desire to make societies better' (Sen,

2010, p 34). The experience of the last 30 years, however, teaches us once again, as Peter recognised, that clear-headed reasoning is not sufficient. Apart from the impossibility of penetrating the extreme of 'unreason' associated with ideological dogma, governments of both main political parties have not been very open to arguments for social justice, regardless of how persuasively they were put. This indicates a limitation of parliamentary democracy in that the chance for public influence is restricted to elections and now, increasingly, subject to the powerful sway of vested interests in business and the media. In between elections there is virtually no opportunity for public influence and, in contrast, the lobby groups representing sectional self-interests have open access to the policy-making process. In addition there is the inevitability that power will corrupt, not necessarily in the financial sense but, more often in the development of dogmatic egoism.

This is why some, such as J.K. Galbraith (1952) and Barbara Wootton (1945, 1955), have pressed the case for social institutions to act as a 'countervailing power' in the exercise of government. In a similar vein Peter argued for social planning and, specifically, for a government department charged with this task. He also made a strong case for such planning at a global level (Chapter Thirteen). We might update this argument and propose that alongside the 'independent' Office for Budget Responsibility should be placed an Office for Social Justice. It would have a remit to promote social justice in policy making across government departments, to subject all major policies to a social justice audit and to prepare an annual plan highlighting progress and the main priorities for action. It may not happen soon but the very proposal serves to contrast the sort of institutional development necessary for social justice with those favoured by free market liberals and, we might add, the other polar extreme of a communist utopia of social ownership of the means of production. Indeed we believe strongly that the flawed certainty of totalitarianism must be rejected in favour of a plural, trial and error, approach.

What matters most is that the goal of social justice is uppermost and that the means adopted to achieve it do not violate that aim. What Peter sought was an open public discourse on social justice, and this book is intended to encourage this to develop. It would not be a discourse among 'impartial spectators' in Adam Smith's (1976) 18th-century formulation but, rather, a very partial one, with the intention of making the case for a broad, inclusive coalition in favour of social justice. In other words, it is not sufficient to make the case to power in the form of clear-headed reasoning, Fabian style, even when armed with the most robust evidence. Ideological certainty is impervious to such reason and, in practice, the neoliberalism that has dominated policy making in Britain and globally for the past 30 years is fundamentally indifferent to social justice. Such efforts are important nonetheless because they can contribute to social progress by, for example, the education of officials and the wider public, and might also have a role to play in coalition building. In addition there is a need for public campaigns, both against policy changes that threaten to worsen poverty, inequality and social injustice, and for an alternative approach aimed at combating those social evils. Every opportunity must be taken, from grass-roots activism to national events, to join up apparently disparate campaigns into a united theme of social justice. There is common cause in universalism and intergenerational solidarity between, for example, campaigners against child and pensioner poverty. This is a tall order and will not yield quick results. It demands time and energy and there may be personal insults to be born, as Peter had to. But a great deal is at stake: what kind of society do we want to live in?

The politics of the deficit

A concrete starting point in the UK is the politics of the deficit. Although this issue overarches public discussion as we go to press, and may well have morphed into another form by the time of publication, it is a useful heuristic focus because the discourses involved are almost identical to those employed by the first Thatcher government and are perennial neoliberal formulations. Back then, in the face of a budget deficit, it was asserted, first, that 'there is no alternative' to public expenditure cuts because 'public expenditure is at the heart of Britain's economic difficulties' (HM Treasury, 1979, p 1). The contemporary version is that deep and immediate cuts in public expenditure in order to reduce the deficit are unavoidable.

Second, the attack on public expenditure by the Thatcher government in 1979 was justified on the spurious economic grounds that investment in the public sector 'crowds out' investment in the private sector. This thesis gained some currency in the mid-1970s (Bacon and Eltis, 1976) but was exposed as merely a new version of the public burden of welfare idea that had no scientific basis (Walker et al, 1979; Walker, 1984). Nonetheless it was seized on by the Thatcher government because it appeared to provide scientific legitimacy for ideological conviction and became an oft-quoted 'truth' in the case for spending cuts. The then Chancellor of the Exchequer, Geoffrey Howe's first Budget speech contains remarkable parallels with the current deficit discourse. For example, the third of his four principles was 'the reduction in the borrowing requirement of the public sector [the deficit in present parlance] that leaves room for the rest of the economy to prosper' (*Hansard*, vol 968, 12 June 1979, vol 240). Today we are told with equal certainty that cuts in the public sector will be compensated for by growth in the private sector (although in the present circumstances, apparently no scientific evidence needs to be adduced). The fact that 30 years ago the cuts discourse was accompanied by an appeal to 'Victorian values' of self and community help, which has parallels with the present 'big society' idea, is beyond the scope of this book. The main focus should be on a re-interpretation of the deficit discourse because that is providing the excuse for a massive attack on public spending, including a serious undermining of universalism.

In response to these ideologically driven assertions it is essential to try to recast the politics of the deficit in a more progressive direction. This is because the public sector is a crucial bastion of social justice and because the social costs of the deficit reduction strategy will not be evenly shared but, instead, fall hardest on those reliant on public services and social security, especially the poor and vulnerable. No amount of soothing rhetoric about fairness can stop this inevitability: the rich always have escape routes and are able to fashion their own good fortune. We are certainly not starry-eyed about the public sector and are aware of its tendencies towards bureau-professional self-interest. But we do believe, with Peter, that it can be reshaped in a form that more consistently empowers citizens.

There are three main avenues by which the politics of the deficit may be recast. First of all, as in the early 1980s, it is essential to question closely the evidence for the scale and speed of the actions being taken to reduce the deficit. This will demonstrate that the driver is an ideological necessity rather than an economic one. For example, we might question the prevailing judgement about the extent of the deficit. The debt threat has been blown out of proportion: it is large but not in historical terms (250% of GDP after the Second World War, never below 100% from 1920 to 1960, and 53% now). The UK has the lowest government debt as a proportion of GDP among the G7 countries (IMF, 2010). The Office for Budget Responsibility stated that the actual deficit was *less* than the previous Chancellor estimated in March 2010, and the rate of growth in the economy was slightly higher. Moreover it noted that the measures proposed in the March 2010 Budget would have halved the deficit in four years. Thus, in 2014/15, the structural deficit would be around 3% of GDP after implementing the cuts and tax increases proposed by the previous Labour government (OBR, 2010). With regard to the overall size of the public sector it is 45.3% of GDP in this country compared with an OECD (Organisation for Economic Co-operation and Development) average of 40.4%, 44.2% in Germany, 52% in Sweden and 52.6% in France. Public expenditure on social protection averages 20.6% in the OECD: 21.1% in the UK, 21.7% in Germany and 29.4% in Sweden (OECD, 2010). In the face of the assertion that there is no alternative, there are many, such as those listed earlier and, for example, a 50% tax rate on incomes over £100,000 (£4.7 billion p.a.), closing tax loopholes (£25 billion), a tax on vacant housing (£5 billion) and a Tobin tax (£20 billion) (Dolphin, 2010). It is also important to highlight the indiscriminate nature of the cuts such as scrapping the Future Jobs Fund, introduced by the previous government to provide guaranteed work for long-term unemployed young people. A less ideologically driven approach might have seen this fund as a tool to prevent a repeat of the 'lost generation' of young unemployed in the 1980s recession.

Second, a key sustained focus must be on the social consequences of the deficit reduction strategy and, in particular, the impact on poverty, inequality and social injustice. This is the route by which the assertion of 'fairness' can be cross-examined and a logical connection built between fairness in terms of allocation according to need or social justice. The first detailed assessment of the Coalition's policies by the Institute for Fiscal Studies (IFS), following the Emergency Budget in June 2010, revealed the harshness of the regressive outcome: the poorest 10% of households will lose 5% of their income as a result of the proposed changes between 2010 and 2014, while the top 10% will lose less than 1% (Browne and Levell, 2010). In the repeat of history as tragedy, it is the same groups of people that will lose the most as did after the 1980s budgets: poor working families with children and those dependent on social security benefits. The IFS reached the same negative conclusion on the Comprehensive Spending Review (CSR): by 2012/13 the impact on the net incomes of the poorest decile will be ten times greater than on the richest one and, by 2014/15, the impact on the former will be three times greater than on the latter (O'Dea, 2010). Treasury analysis of the CSR suggesting progressivity omitted reforms likely to fall heaviest on the poor, such as those to Housing Benefit, Employment and Support Allowance, Disability Living Allowance and Council Tax Benefit. In contrast to the heaviest burden of the deficit reduction strategy being imposed on the poorest, the total pay awarded to the top executives in the FTSE 100 companies rose by 55% between June 2009 and June 2010, a period in which the FTSE 100 rose by less than 20% (IDS, 2010). In the last decade these companies lost 19% in value but their chief executives' pay rose by 160% on average.

The third focus of attention must be the deficit discourse itself. As in previous eras the present discourse is designed to perform important political functions in terms of both legitimation and diverting attention from fundamental questions of causation and just deserts in financing the deficit. Thus, when attention is focused on the deficit, there is little opportunity to question the role of financial institutions in causing the global debt crisis and the need for radical reform of the international finance system. For example, the role of the credit rating agencies, held to be the arbiters of Britain's economic strategy, must be questioned. Rather than subjecting the banks' sub-prime mortgages to close scrutiny, or due diligence, in the lead-up to the financial collapse, they awarded them their highest market rating

– triple A. The question is why these private sector organisations, which are deeply implicated in the debt crisis, are suitable to assess the UK's credit worthiness rather than an international public authority. Similar questions should be directed at the deficit rhetoric. For example, the assertion that public investment will be replaced by private investment does not hold water. The National Institute of Economic and Social Research (NIESR) (Barrell, 2010) concludes that government spending cuts will reduce potential growth in every year from 2011 to 2015. The real driving force is a reprise of the Thatcher dogma that the public sector is too large. As the Treasury minister put it when winding up the debate on the 2010 Finance Bill, 'we cannot afford a public sector of the size to which it has grown'. Thus, in a stunning political sleight of hand, the government has turned a private financial crisis into a public sector one. Finally we must keep alive the alternative discourse on the purposes of growth, which had just got under way in the wake of the global debt crisis but was swamped by deficit reduction rhetoric (Stiglitz et al, 2009).

In sum we see possibilities for the politics of the deficit to be recast, first, to restate the importance of public investment as the basis for social justice and a decent society, as well as a growth stimulator; second, to question the purposes of economic change: the need for well-being rather than growth *per se*; third, to employ the discourse of national interest to try to emphasise common wealth and the shared nature of human welfare; and finally, to open up the argument towards *Building decent societies* worldwide, as Peter argued in his last book.

Challenges for social policy

Finally we turn to our own discipline, or area of study, social policy. In doing so we do not want to be exclusive and intend these comments for everyone with a policy interest. Peter's work has been woefully neglected in sociology especially but also in economics, political science, law and the humanities. What contribution should social policy be making to the creation of a socially just society? Peter's approach to social policy was a sociological one. Like his mentor Richard Titmuss, he was more interested in the functions that institutions perform rather than their particular administrative labels. He went further than Titmuss in articulating a thoroughly sociological definition of social policy, pointing to implicit as well as explicit social ends (1974, p x). This is the first challenge to social policy: to follow the vision that Peter articulated of a comprehensive social policy, not limited to government action, and global as well as national and local. Despite some exceptions, the mainstream remains largely confined within a rather narrow administrative paradigm. Peter himself might have done more to assist succeeding generations of students by expanding his initial ideas on the nature of social policy into a fully formulated model. But he directed his commitment to social policy as a vehicle for social change – to achieve social justice or 'a society for people' – rather than as an academic endeavour, and in this he proved to be outstanding, gaining many more than his share of important policy reforms. The challenge is to move out of the comfort zone of the welfare state and to grapple with social policy as, first, an analysis of social change, and then only second, as entailing administrative and institutional questions. In Peter's own words, there is a need for an 'articulation of social policy not as a fragmented, marginalised form of analysis, but as an analysis of social change, from which practical conclusions may be drawn' (Townsend, 1996, p 4). Here is an implicit challenge to sociologists to respond to Peter's sociological analysis of social policy because it conveys social rationales and has a direct impact on social structure.

The second related challenge concerns the subordination of social policy to economic policy. Peter started the analysis of the relationship between economic and social policy: 'it is impossible to have an economic policy which is not also a social policy' (Townsend, 1975, p 23). This critical insight might have been the basis for a close examination of this relationship not only from within social policy but in economics as well. Alas it has not been and still stands as an open challenge to social policy and the wider social sciences. It is straightforward to explain the subordination of social policy to economic policy (Townsend, 1975; Walker, 1984) but less so to construct an alternative relationship in both theoretical and practical terms. The challenge to economists is clear and is implicit in Tony Atkinson's analytical case study in Chapter Four. They need to be open about the social and especially the distributional consequences of their models, rather than leaving them in a separate box labelled 'all other things being equal'. They might also question the absence of social variables in many of the mathematical formulae that are the essence of contemporary economics.

The task for social policy is equally challenging. It is to articulate a rationale for the subject that extends beyond a minimalist construction concerned with government action in the field of welfare. If it stays there it will remain subordinate to economic policy and almost everything else. Again we do not want to be prescriptive because social policy is a broad church and there may be multiple paths towards a similar end. Some have tried to advance a 'productionist' perspective in which social policy is positioned as a factor of production (Berghman, 1998). The European Commission lent its weight to this endeavour to create legitimacy for social policy in the face of neoliberal economic policies (European Commission, 2000). Despite the progressive intentions, this approach appears to have had little tangible impact on the unequal relationship between the economic and the social, and there are fears that to reduce the defence of the welfare state to crude utilitarianism is to sacrifice the moral case for it (Bauman, 2000).

An alternative approach is that of social quality which, rather than trying to bolt social policy onto the side of economic policy, starts from first principles by asking what the meaning is of the 'social' in social policy. This direction was partly inspired by Peter's questioning of the nature of the social (Townsend, 1975). It comprises a complex sociological understanding of the social sphere – the tension between individual self-realisation and membership of the various collectivities that create identity – as well as practical yardsticks for measuring the extent of social quality, in terms of the extent of socioeconomic security, social cohesion, social inclusion and social empowerment (Beck et al, 1997, 2001). In this model the economic is subsumed within the social because all economic relations are also social ones. This opens the way for a possible re-alignment between economics and social policy, if not a re-fusion in the form of a new political economy then a re-awakening of social economics.

Social quality is not a neutral policy tool. It is underpinned by clear normative guidelines – social justice, solidarity, equal value and human dignity – and was spurred into existence as part of the reaction to the neoliberal-inspired attack on European welfare states in the 1990s. Perhaps most importantly, for social policy students seeking to enlarge their understanding of the scope and potential of this subject, the social quality approach provides a vision of society that reaches beyond minimum welfare or the solution to dire social problems such as poverty, a vision that is very much in the mould created by Peter Townsend:

> ... the extent to which people are able to participate in the social and economic life of their communities under conditions which enhance their well-being and individual potential. (Beck et al, 1997, p 2)

Following this formulation social justice becomes a matter of social participation.

The third challenge for social policy is to rehabilitate social planning. Peter's work, once again, is potentially inspirational in this regard. As he noted, in countless places, if major social problems such as poverty are to be eradicated, there must be a plan to do so. Unfortunately planning was given a bad name by the Soviet Union, with the often correct caricatures of rigid and unrealisable five-year plans seemingly damning the pursuit forever. Thus, although governments set targets, with identified actions and milestones, such as for the abolition of child poverty in the UK, they shy away from calling them 'plans'. Moreover they resemble the old Soviet documents in one respect and that is that they are invariably top-down in orientation. Social policy occupies a special place in this discourse because social plans, however euphemistically they are described, are very much the business of this discipline. A concerted effort is required by social policy analysts, therefore, to re-establish the importance of social planning as a means both to articulate aspects of social progress and to ensure that the resources necessary for their achievement are identified and the public plays as full a role as possible in this process. In other words, what is needed is the development of an open, democratic approach to social planning in which citizens are empowered with knowledge about needs and available resources.

The fourth challenge to social policy and those in other disciplines with a policy focus is to embed a global perspective in their analyses (see Chapter Thirteen). Peter did so increasingly with his last book, setting out the case for international social insurance (Townsend, 2009). It was a response to the urgent need to tackle poverty in less developed countries and a sociological understanding of the role of global processes and institutions in determining the distribution of resources between countries and between the Global North and South. The 2008–09 debt crisis is only the latest illustration of global interdependency and the devastating impact that this may have on ordinary people's lives. It also underlined the inadequacy of the world's regulatory framework and the absence of a forceful representation of the public interest at a global level. International social policy, including the analysis of globalisation and international governmental organisations and the articulation of the case for global social justice, must move to the centre stage of social policy (Deacon, 2007).

The fifth and final challenge to social policy and related subjects concerns the public role of the intellectual. With notable exceptions, among whom Peter was the leading light, some social policy analysts appear to prefer quiet scholarly pursuits to active public campaigning. This might be easy to justify in some disciplines but it is harder to do so in such a public discipline as social policy. On the one hand, there is the general duty of the intellectual, paid for by taxes on the public, to contribute to public debates and 'to tell the truth to power'. The conviction that intellectuals should be 'public' and that one of their leading tasks is to improve the world, and especially the conditions of the poorest, burns with a passionate intensity in most of what Peter wrote. On the other hand, there is the special nature of social policy:

> We all have our values and our prejudices; we all have our rights and duties as citizens, and our rights and duties as teachers and students. At the very least, we have a responsibility for making our values clear; and we have a special duty to do so when we are discussing such a subject as social policy which, quite clearly, has no

meaning at all if it is to be considered neutral in terms
of values. (Titmuss, 1974, p 27)

If Titmuss may be characterised, in terms of values, by a commitment
to welfare, Townsend nailed his colours to the mast of social justice.
Those working in the field of social policy have an unusually close
proximity to values and, obviously, to public policy. This close
relationship with public policy may lead to personal attacks when
the self-interested neoliberal policy elite feels threatened. Witness
the opprobrium heaped on Richard Wilkinson and Kate Pickett by
right-wing commentators following the publication of *The spirit level*.
Despite this and the obvious threats to future funding for individual
research, the concerted voices of social policy and related subjects
will be increasingly needed nationally and globally to replace the
present widespread approach to deficit politics and deference to
market forces, to defend those institutions that promote social justice
and to articulate an alternative vision of a society without poverty,
gross inequalities and social injustices.

We will end on a positive note of hope inspired by Seamus Heaney
(quoted in Sen, 2010, p 26), and urge all who believe in social justice
to campaign for it in whatever spheres of life they occupy:

> History says, Don't hope
> On this side of the grave,
> But then, once in a lifetime
> The longed for tidal wave
> Of justice can rise up,
> And hope and history rhyme.

Acknowledgement

We are very grateful to Adrian Sinfield for his comments on the draft
version of this chapter and for the section on fair taxation.

References

Bacon, R. and Eltis, W. (1976) *Britain's economic problems*, Oxford: Oxford
University Press.

Barnard, A. (2010) *The effect of taxes and benefits on household income 2008-09*, Newport: ONS (www.statistics.gov.uk/taxesbenefits).

Barrell, R. (2010) *What are the effects on growth of increases in taxes and cuts in spending?*, London: National Institute of Economic and Social Research, June.

Bauman, Z. (2000) 'Am I my brother's keeper?', *European Journal of Social Work*, vol 3, no 1, pp 5-11.

Beck, W., van der Maesen, L. and Walker, A. (eds) (1997) *The social quality of Europe*, Bristol: The Policy Press.

Beck, W., van der Maesen, L., Thomese, F. and Walker, A. (eds) (2001) *Social quality: A vision for Europe*, The Hague: Kluwer International.

Berghman, J. (ed) (1998) *Social protection as a productive factor*, Leuven: EISS.

Beveridge, Sir W. (1942) *Social insurance and allied services*, Cmd 6404, London: HMSO.

Bosanquet, N. and Townsend, P. (1980) *Labour and equality: A Fabian study of Labour in power, 1974–79*, London: Heinemann.

Brewer, M., Sibieta, L. and Wren-Lewis, L. (2008) *Racing away? Income inequality and the evolution of high incomes*, IFS Briefing Note No 76, London: Institute for Fiscal Studies.

Browne, J. and Levell, P. (2010) *The distributional effect of tax and benefit reforms to be introduced between June 2010 and April 2014: A revised assessment*, London: Institute for Fiscal Studies.

Coote, A. and Lenaghan, J. (1997) *Citizens' juries: Theory and practice*, London: Institute for Public Policy Research.

Cripps, F., Griffiths, J., Morrell, F., Reid, J., Townsend, P. and Weir, S. (1981) *Manifesto – A radical strategy for Britain's future*, London: Fontana.

Deacon, B. (2007) *Global social policy and governance*, London: Sage Publications.

Dolphin, J. (2010) *Financial sector taxes*, London: Institute for Public Policy Research.

Dorling, D. (2010) *Injustice: Why social inequality persists*, Bristol: The Policy Press.

Esping-Andersen, G. (1990) *The three worlds of welfare capitalism*, Cambridge: Polity Press.

European Commission (2000) *The social policy agenda*, Brussels: European Commission.

Galbraith, J.K. (1952) *American capitalism*, London: Hamish Hamilton.

HM Treasury (1979) *The government's expenditure plans 1979–80 to 1982––83*, Cmnd 7439, London: HMSO.

Hutton, W. (2010) *Them and us: Changing Britain – why we need a fair society*, London: Littlebrown.

IDS (Income Data Services) (2010) *Directors' pay report*, London: IDS.

IMF (International Monetary Fund) (2010) *World Economic Outlook database*, Washington, DC: IMF.

Lister, R. (2004) *Poverty*, Cambridge: Polity Press.

Marmot, M. (2010) *Fair society, healthy lives*, London: Department of Health.

OBR (Office for Budget Responsibility) (2010) *Pre-budget forecast*, London: The Stationery Office, June.

O'Dea, C. (2010) *Who loses most from public service cuts?*, London: IFS (www.ifs.org.uk/publications/5314).

OECD (Organisation for Economic Co-operation and Development) (2010) *OECD world factbook*, Paris: OECD.

Park, A., Curtis, J., Thomson, K., Phillips, M. and Clery, E. (eds) (2009) *British social attitudes*, London: Sage.

Rawls, J. (1973) *A theory of justice*, Oxford: Oxford University Press.

Sen, A. (2010) *The idea of justice*, Harmondsworth: Penguin.

Smith, A. (1976) *Theory of moral sentiments*, Oxford: Clarendon Press.

Stiglitz, J., Sen A. and Fitoussi, J. (2009) *Report of the Commission on the Measurement of Economic Performance and Social Progress* (www.stiglitz-sen-fitoussi.fr).

Tawney, R.H. (1964) *Equality*, London: Allen & Unwin.

Taylor-Gooby, P. (1998) 'Commitment to the welfare state', in R. Jowell et al (eds) *British and European social attitudes*, Aldershot: Ashgate, pp 57-76.

Timmins, N. (1995) *The five giants*, London: Fontana.

Titmuss, R.M. (1974) *Social policy*, London: Allen & Unwin.

Townsend, P. (1958) 'A society for people', in N. Mackenzie (ed) *Conviction*, London: MacGibbon & Kee, pp 93-120 [shortened in *New Statesman*, 18 October, pp 523-30, reprinted in (2009) *Social Policy and Society*, vol 8, no 2, pp 147-58].

Townsend, P. (1975) *Sociology and social policy*, London: Allen Lane.

Townsend, P. (1979) *Poverty in the United Kingdom*, London: Penguin Books and Allen Lane.

Townsend, P. (1996) 'Concluding comments', Conference on the Social Quality of Europe, Amsterdam, 28 November (handwritten).

Townsend, P. (ed) (2009) *Building decent societies: Rethinking the role of social security in state building*, Geneva: International Labour Organization/ Palgrave Macmillan.

Townsend, P. and Bosanquet, N. (1972) *Labour and inequality: Sixteen Fabian essays*, London: Fabian Society.

Walker, A. (1984) *Social planning*, Oxford: Blackwell.

Walker, A. (1990) 'The strategy of inequality', in I. Taylor (ed) *The social effects of free market policies*, Hemel Hempstead: Harvester Wheatsheaf, pp 29–48.

Walker, A. and Walker, C. (eds) (1987) *The growing divide*, London: Child Poverty Action Group.

Walker, A. and Walker, C. (eds) (1997) *Britain divided*, London: Child Poverty Action Group.

Walker, A., Ormerod, P. and Whitty, L. (1979) *Abandoning social priorities*, London: Child Poverty Action Group.

Wilkinson, R. and Pickett, R. (2009) *The spirit level: Why more equal societies almost always do better*, London: Allen Lane.

Wootton, B. (1945) *Freedom under planning*, London: Allen & Unwin.

Wootton, B. (1955) *The social foundations of wage policy*, London: Allen & Unwin.

Wright, E.O. (2010) *Envisioning real utopias*, London: Verso.

INDEX

Page references for notes are followed by n